SECOND EDITION

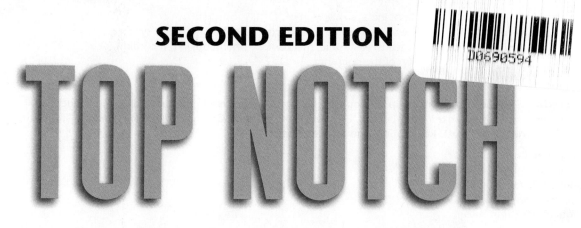

TOP NOTCH

English for Today's World

2

Joan Saslow • Allen Ascher

With *Top Notch Pop Songs and Karaoke*
by Rob Morsberger

Top Notch: English for Today's World 2, Second Edition

Pearson Education, 10 Bank Street, White Plains, NY 10606

Staff credits: The people who made up the Top Notch 2 team—representing editorial, design, production, and manufacturing—are Rhea Banker, Peter Benson, Elizabeth Carlson, Aerin Csigay, Dave Dickey, Warren Fischbach, Shelley Gazes, Aliza Greenblatt, Ray Keating, and Mike Kemper.

Cover design: Rhea Banker
Cover photo: Sprint/Corbis
Text design: Elizabeth Carlson
Text composition: Quarasan!
Text font: 9/10 Stone Sans

Library of Congress Cataloging-in-Publication Data

Saslow, Joan M.
  Top notch: English for today's world / Joan Saslow, Allen Ascher; with Top Notch pop songs and Karaoke by Rob Morsberger. — 2nd ed.
     p. cm.
  ISBN 0-13-246988-X (set) — ISBN 0-13-247038-1 (v. 1) — ISBN 0-13-247048-9 (v. 2) — ISBN 0-13-247027-6 (v. 3) 1. English language — Textbooks for foreign speakers. 2. English language — Problems, exercises, etc. I. Ascher, Allen. II. Title.
  PE1128.S2757 2011
  428.2'4 — dc22

                                        2010019162

Photo credits: All original photography by Sharon Hoogstraten and David Mager. Page 2 (background) Shutterstock.com, (top left) Will & Deni McIntyre/Getty Images, (top middle left) Kim Steele/Blend RF/Glow Images, (top middle right) Michael Goldman/Masterfile, (top right) Jeff Greenberg/PhotoEdit Inc., (bottom left) Michael Newman/PhotoEdit Inc., (bottom middle left) Dorling Kindersley; p. 5 Shutterstock.com; p. 7 (Egypt) Dallas & John Heaton/Corbis, (Mexico) John Neubauer/PhotoEdit Inc., (China) Picture Finders Ltd./eStock Photo, (Peru) Fotolia.com, (Japan) Dallas & John Heaton/Corbis, (Rio) Mathias Oppersdorff/Photo Researchers, Inc., (Feijoada) Fotolia.com; p. 8 (middle) Shutterstock.com, (bottom) Shutterstock.com; p. 10 (middle) Shutterstock.com, (1) Shutterstock.com, (2) Shutterstock.com, (3) Shutterstock.com; p. 11 Sunstar/Photo Researchers, Inc.; p. 12 (1) Fotolia.com, (2) Steve Vidler/eStock Photo, (3) Superstock, (4) Rafael Macia/Photo Researchers, Inc.; p. 14 (left) Warner Bros/Photofest, (middle left) Photofest, (middle right) DreamWorks/Photofest, (right) Paramount Pictures/Photofest; p. 16 Stephane Cardinale/People Avenue/Corbis; p. 18 (action) Original Films/Bob Marshak/The Kobal Collection, (horror) Warner Bros/The Kobal Collection, (sci-fi) MGM/The Kobal Collection, (animated) Globe Photos, (comedy) Morgan Creek/The Kobal Collection, (drama) Paramount/The Kobal Collection, (documentary) Les Gibbon/Alamy, (musical) Simon Fergusson/Getty Images; p. 20 Shutterstock.com; p. 21 (top left) Shutterstock.com, (top right) Shutterstock.com, (bottom left) Shutterstock.com, (bottom right) Shutterstock.com; p. 22 Shutterstock.com; p. 23 Miramax Films/Photofest; p. 26 (top right logos) Shutterstock.com, (single) Jeff Greenberg/PhotoEdit Inc., (double) Jeff Greenberg/PhotoEdit Inc.; p. 28 Shutterstock.com; p. 30 Shutterstock.com, (top right) Inspirestock RF/Getty Images; p. 32 (towels) Comstock.com, (hangers) Murat Sentürk/Fotolia, (iron) Michael Matisse/Getty Images, (dryer) Getty Images, (make up) Jeff Greenberg/Index Stock Imagery, (turn down) Comstock.com, (bring up) David Bartruff Inc.; p. 33 Shutterstock.com; p. 34 (left) Dorling Kindersley, (middle) Rudy Van Briel/PhotoEdit Inc., (right) LOOK Die Bildagentur der Fotogafen GmbH/Alamy; p. 37 (left) Shutterstock.com, (right) Shutterstock.com; p. 38 (left) Shutterstock.com, (sedan) Courtesy DaimlerChrysler Corporation, (compact) Shutterstock.com, (wagon) Dorling Kindersley, (van) Oleksiy Maksymenko/Alamy, (convertible) Motoring Picture Library/Alamy, (SUV) Kurt Wittman/Corbis, (sports) Adam Woolfitt/Corbis, (luxury) Ron Kimball Photography; p. 44 (bottom right) Shutterstock.com;p. 45 (Lexor) Photolibrary.com, (Sea) Ron Kimball Photography, (Outing) Izmostock/Alamy, (Invocation) Photolibrary.com, (Turbo) Photolibrary.com, (Micro) Dreamstime.com, (Amigo) Shutterstock.com, (Overland) Izmostock/Alamy; p. 46 iStockphoto.com; p. 47 Shutterstock.com; p. 50 (top left) Shutterstock.com, (top middle) Shutterstock.com, (top right) Shutterstock.com, (bottom left) Shutterstock.com, (bottom middle) Photolibrary.com, (bottom right) Shutterstock.com; p. 52 (2) Shutterstock.com, (4) Aina Zimnika/Fotolia, (6) Shutterstock.com, (7) Shutterstock.com, (8) Shutterstock.com, (10) Shutterstock.com, (12) Shutterstock.com, (13) Shutterstock.com, (14) Shutterstock.com, (15) Shutterstock.com, (16) Shutterstock.com, p. 56 (left) Shutterstock.com, (right) Michael Bermant, MD, Board Certified, American Board of Plastic Surgery, www.plasticsurgery4u.com; p. 57 Bill Losh/Getty Images; p. 58 (left) Shutterstock.com, (right) Shutterstock.com; p. 59 (1) Shutterstock.com, (2) Shutterstock.com, (3) Shutterstock.com, (4) Shutterstock.com; p. 62 (fats) Shutterstock.com, (meat) Shutterstock.com, (dairy) Shutterstock.com, (fruit) Shutterstock.com, (vegetables) Shutterstock.com, (breads) Shutterstock.com; p. 64 (sushi) Vito Arcomano/eStock Photo, (mangoes) Fotolia.com, (pasta) Fotolia.com, (ice cream) Judd Pilossof/FoodPix, (asparagus) Shutterstock.com; p. 67 (shellfish) Fotolia.com, (chocolates) Fotolia.com, (tofu) Gary Conner/PhotoEdit Inc., (steak) Fotolia.com, (fries) Fotolia.com, (noodles) Fotolia.com, (sardines) Fotolia.com; p. 68 (left) Photolibrary.com, (right) Photolibrary.com; p. 69 Shutterstock.com; p. 70 (a left) Jimmy Dorantes/LatinFocus.com, (a right) George D. Lepp/Corbis, (b) Michael Newman/PhotoEdit Inc., (c) Steve Cohen/FoodPix, (d) Fotolia.com, (e) Richard McDowell/Alamy, (f left) Cathy Melloan/PhotoEdit Inc., (f right) Fotolia.com; p. 71 (top) Dorling Kindersley, (right) Michael Newman/PhotoEdit, Inc.; p. 73 (background) Tyson Foods, Inc., (Thailand) Stephen Mark Needham/Foodpix, (Korea) James Baigrie/Foodpix, (Mexico) Jimmy Dorantes/LatinFocus.com, (Colombia) Henry Rodríguez Bohórquez, (Lebanon) James Baigrie/Getty Images, (China) Shutterstock.com, (Peru) Veronica Vallarino; p. 74 Shutterstock.com; p. 76 Photolibrary.com; p. 80 Shutterstock.com; p. 81 (top) David Muir/Masterfile, (bottom right) Shutterstock.com; p. 82 Ken Weingart/ImageState; p. 83 (top) Tony Freeman/PhotoEdit Inc., (bottom) Anthony Redpath/Corbis; p. 85 (background) Dimitri Vervitsiotis/Getty Images, (middle) Photos.com, (bottom) David Butlow/Corbis; p. 86 (drawing) A. Ascher "Talavera", (jewelry) Wendy Wolf "tagua nut, Bayong wood, and lava rock necklace", (fashion) Shutterstock.com, (sculpture) Vivian Nash "La Rueda", (pottery) Matthew J. Sovjani "Wave Vase", (painting) Jessica Miller-Smith "Rockefeller Preserve", (photography) Peter C. Benson "Sagamore"; p. 87 (top) Mrs. Simon Guggenheim Fund. (163.1945). ®2004 Successio Miro/Artist Rights Society ARS, NY. The Museum of Modern Art/Licensed by Scala-Art Resource, NY, (bottom) Historical Picture Archive/Corbis; p. 89 (top) Francis G. Mayer/Corbis, (David) Copyright ©2001 by Martin Yu, (K'uan) Collection of the National Palace Museum, Taiwan, Republic of China, (Rivera) Reproduction authorized by the Instituto Nacional de Bellas Artes y Literatura. Courtesy of Art Resource, NY; p. 90 (wood) Paul A. Souders/Corbis, (glass) Susan Van Etten/PhotoEdit Inc., (silver) Charles Edenshaw. Photograph by Paul Macapia. Seattle Art Museum, (gold) Art Resource, NY, (cloth) Iconotec/Alamy, (clay) Stockbyte, (stone) Banco Mexicano de Imagenes/The Bridgeman Art Library International Ltd., p. 91 (top) Lizz Carlson, (pot) Shutterstock.com, (vase) Picture Desk, Inc./Kobal Collection (dolls) Dave G. Houser/Corbis, (figure) Claudia Obrocki/Art Resource, NY, (cups) Shutterstock.com; p. 92 Audrey Benson; p. 94 (top left) The Newark Museum/Art Resource, NY, (top right) Art Resource, NY, (middle) Reuters NewMedia Inc./Corbis, (bottom left) Bettmann/Corbis, (bottom middle) Reuters/Corbis, (bottom right) Stephane Cardinale/People Avenue/Corbis; p. 95 (right) Shutterstock.com; p. 96 (a) Collier Campbell Lifeworks/Corbis, (b) Heini Schneebeli/The Bridgeman Art Library International Ltd., (c) Erich Lessing/Art Resource, NY, (d) Archivo Iconografico, S.A./Corbis, (e) Picture Desk, Inc./Kobal Collection; p. 97 (background) Shutterstock.com, (Louvre) Richard List/Corbis, (Mona) Gianni Dagli Orti/Corbis, (Tate) Shutterstock.com, (Mustard) Tate Gallery, London/Art Resource, NY, (Japan) Sakamoto Photo Research Laboratory/Corbis, (Peru) Mireille Vautier/Alamy, (France) Picture Desk, Inc./Kobal Collection, (Mexico) Corbis; p. 98 (top) Shutterstock.com, (monitor) Burke/Triolo/Jupiterimages, (keyboard) Shutterstock.com, (mouse) Shutterstock.com, (touchpad) Shutterstock.com; p. 100 (background) Shutterstock.com, (hand) Shutterstock.com; p. 101 Fotolia.com; p. 102 Logitech, Inc.; p. 104 (4) Shutterstock.com; p. 106 Burke/Triolo/Jupiterimages, p. 109 (background) Shutterstock.com, (family photo) Shutterstock.com; p. 115 (wallet) Dorling Kindersley, (books) Myrleen Ferguson Cate/PhotoEdit Inc., (phone) Shutterstock.com, (jacket) Dorling Kindersley, (glove) Dorling Kindersley, (umbrella) Shutterstock.com, (suitcase) Dorling Kindersley; p. 116 (left) Robert Rathe/Mira.com, (middle) Shutterstock.com, (right) Shutterstock.com; p. 117 Library of Congress; p. 118 Shutterstock.com.

Illustration credits: Steve Attoe, pp. 6, 64; Sue Carlson, p. 35; John Ceballos, pp. 25, 37, 49, 121; Mark Collins, pp. 27, 42 (left); John Hovell, p. 9; Brian Hughes, pp. 24 (bottom), 41, 71; Adam Larkum, p. 61; Pat Lewis, p. 10; Andy Myer, pp. 16 (left, center), 66, 106; Dusan Petricic, pp. 8, 33, 41, 70, 78, 79, 113; Jake Rickwood, p. 24 (top); Neil Stewart, p. 119 (center, bottom); Anne Veltfort, pp. 16 (right), 29, 42 (right), 66 (top-right), 119 (top); Jean Wisenbaugh, p. 13.

Text credits: Page 46 (article) Teens Health.org, (c) 2007–2009, Adapted with permission; p.74 Information Please® 2009 Pearson, Inc. All rights reserved.

Printed in the United States of America

ISBN 10: 0-13-245558-7
ISBN 13: 978-0-13-245558-9
9 10 11 12 – V082 – 17 16 15 14 13

ISBN 10: 0-13-247048-9 (with MyEnglishLab)
ISBN 13: 978-0-13-247048-3 (with MyEnglishLab)
4 5 6 7 8 9 10 – V082 – 17 16 15 14 13

About the Authors

Joan Saslow

Joan Saslow has taught in a variety of programs in South America and the United States. She is author of a number of multi-level integrated-skills courses for adults and young adults: *Ready to Go: Language, Lifeskills, and Civics; Workplace Plus: Living and Working in English;* and of *Literacy Plus.* She is also author of *English in Context: Reading Comprehension for Science and Technology.* Ms. Saslow was the series director of *True Colors* and *True Voices.* She participates in the English Language Specialist Program in the U.S. Department of State's Bureau of Educational and Cultural Affairs.

Allen Ascher

Allen Ascher has been a teacher and a teacher trainer in China and the United States and taught in the TESOL Certificate Program at the New School in New York. He was also academic director of the International English Language Institute at Hunter College. Mr. Ascher is author of the "Teaching Speaking" module of *Teacher Development Interactive*, an online multimedia teacher-training program, and of *Think about Editing: A Grammar Editing Guide for ESL.*

Both Ms. Saslow and Mr. Ascher are frequent and popular speakers at professional conferences and international gatherings of EFL and ESL teachers.

Authors' Acknowledgments

The authors are indebted to these reviewers who provided extensive and detailed feedback and suggestions for the second edition of *Top Notch* as well as the hundreds of teachers who participated in surveys and focus groups.

Manuel Aguilar Díaz, El Cultural Trujillo, Peru • **Manal Al Jordi,** Expression Training Company, Kuwait • **José Luis Ames Portocarrero,** El Cultural Arequipa, Peru • **Vanessa de Andrade,** CCBEU Inter Americano, Curitiba, Brazil • **Rossana Aragón Castro,** ICPNA Cusco, Peru • **Jennifer Ballesteros,** Universidad del Valle de México, Campus Tlalpan, Mexico City, Mexico • **Brad Bawtinheimer,** PROULEX, Guadalajara, Mexico • **Carolina Bermeo,** Universidad Central, Bogotá, Colombia • **Zulma Buitrago,** Universidad Pedagógica Nacional, Bogotá, Colombia • **Fabiola R. Cabello,** Idiomas Católica, Lima, Peru • **Emma Campo Collante,** Universidad Central Bogotá, Colombia • **Viviane de Cássia Santos Carlini,** Spectrum Line, Pouso Alegre, Brazil • **Fanny Castelo,** ICPNA Cusco, Peru • **José Luis Castro Moreno,** Universidad de León, Mexico • **Mei Chia-Hong,** Southern Taiwan University (STUT), Taiwan • **Guven Ciftci,** Faith University, Turkey • **Freddy Correa Montenegro,** Centro Colombo Americano, Cali, Colombia • **Alicia Craman de Carmand,** Idiomas Católica, Lima, Peru • **Jesús G. Díaz Osío,** Florida National College, Miami, USA • **Ruth Domínguez,** Universidad Central Bogotá, Colombia • **Roxana Echave,** El Cultural Arequipa, Peru • **Angélica Escobar Chávez,** Universidad de León, Mexico • **John Fieldeldy,** College of Engineering, Nihon University, Aizuwakamatsu-shi, Japan • **Herlinda Flores,** Centro de Idiomas Universidad Veracruzana, Mexico • **Claudia Franco,** Universidad Pedagógica Nacional, Colombia • **Andrea Fredricks,** Embassy CES, San Francisco, USA • **Chen-Chen Fu,** National

Kaoshiung First Science Technology University, Taiwan • **María Irma Gallegos Peláez,** Universidad del Valle de México, Mexico City, Mexico • **Carolina García Carbajal,** El Cultural Arequipa, Peru • **Claudia Gavancho Terrazas,** ICPNA Cusco, Peru • **Adriana Gómez,** Centro Colombo Americano, Bogotá, Colombia • **Raphaël Goossens,** ICPNA Cusco, Peru • **Carlo Granados,** Universidad Central, Bogotá, Colombia • **Ralph Grayson,** Idiomas Católica, Lima, Peru • **Murat Gultekin,** Fatih University, Turkey • **Monika Hennessey,** ICPNA Chiclayo, Peru • **Lidia Hernández Medina,** Universidad del Valle de México, Mexico City, Mexico • **Jesse Huang,** National Central University, Taiwan • **Eric Charles Jones,** Seoul University of Technology, South Korea • **Jun-Chen Kuo,** Tajen University, Taiwan • **Susan Krieger,** Embassy CES, San Francisco, USA • **Robert Labelle,** Centre for Training and Development, Dawson College, Canada • **Erin Lemaistre,** Chung-Ang University, South Korea • **Eleanor S. Leu,** Soochow University, Taiwan • **Yihui Li (Stella Li),** Fooyin University, Taiwan • **Chin-Fan Lin,** Shih Hsin University, Taiwan • **Linda Lin,** Tatung Institute of Technology, Taiwan • **Kristen Lindblom,** Embassy CES, San Francisco, USA • **Ricardo López,** PROULEX, Guadalajara, Mexico • **Neil Macleod,** Kansai Gaidai University, Osaka, Japan • **Robyn McMurray,** Pusan National University, South Korea • **Paula Medina,** London Language Institute, Canada • **María Teresa Meléndez de Elorreaga,** ICPNA Chiclayo, Peru • **Sandra Cecilia Mora Espejo,** Universidad del Valle de México, Campus Tlalpan, Mexico City, Mexico •

Ricardo Nausa, Centro Colombo Americano, Bogotá, Colombia • **Tim Newfields,** Tokyo University Faculty of Economics, Tokyo, Japan • **Mónica Nomberto,** ICPNA Chiclayo, Peru • **Scarlett Ostojic,** Idiomas Católica, Lima, Peru • **Ana Cristina Ochoa,** CCBEU Inter Americano, Curitiba, Brazil • **Doralba Pérez,** Universidad Pedagógica Nacional, Bogotá, Colombia • **David Perez Montalvo,** ICPNA Cusco, Peru • **Wahrena Elizabeth Pfeister,** University of Suwon, South Korea • **Wayne Allen Pfeister,** University of Suwon, South Korea • **Cecilia Ponce de León,** ICPNA Cusco, Peru • **Andrea Rebonato,** CCBEU Inter Americano, Curitiba, Brazil • **Elizabeth Rodríguez López,** El Cultural Trujillo, Peru • **Olga Rodríguez Romero,** El Cultural Trujillo, Peru • **Timothy Samuelson,** BridgeEnglish, Denver, USA • **Enrique Sánchez Guzmán,** PROULEX, Guadalajara, Mexico • **Letícia Santos,** ICBEU Ibiá, Brazil • **Lyndsay Shaeffer,** Embassy CES, San Francisco, USA • **John Eric Sherman,** Hong Ik University, South Korea • **João Vitor Soares,** NACC, São Paulo, Brazil • **Elena Sudakova,** English Language Center, Kiev, Ukraine • **Richard Swingle,** Kansai Gaidai College, Osaka, Japan • **Sandrine Ting,** St. John's University, Taiwan • **Shu-Ping Tsai,** Fooyin University, Taiwan • **José Luis Urbina Hurtado,** Universidad de León, Mexico • **Monica Urteaga,** Idiomas Católica, Lima, Peru • **Juan Carlos Villafuerte,** ICPNA Cusco, Peru • **Dr. Wen-hsien Yang,** National Kaohsiung Hospitality College, Kaohsiung, Taiwan • **Holger Zamora,** ICPNA Cusco, Peru.

Learning Objectives

Unit	Communication Goals	Vocabulary	Grammar
1 **Greetings and Small Talk** page 2	• Get reacquainted with someone • Greet a visitor to your country • Discuss gestures and customs • Describe an interesting experience	• Tourist activities • Participial adjectives to describe experiences	• The present perfect ◦ Statements and yes / no questions ◦ Form and usage ◦ Past participles of irregular verbs ◦ With already, yet, ever, and before ◦ Common errors **GRAMMAR BOOSTER** • The present perfect ◦ Past participles: regular and irregular ◦ Questions with What or Which ◦ Yet and already: expansion ◦ Ever, never, and before ◦ Common errors
2 **Movies and Entertainment** page 14	• Apologize for being late • Discuss preferences for movie genres • Describe and recommend movies • Discuss effects of movie violence on viewers	• Explanations for being late • Movie genres • Phrases to describe preferences • Adjectives to describe movies	• The present perfect ◦ With for and since ◦ Other uses • Would rather + base form ◦ Form and usage ◦ Statements, questions, and answers ◦ Common errors **GRAMMAR BOOSTER** • The present perfect continuous • The present participle: spelling • Expressing preferences: review
3 **Staying in Hotels** page 26	• Check into a hotel • Leave and take a telephone message • Request hotel housekeeping services • Choose hotels and explain reasons for choices	• Hotel room types and features • Hotel services • Hotel room amenities and services	• Had better ◦ Usage ◦ Vs. should ◦ Contractions • The future with will ◦ Form and usage ◦ Contractions **GRAMMAR BOOSTER** • Obligation: have to / must • Suggestions and advice: could / should / ought to / had better • Expectation: be supposed to • Will: other uses; vs. be going to
4 **Cars and Driving** page 38	• Describe a car accident • Report a problem with a car • Rent a car • Discuss good and bad driving	• Car types • Car parts • Ways to show concern • Causes of car accidents • Phrasal verbs for talking about cars • Aggressive driving behavior	• The past continuous ◦ Form and usage ◦ Vs. the simple past tense • Direct objects with phrasal verbs **GRAMMAR BOOSTER** • The past continuous: other uses • Nouns and pronouns: review
5 **Personal Care and Appearance** page 50	• Ask for something in a store • Request salon services • Discuss ways to improve one's appearance • Define and discuss the meaning of beauty	• Salon services • Personal care products • Ways to discuss beauty	• Indefinite quantities and amounts ◦ Some and any ◦ A lot of, many, and much • Indefinite pronouns: someone / no one / anyone **GRAMMAR BOOSTER** • Some and any: indefiniteness • Too many, too much, and enough • Indefinite pronouns: something, anything, and nothing

Conversation Strategies	Listening/ Pronunciation	Reading	Writing
• Use "I don't think so." to soften a negative answer • Say "I know!" to exclaim that you've discovered an answer • Use "Welcome to ___." to greet someone to a new place • Say "That's great." to acknowledge someone's positive experience	**Listening Skills:** • Listen to associate • Listen for details **Pronunciation:** • Sound reduction in the present perfect	**Texts:** • A poster about customs • A magazine article about non-verbal communication • A geographical map • A photo story **Skills/Strategies:** • Identify supporting details • Personalize information	**Task:** • Write a description of a fascinating, strange, thrilling, or frightening experience **WRITING BOOSTER** • Avoiding run-on sentences
• Apologize and provide a reason when late • Say "That's fine." to reassure • Offer to repay someone with "How much do I owe?" • Use "What would you say to ___?" to propose an idea • Soften a negative response with "To tell you the truth, …"	**Listening Skills:** • Listen for main ideas • Listen to infer meaning • Dictation **Pronunciation:** • Reduction of <u>h</u>	**Texts:** • A movie website • Movie reviews • A textbook excerpt about violence in movies • A photo story **Skills/Strategies:** • Confirm content • Evaluate ideas	**Task:** • Write an essay about violence in movies and on TV **WRITING BOOSTER** • Paragraphs • Topic sentences
• Say "Let's see." to indicate you're checking information • Make a formal, polite request with "May I ___?" • Say "Here you go." when handing someone something • Use "By the way, …" to introduce new information • Say "Would you like to leave a message?" if someone isn't available	**Listening Skills:** • Listen to take phone messages • Listen for main ideas • Listen for details **Pronunciation:** • Contractions with <u>will</u>	**Texts:** • A hotel website • Phone message slips • A hotel guide book • A city map • A photo story **Skills/Strategies:** • Draw conclusions • Identify supporting details • Interpret a map	**Task:** • Write a paragraph explaining the reasons for choosing a hotel **WRITING BOOSTER** • Avoiding sentence fragments with <u>because</u> or <u>since</u>
• Express concern about another's condition after an accident • Express relief when hearing all is OK • Use "only" to minimize the seriousness of a situation • Use "actually" to soften negative information • Empathize with "I'm sorry to hear that."	**Listening Skills:** • Listen to summarize • Listen to infer outcomes • Listen for main ideas **Pronunciation:** • Stress of particles in phrasal verbs	**Texts:** • A rental car brochure • Rental car case studies • A feature article about defensive driving • A driving behavior survey • A photo story **Skills/Strategies:** • Understand from context • Critical thinking	**Task:** • Write a paragraph comparing good and bad drivers **WRITING BOOSTER** • Connecting words and sentences: <u>and</u>, <u>in addition</u>, <u>furthermore</u>, and <u>therefore</u>
• Use "Excuse me." to initiate a conversation with a salesperson • Confirm information by repeating it with rising intonation • Use "Not at all." to show you don't mind an inconvenience	**Listening Skills:** • Listen to summarize • Listen to take notes **Pronunciation:** • Pronunciation of unstressed vowels	**Texts:** • A hotel spa advertisement • A health advice column • A photo story **Skills/Strategies:** • Predict • Confirm content • Apply information	**Task:** • Write a letter on how to improve appearance **WRITING BOOSTER** • Writing a formal letter

Unit	Communication Goals	Vocabulary	Grammar
6 **Eating Well** page 62	• Talk about food passions • Make an excuse to decline food • Discuss lifestyle changes you have made • Describe local dishes	• Nutrition terminology • Food passions • Excuses for not eating something • Food descriptions	• <u>Use to</u> / <u>used to</u> • Negative <u>yes</u> / <u>no</u> questions • Offers and suggestions with <u>Why don't</u> ... ? **GRAMMAR BOOSTER** • <u>Use to</u> / <u>used to</u>: expansion ◦ <u>Be used to</u> vs. <u>get used to</u> ◦ <u>Would</u> + base form • More about negative <u>yes</u> / <u>no</u> questions; <u>Why don't</u> ... ?
7 **About Personality** page 74	• Get to know someone's likes and dislikes • Cheer someone up • Discuss personality and its origin • Examine the impact of birth order on personality	• Positive and negative adjectives • Terms to discuss psychology and personality	• Gerunds and infinitives as direct objects • Gerunds as objects of prepositions **GRAMMAR BOOSTER** • Gerunds and infinitives: other functions • Negative gerunds
8 **The Arts** page 86	• Recommend a museum • Ask about and describe art objects • Talk about artistic talent and where it comes from • Discuss your favorite artists and the reasons you like them	• Kinds of art • Positive adjectives • Materials and objects • Describing how art affects us	• The passive voice ◦ Form, meaning, and usage ◦ Statements and questions **GRAMMAR BOOSTER** • Transitive and intransitive verbs • The passive voice: form in all tenses
9 **Living with Computers** page 98	• Troubleshoot computer problems • Recommend a better deal • Describe how you use computers • Discuss the social impact of the Internet	• Computer parts • Ways to reassure someone • Computer terms and commands • Internet activities	• The infinitive of purpose • Comparisons with <u>as</u> ... <u>as</u> ◦ Meaning and usage ◦ <u>Just</u>, <u>almost</u>, <u>quite</u>, <u>nearly</u> **GRAMMAR BOOSTER** • Expressing purpose with <u>in order to</u> and <u>for</u> • <u>As</u> ... <u>as</u> to compare adverbs • Comparatives / superlatives: review
10 **Ethics and Values** page 110	• Discuss ethical choices • Return someone else's property • Express personal values • Discuss acts of kindness and honesty	• Ways to confirm a response • Ethical choices • Ways to acknowledge thanks • Personal values	• The real and unreal conditional ◦ Form, usage, common errors • Possessive pronouns / <u>Whose</u> ◦ Form, usage, common errors **GRAMMAR BOOSTER** • Present and future factual conditionals: usage and common errors • Order of clauses: punctuation • Possessive nouns: review and expansion • Pronouns: summary

Conversation Strategies	Listening/Pronunciation	Reading	Writing
• Provide an emphatic affirmative response with "Definitely." • Offer food with "Please help yourself." • Acknowledge someone's efforts by saying something positive • Soften the rejection of an offer with "I'll pass on the ___." • Use a negative question to express surprise • Use "It's not a problem." to downplay inconvenience	**Listening Skills:** • Listen for details • Listen to personalize **Pronunciation:** • Sound reduction: <u>use to</u> / <u>used to</u>	**Texts:** • A healthy eating pyramid • Descriptions of types of diets • A magazine article about eating habits • A lifestyle survey • Menu ingredients • A photo story **Skills/Strategies:** • Understand from context • Summarize • Compare and contrast	**Task:** • Write a persuasive paragraph about the differences in present-day and past diets **WRITING BOOSTER** • Connecting ideas: subordinating conjunctions
• Clarify an earlier question with "Well, for example, ..." • Buy time to think with "Let's see." • Use auxiliary <u>do</u> to emphasize a verb • Thank someone for showing interest • Offer empathy with "I know what you mean."	**Listening Skills:** • Listen for main ideas • Listen for specific information • Synthesize information • Infer information **Pronunciation:** • Reduction of <u>to</u> in infinitives	**Texts:** • A pop psychology website • A textbook excerpt about the nature / nurture controversy • Personality surveys • A photo story **Skills/Strategies:** • Support reasoning with details • Understand from context • Make personal comparisons	**Task:** • Write an essay describing someone's personality **WRITING BOOSTER** • Parallel structure
• Say "Be sure not to miss ___." to emphasize the importance of an action • Introduce the first aspect of an opinion with "For one thing, ..." • Express enthusiasm for what someone has said with "No kidding!" • Invite someone's opinion with "What do you think of ___?"	**Listening Skills:** • Understand from context • Listen to take notes • Infer point of view **Pronunciation:** • Emphatic stress	**Texts:** • Museum descriptions • A book excerpt about the origin of artistic talent • An artistic survey • A photo story **Skills/Strategies:** • Recognize the main idea • Identify supporting details • Paraphrase	**Task:** • Write a detailed description of a decorative object **WRITING BOOSTER** • Providing supporting details
• Ask for assistance with "Could you take a look at ___?" • Introduce an explanation with "Well, ..." • Make a suggestion with "Why don't you try ___ing?" • Express interest informally with "Oh, yeah?" • Use "Everyone says ..." to introduce a popular opinion • Say "Well, I've heard ___." to support a point of view	**Listening Skills:** • Infer meaning • Listen for the main idea • Listen for details **Pronunciation:** • Stress in <u>as</u> ... <u>as</u> phrases	**Texts:** • A computer troubleshooting website • A computer user survey • Newspaper clippings about the Internet • A photo story **Skills/Strategies:** • Understand from context • Relate to personal experience	**Task:** • Write an essay evaluating the benefits and problems of the Internet **WRITING BOOSTER** • Organizing ideas
• Say "You think so?" to reconfirm someone's opinion • Provide an emphatic affirmative response with "Absolutely." • Acknowledge thanks with "Don't mention it."	**Listening Skills:** • Listen to infer information • Listen for main ideas • Understand vocabulary from context • Listen to apply new vocabulary • Support reasoning with details **Pronunciation:** • Assimilation of <u>d</u> + <u>y</u> in <u>would you</u>	**Texts:** • A personal values self-test • Print and online news stories about kindness and honesty • A photo story **Skills/Strategies:** • Predict • Infer meaning • Summarize • Interpret information • Relate to personal experience	**Task:** • Write an essay about someone's personal choice **WRITING BOOSTER** • Introducing conflicting ideas

What is *Top Notch*?

Top Notch is a six-level* communicative course that prepares adults and young adults to interact successfully and confidently with both native and non-native speakers of English.

The goal of the *Top Notch* course is to make English unforgettable through:

► Multiple exposures to new language
► Numerous opportunities to practice it
► Deliberate and intensive recycling

The *Top Notch* course has two beginning levels: *Top Notch* Fundamentals for true beginners and *Top Notch* 1 for false beginners.

Each full level of *Top Notch* contains enough material for 60 to 90 hours of classroom instruction. A wide choice of supplementary components makes it easy to tailor *Top Notch* to the needs of your classes.

*Summit 1 and *Summit* 2 are the titles of the fifth and sixth levels of the *Top Notch* course. All Student's Books are available in split editions with bound-in workbooks.

The *Top Notch* instructional design

Daily confirmation of progress

Each easy-to-follow two-page lesson begins with a clearly stated communication goal. All lesson activities are integrated with the goal and systematically build toward a final speaking activity in which students demonstrate achievement of the goal. "Can-do" statements in each unit ensure students' awareness of the continuum of their progress.

A purposeful conversation syllabus

Memorable conversation models provide essential and practical social language that students can carry "in their pockets" for use in real life. Guided conversation pair work enables students to modify, personalize, and extend each model so they can use it to communicate their own thoughts and needs. Free discussion activities are carefully crafted so students can continually retrieve and use the language from the models. All conversation models are informed by the Longman Corpus of Spoken American English.

An emphasis on cultural fluency

Recognizing that English is a global language, *Top Notch* actively equips students to interact socially with people from a variety of cultures and deliberately prepares them to understand accented speakers from diverse language backgrounds.

Intensive vocabulary development

Students actively work with a rich vocabulary of high-frequency words, collocations, and expressions in all units of the Student's Book. Clear illustrations and definitions clarify meaning and provide support for independent study, review, and test preparation. Systematic recycling promotes smooth and continued acquisition of vocabulary from the beginning to the advanced levels of the course.

A dynamic approach to grammar

An explicit grammar syllabus is supported by charts containing clear grammar rules, relevant examples, and explanations of meaning and use. Numerous grammar exercises provide focused practice, and grammar usage is continually activated in communication exercises that illustrate the grammar being learned.

A dedicated pronunciation syllabus

Focused pronunciation, rhythm, and intonation practice is included in each unit, providing application of each pronunciation point to the target language of the unit and facilitating comprehensible pronunciation.

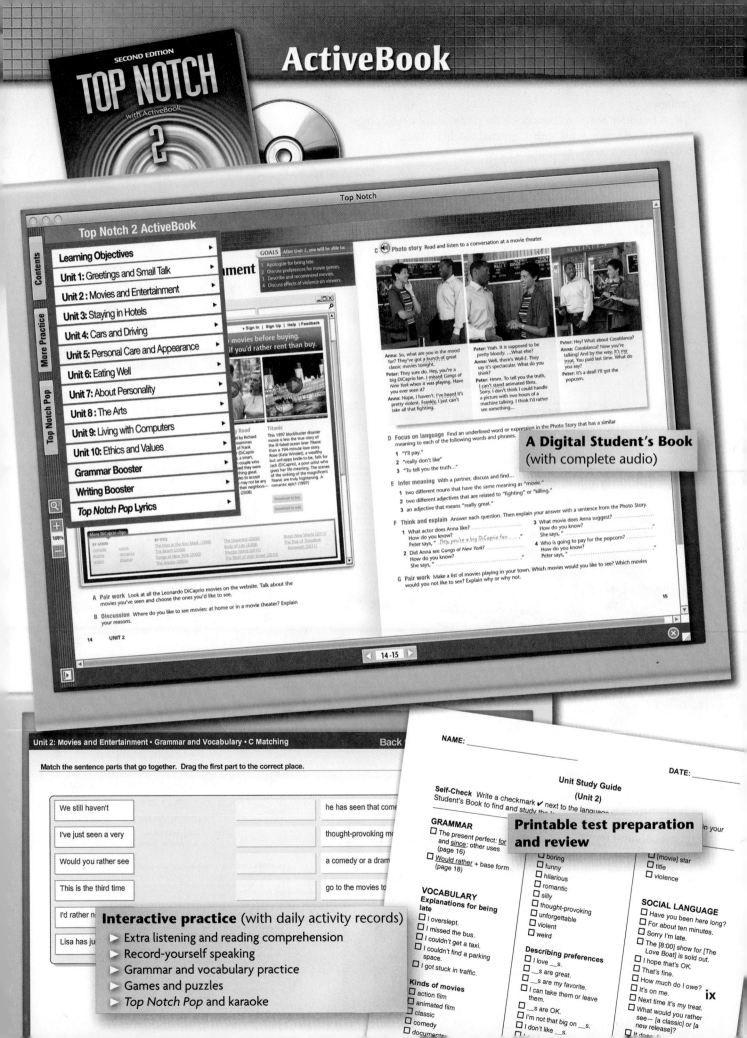

The Teacher's Edition and Lesson Planner

Includes:
- ► A bound-in Methods Handbook for professional development
- ► Detailed lesson plans with suggested teaching times
- ► Language, culture, and corpus notes
- ► Student's Book and Workbook answer keys
- ► Audioscripts
- ► *Top Notch TV* teaching notes

► ActiveTeach

- ► A Digital Student's Book with interactive whiteboard (IWB) software
- ► Instantly accessible audio and *Top Notch TV* video
- ► Interactive exercises from the Student's *ActiveBook* for in-class use
- ► A complete menu of printable extension activities

Teacher's Edition and Lesson Planner with ActiveTeach
SECOND EDITION
TOP NOTCH 2
Joan Saslow · Allen Ascher

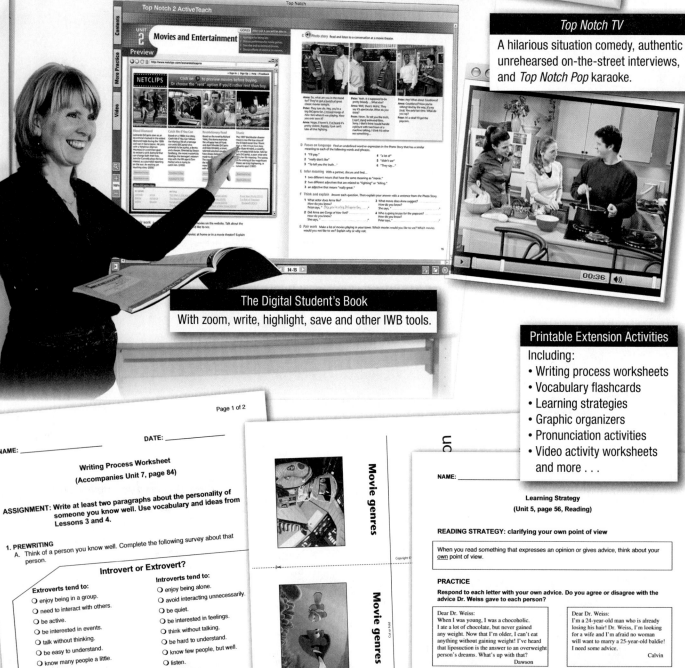

Top Notch TV

A hilarious situation comedy, authentic unrehearsed on-the-street interviews, and *Top Notch Pop* karaoke.

The Digital Student's Book
With zoom, write, highlight, save and other IWB tools.

Printable Extension Activities
Including:
- • Writing process worksheets
- • Vocabulary flashcards
- • Learning strategies
- • Graphic organizers
- • Pronunciation activities
- • Video activity worksheets and more . . .

Page 1 of 2

NAME: _____   DATE: _____

Writing Process Worksheet
(Accompanies Unit 7, page 84)

ASSIGNMENT: Write at least two paragraphs about the personality of someone you know well. Use vocabulary and ideas from Lessons 3 and 4.

1. PREWRITING
A. Think of a person you know well. Complete the following survey about that person.

Introvert or Extrovert?

Extroverts tend to:	Introverts tend to:
○ enjoy being in a group.	○ enjoy being alone.
○ need to interact with others.	○ avoid interacting unnecessarily.
○ be active.	○ be quiet.
○ be interested in events.	○ be interested in feelings.
○ talk without thinking.	○ think without talking.
○ be easy to understand.	○ be hard to understand.
○ know many people a little.	○ know few people, but well.
○ talk.	○ listen.
○ seek excitement.	○ seek peace.
○ express their opinions openly.	○ keep their ideas to themselves.

Total introvert selections: _____

Movie genres

Movie genres

NAME: _____

Learning Strategy
(Unit 5, page 56, Reading)

READING STRATEGY: clarifying your own point of view

When you read something that expresses an opinion or gives advice, think about your own point of view.

PRACTICE

Respond to each letter with your own advice. Do you agree or disagree with the advice Dr. Weiss gave to each person?

Dear Dr. Weiss:
When I was young, I was a chocoholic. I ate a lot of chocolate, but never gained any weight. Now that I'm older, I can't eat anything without gaining weight! I've heard that liposuction is the answer to an overweight person's dreams. What's up with that?
Dawson

Dear Dr. Weiss:
I'm a 24-year-old man who is already losing his hair! Dr. Weiss, I'm looking for a wife and I'm afraid no woman will want to marry a 25-year-old baldie! I need some advice.
Calvin

Your advice:

Your advice:

Other components

Workbook
Workbook
Daily assignments that reinforce each lesson.

Classroom Audio Program
Classroom Audio Program
Includes a variety of authentic regional and non-native accents.

Complete Assessment Package
Complete Assessment Package
Ready-made achievement tests. Software provides option to edit, delete, or add items.

Full-Course Placement Tests
Full-Course Placement Tests
Choose printable or online version.

Copy & Go
Copy & Go
Board games, role plays, information gaps, and "find someone who. . ." for every lesson.

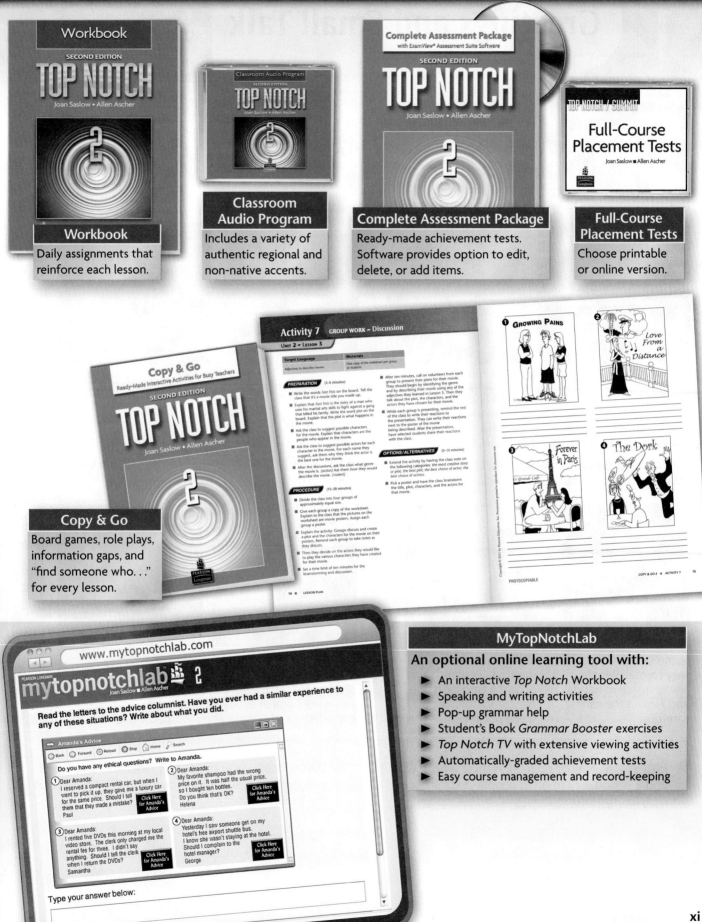

MyTopNotchLab
An optional online learning tool with:
► An interactive *Top Notch* Workbook
► Speaking and writing activities
► Pop-up grammar help
► Student's Book *Grammar Booster* exercises
► *Top Notch TV* with extensive viewing activities
► Automatically-graded achievement tests
► Easy course management and record-keeping

Greetings and Small Talk

GOALS After Unit 1, you will be able to:

1 Get reacquainted with someone.
2 Greet a visitor to your country.
3 Discuss gestures and customs.
4 Describe an interesting experience.

Customs Around the World

Greetings People greet each other differently around the world.

Some people bow.

Some people kiss once.
Some kiss twice.

Some shake hands.

And some hug.

Exchanging Business Cards

People have different customs for exchanging business cards around the world.

Some customs are very formal. People always use two hands and look at the card carefully.

Other customs are informal. People accept a card with one hand and quickly put it in a pocket.

Small Talk

What about small talk—the topics people talk about when they don't know each other well?

In some places, it's not polite to ask about someone's age or salary. In others, it's considered rude to ask about someone's family.

A Pair work In your opinion, is there a right way and a wrong way to greet people? Explain.

B Discussion In your country, are there any topics people should avoid during small talk? What about the topics below?

- the weather
- someone's job
- someone's religion
- someone's family
- someone's home
- (other) _____

C 🔊 1:02 **Photo story** Read and listen to two people meeting in a hotel lobby.

ENGLISH FOR TODAY'S WORLD
connecting people from different cultures
and language backgrounds

Leon: You look familiar. Haven't we met somewhere before?

Taka: I don't think so. I'm not from around here.

Leon: I know! Aren't you from Japan? I'm sure we met at the IT conference last week.

Taka: Of course! You're from Mexico, right?

Leon: That's right. I'm sorry. I've forgotten your name.

Taka: Kamura Takashi. But you can call me Taka.

Leon: Hi, Taka. Leon Prieto. Please call me Leon. So, what have you been up to since the conference?

Taka: Not much. Actually, I'm on my way to the airport now. I'm flying back home.

Leon: Hey, we should keep in touch. Here's my card. The conference is in Acapulco next year and I could show you around.

Taka: That would be great. I hear Acapulco's beautiful.

Leon: It was nice to see you again, Taka.

Taka: You, too.

Leon: Spanish speaker / Taka: Japanese speaker

D **Focus on language** Find an underlined expression in the Photo Story to match each of the following explanations.

1 You say this when you want to offer to introduce someone to a new place.
2 You say this to suggest that someone call or e-mail you in the future.
3 You say this when you're not sure if you know someone, but you think you might.
4 You say this when you want to ask about someone's recent activities.

E **Think and explain** Answer the questions, according to the Photo Story. Explain your answers.

1 Why does Leon begin speaking with Taka?
2 Has Taka been busy since the conference?
3 Why does Leon give Taka his business card?
4 What does Leon offer to do at the next conference?

F **Pair work** Write suggestions to a visitor about how to behave in your country. Then share your advice with the class.

❝Never ask about a person's age or salary!❞

❝Please don't exchange business cards with one hand!❞

Your advice
1
2
3

3

GOAL   **Get reacquainted with someone**

CONVERSATION MODEL

A 🔊 1:03 Read and listen to people getting reacquainted.

A: Audrey, have you met Hanah?

B: No, I haven't.

A: Hanah, I'd like you to meet Audrey.

C: Hi, Audrey. You look familiar. Have we met before?

B: I don't think so.

C: I know! Last month. You were at my sister Nicole's party.

B: Oh, that's right! How have you been?

B 🔊 1:04 **Rhythm and intonation** Listen again and repeat.
Then practice the Conversation Model with a partner.

> **Contractions**
> have met = **'ve** met
> has met = **'s** met
> have not met = **haven't** met
> has not met = **hasn't** met

GRAMMAR   *The present perfect*

**Use the present perfect to talk about an indefinite time in the past.
Use the simple past tense to talk about a definite or specific time.**

present perfect: indefinite time   simple past tense: definite time
I**'ve met** Bill twice.   We **met** in 1999 and again in 2004.

Form the present perfect with <u>have</u> **or** <u>has</u> **and a past participle.
For regular verbs, the past participle form is the same as the
simple past form:** (open → open**ed**, study → stud**ied**)

We { **'ve** / **haven't** } **met** them.   She { **'s** / **hasn't** } **called** him.

Have you **met** them?   **Has** she **called** him?
Yes, we **have**. / No, we **haven't**.   Yes, she **has**. / No, she **hasn't**.

> **Irregular verbs**
>
> | base form | simple past | past participle |
> |---|---|---|
> | be | was / were | been |
> | come | came | come |
> | do | did | done |
> | eat | ate | eaten |
> | fall | fell | fallen |
> | go | went | gone |
> | have | had | had |
> | make | made | made |
> | meet | met | met |
> | see | saw | seen |
> | speak | spoke | spoken |
> | take | took | taken |
> | write | wrote | written |
>
> For more irregular verb forms,
> open **Reference Charts** on your
> *ActiveBook* Self-Study Disc.

A Pair work Complete the conversations with the present
perfect or the simple past tense. Then practice the
conversations with a partner.

GRAMMAR BOOSTER ▸ p. 122
• *The present perfect:
information questions*

1 A: .... our new teacher?
         Jake / meet
   B: Yes, ... He .... her in the office this morning.
                                             meet

2 A: .... to this class before?
         they / be
   B: No, ... They're new at this school.

3 A: .... in the new school restaurant?
         you / eat
   B: No, ... Is it good?

4 A: .... with the school director?
         your classmates / speak
   B: Yes, ... They .... with her yesterday.
                                             speak

5 A: .... the new language lab?
         Beth / see
   B: No, ... But she .... the library.
                                             see

B Grammar practice Complete the message with the present perfect or the simple past tense.

FaceSpace

| SAVE | DELETE | REPLY | ATTACH |

August 29 at 10:50 AM

Hi, Emilie:

I have always remembered your wonderful English classes in Rome, and when I (1 see) _____ you on FaceSpace yesterday, I (2 decide) _____ to send you a message to say hello. We (3 not see) _____ each other in years! So let me tell you what I've been up to. In 2006, I (4 move) _____ to Canada, and I'm living in Montreal right now. I'm still studying English, and I recently (5 enroll) _____ in a great language school here. I (6 travel) _____ a lot in Canada and the US, too. I (7 be) _____ to Toronto, Halifax, Boston, and New York. I (8 go) _____ back home to Rome to visit my parents last September. Sorry I (9 not call) _____ you then! Do you think my English is better now? I'm going to keep studying until I can speak as well as you! After more than three years here, I (10 fall) _____ in love with this city! Let's keep in touch. If you come to Montreal, I'd love to show you around.

Antoinetta

Antoinetta

Birthday: June 3

Current city: Montreal

Hometown: Rome

🔍 SEARCH

✉ INBOX

➡ SENT

1:05

PRONUNCIATION *Sound reduction in the present perfect*

A 🔊 Listen to how the sound /t/ of the negative contraction "disappears." Then listen again and repeat.

1 I haven't been to that class.

2 He hasn't met his new teacher.

3 They haven't taken the test.

4 She hasn't heard the news.

B Now practice saying the sentences on your own.

NOW YOU CAN **Get reacquainted with someone**

Group work Adapt the Conversation Model. With two other students, make introductions and get reacquainted. Use the present perfect. Then change the situation and roles.

A: ...., have you met ....?

B: No, I haven't.

A: ...., I'd like you to meet ....

C: .... You look familiar. Have we met before?

B: ....

Ideas
You met...
• at a party
• at a meeting
• at a friend's house
• in a class
• (your own idea) ___

Don't stop!
Engage in small talk.
Talk about how the weather has been.
Ask what your partners did before class began.
Introduce other classmates.

GOAL **Greet a visitor to your country**

VOCABULARY *Tourist activities around the world*

A 🔊 1:06 Read and listen. Then listen again and repeat.

climb Mt. Fuji

go sightseeing in New York

go to the top of the Eiffel Tower

try Korean food

take a tour of the Tower of London

take pictures of the Great Wall

B **Pair work** What tourist activities have you done? Which haven't you done? Use the Vocabulary and the present perfect.

> ❝ I've climbed two famous mountains. ❞

> ❝ I haven't gone to the top of the Empire State Building in New York. ❞

GRAMMAR *The present perfect: already, yet, ever, and before*

Use yet or already in questions about recent experiences.
Have you toured Quito **yet**?   Has she **already** tried Korean barbecue?

Use already in affirmative statements. Use yet in negative statements.
I've **already** tried sushi.   I haven't tried sashimi **yet**.

Use ever or before in questions about life experiences.
Have you **ever** eaten Indian food?   Has she **ever** been to London?
Have you eaten Thai food **before**?   Has she been to Paris **before**?

Use already or before in affirmative statements. Use have never or haven't ever in negative statements.
I've **already** tried Indian food three times, but I**'ve never** tried Thai food.
I've tried Indian food **before**, but I **haven't ever** tried Thai food.

> **Be careful!**
> You can use before in affirmative statements. But don't use ever.
> Don't say:
> I've ever been to London before.

> **GRAMMAR BOOSTER** ▸ p. 122
> • *Yet* and *already*: expansion, common errors
> • *Ever*, *never*, and *before*: use and placement

A **Grammar practice** On a separate sheet of paper, use the words to write statements or questions in the present perfect.

1 (you / go sightseeing / in London / before)
2 (she / already / try / Guatemalan food)
3 (they / ever / be / to Buenos Aires)
4 (we / not take a tour of / Prague / yet)

B ◀》 **Listening comprehension** Listen to each conversation and complete the questions. Then listen again and complete the short answers.

The Great Pyramids • Egypt

The Pyramid of the Sun • Mexico City

Questions	Short Answers
1 Has she .... of the Great Pyramids yet?	............, she ....
2 Has he .... in Kyoto yet?	............, he ....
3 Has she ever .... ceviche?	............, she ....
4 Has he already .... the Pyramid of the Sun?	............, he ....
5 Has she ever .... to Beijing before?	............, she ....
6 Has she .... of the Forbidden City yet?	............, she ....

C Write five questions about tourist activities in your city or country. Use <u>yet</u>, <u>already</u>, <u>ever</u>, and <u>before</u>.

Have you ever tried our seafood dishes?

The Forbidden City • Beijing, China

Ceviche • Peru

A temple • Kyoto, Japan

CONVERSATION MODEL

A ◀》 Read and listen to someone greeting a visitor.

A: Welcome to Rio. Have you ever been here before?

B: No, it's my first time. But yesterday I went to Sugarloaf. It was really beautiful.

A: That's great. Have you tried feijoada yet?

B: Feijoada? No, I haven't. What's that?

A: It's a famous Brazilian dish. I think you'll like it.

B ◀》 **Rhythm and intonation** Listen again and repeat. Then practice the Conversation Model with a partner.

Sugarloaf, Rio de Janeiro

Feijoada

NOW YOU CAN Greet a visitor to your country

A Notepadding On the notepad, write at least five activities for a tourist in your city or country.

B Pair work Change the Conversation Model to greet a visitor to <u>your</u> country. Use the present perfect. Suggest tourist activities in your city. Use your notepad. Then change roles.

A: Welcome to .... Have you ever been here before?

B: No, it's my first time. But yesterday I ....

A: .... Have you ....yet?

B: ....

Don't stop!
Ask about other places and tourist activities.

C Change partners Practice the conversation again, asking about other tourist activites on your notepad.

Activity	Description
try feijoada	It's a famous Brazilian dish.

Activity	Description

BEFORE YOU READ

Pair work Discuss which hand gestures people use in your country for the expressions below.
Are there any other gestures you can think of that people often use?

a	b
"Come with me."	

c	d
"There he is."	

e	f
"Six."	

READING 1:10

Body Talk

By Kelly Garbo

To communicate well with people of other countries, you must learn to speak well, right? Yes, but speaking isn't everything. Some experts say only thirty percent of communication comes from talking. Your gestures and other non-verbal actions matter, too.

But in different cultures, the same action can have different meanings. When you have to meet someone from a different culture, be prepared. Do you know what kind of gestures and customs are appropriate?

Let's look at shaking hands. North Americans like a firm handshake. But the French prefer a light, short handshake. If you shake a French person's hand the North American way, he or she may not like it. People in Eastern European countries and some Latino cultures prefer shorter handshakes, too. Hugging after shaking hands is also a common introduction there. Don't be surprised if a Brazilian gives you a hug. If you misinterpret gestures of introduction, your friendship may get off on the wrong foot!

Everyone around the world knows the "OK" hand gesture don't they? But in Spain, parts of South America, and Eastern Europe, the OK sign is considered rude. And if you go shopping in Japan, it means you'd like your change in coins instead of bills. In France, making the OK sign means "zero" or that something is worthless. So check before you use the OK sign to be sure it's OK!

Understanding even a few key gestures from different cultures can make you a better communicator. So next time you travel, try being culturally sensitive. Find out the local gesture and let your body talk.

Source: bellaonline.com

A Identify supporting details Check the statements that are true, according to the article.
Explain your answers.

☐ **1** Seventy percent of communication comes from non-verbal actions.
☐ **2** If you don't speak someone's language, it's always safe to use gestures from your own culture.
☐ **3** Eastern Europeans generally don't like long handshakes.
☐ **4** Hugging is common during introductions in Brazil.
☐ **5** Japanese people think the OK sign is rude.

B Relate to personal experience Discuss the questions:
Have you ever been surprised by someone's body language on TV, in the movies, or in real life? What was the non-verbal action? What do you think it meant? Why were you surprised?

> On your *ActiveBook* Self-Study Disc:
> **Extra Reading Comprehension Questions**

NOW YOU CAN Discuss gestures and customs

A Pair work Read the travel tips about gestures and customs around the world.
Compare your own customs with those described.

Travel Tips

If someone gives you a gift, thank the person and open it right away. (Ecuador)

If you want to get a server's attention, it's more polite to use eye contact rather than hand gestures. (Kenya)

If you are going to be more than 15 minutes late for a party, lunch, or dinner, you should call to explain. (United States)

If you invite someone to go to a restaurant, you should always pay for the meal. (India)

Before you enter someone's home, you should take off your shoes. (Ukraine)

When a visitor is leaving your home, you should walk with that person out the door. (Korea)

When greeting people, older people should always be greeted first. (Mongolia)

B Notepadding With a partner, choose a topic and discuss your country's customs.
Then write notes about your country on the notepad.

Topic: *showing respect for older people.*
Customs: *It's not polite to disagree with an older person.*

Topic:

Customs:

Are the rules the same for both men and women? How about for young people or older people? Explain.

Topics
- showing respect to older people
- do's and don'ts for gestures
- invitations
- visiting someone's home
- giving gifts
- offering or refusing food
- touching or not touching
- (your own topic) ___

C Discussion Tell your classmates about the customs you described on your notepad. Does everyone agree?

Text-mining (optional)
Underline language in the Reading on page 8 to use in the Discussion.
For example:
"Don't be surprised if …"

GOAL Describe an interesting experience

A 🔊 1:11 **Vocabulary • *Participial adjectives*** Read and listen. Then listen again and repeat.

The safari was **fascinating**.
(They were **fascinated**.)

The ski trip was **thrilling**.
(They were **thrilled**.)

The sky-dive was **frightening**.
(They were **frightened**.)

The food was **disgusting**.
(They were **disgusted**.)

B On a separate sheet of paper, write lists of things you think are fascinating, thrilling, frightening, and disgusting.

C **Pair work** Compare your lists.

> ❝I think eating snails is disgusting.❞

> ❝Really? I've tried them and I wasn't disgusted at all.❞

A 🔊 1:12 **Listen to associate** Listen to the three interviews. Then listen again and write the number of the speaker described by each statement.

...3... **a** travels to have thrilling experiences

.... **b** describes differences in body language

.... **c** was disgusted by something

.... **d** is fascinated by other cultures

.... **e** tries to be polite

.... **f** does some things that are scary

.2
Andrew Barlow

1
Nancy Sullivan

3
Mieko Nakamura

B ◀))) **Listen for details** Listen again and answer the questions in complete sentences.

1 Nancy Sullivan

    a How many countries has she visited? ....

    b What did she notice about gestures in India? ....

2 Andrew Barlow

    c What did the people in the village do to thank him? ....

    d Why did he eat something he didn't want to? ....

3 Mieko Nakamura

    e What has she done twice? ....

    f How did she get to "the top of the world"? ....

NOW YOU CAN Describe an interesting experience

A Notepadding Answer the questions. Explain what happened. Write as many details as you can.

Have you ever been someplace that was really fascinating?

Have you ever eaten something that was really strange or disgusting?

Have you ever done something that was really thrilling or frightening?

B Pair work Ask your partner about the experiences on his or her notepad.

Don't stop!
Ask more questions.
Ask about other experiences.
  "Have you ever ..."

♻ **Be sure to recycle this language.**

climb ___
go sightseeing in ___
go to the top of ___
try ___
take a tour of ___
take pictures of ___

C Group work Choose one of the experiences your partner told you about. Tell your classmates about your partner's experience.

❝ My partner went hang gliding last year. She was frightened but it was really thrilling. ❞

hang gliding

11

Review

A 🔊 1:14 **Listening comprehension** Listen to the conversation with a tourist in Vancouver and check <u>Yes</u> or <u>No</u>. Then listen again and write the answers to the questions, using <u>yet</u> or <u>already</u>.

Has she...	Yes	No	
1 been to the Vancouver Aquarium?	☑	☐	*Yes. She's already been to the . . . .*
2 visited Gastown?	☐	☐	
3 been to the top of Grouse Mountain?	☐	☐	
4 seen the Capilano Suspension Bridge?	☐	☐	
5 tried dim sum?	☐	☐	
6 gone to the top of the Harbour Centre Tower?	☐	☐	

B Use the photos to write questions using the present perfect with <u>ever</u> or <u>before</u>. Don't use the same verb more than once.

1 Thai food

2 LONDON THE UNITED KINGDOM

3 Mount Aconcagua Argentina

4 The Tower of Pisa Italy

1 ....

2 ....

3 ....

4 ....

C On a separate sheet of paper, write sentences about the topics below, using the present perfect.

> **1** I've been to the top of the Taipei 101 Building.

1 tall buildings you've been to the top of

2 cities or countries you've visited

3 foods you've tried

4 mountains or high places you've climbed

D Writing On a separate sheet of paper, write about one of the experiences you talked about in Lesson 4. Describe what happened, where you were, who you were with, and how you felt.

> I've had a few frightening experiences in my life.
>
> Last year, I was on vacation in . . .

🎵 1:15/1:16 **Top Notch Pop**
"Greetings and Small Talk"
Lyrics p. 149

WRITING BOOSTER ▸ p. 139

- *Avoiding run-on sentences*
- *Preparation for Exercise D*

Pair work

1 Create a conversation for the man and woman. Imagine the man is welcoming the woman to his city. (Choose one of the cities on the map.)

Welcome to Paris. Have you been here before?

2 Create a conversation for the three people below. Imagine they get reacquainted during a tour of Europe.

A: Have you met ___ ?
B: Actually, you look familiar. Have we met before?
C: Yes, I think we have. You were on the tour of . . .

3 Imagine that you are on a tour of Europe. Ask and answer questions, using the present perfect.

Have you tried crepes yet?

EUROPE

UNITED KINGDOM

Buckingham Palace

London

the Millennium Wheel

Paris

the Eiffel Tower

crepes

FRANCE

the Prado Museum

● Madrid

tapas

SPAIN

ATLANTIC OCEAN

the Campanile Tower

Venice

a gondola

ITALY

Mozart's house

Vienna Boys' Choir

Vienna

AUSTRIA

GREECE

the Parthenon

moussaka

Athens

NOW I CAN...

☐ Get reacquainted with someone.
☐ Greet a visitor to my country.
☐ Discuss gestures and customs.
☐ Describe an interesting experience.

13

Movies and Entertainment

GOALS   After Unit 2, you will be able to

1 Apologize for being late.
2 Discuss preferences for movie genres.
3 Describe and recommend movies.
4 Discuss effects of violence on viewers.

— □ ✕

🔍

» Sign In | Sign Up | Help | Feedback

NETCLIPS

Click on ▶ to preview movies before buying.
Or choose the "rent" option if you'd rather rent than buy.

Blood Diamond

Leonardo DiCaprio stars as an ex-criminal involved in the violent diamond trade during the 1999 civil war in Sierra Leone. He joins with a fisherman (Djimon Hounsou) in a common goal: to recover a pink diamond that can change both their lives. Jennifer Connelly plays the love interest as a journalist reporting on the war. An exciting yet touching story. (2006)

    Download to buy

    Download to rent

Catch Me if You Can

Based on a 1960s true story, *Catch Me if You Can* follows the hilarious life of a teenage con artist (DiCaprio) who pretends to be a pilot, a doctor, and a lawyer. Directed by Steven Spielberg, the movie masterfully develops the teenager's relationship with the FBI agent (Tom Hanks) who is trying to catch him. (2002)

    Download to buy

    Download to rent

Revolutionary Road

Based on the novel by Richard Yates, this drama examines the unhappy lives of Frank and April Wheeler (DiCaprio and Kate Winslet), a smart, talented suburban couple who have always believed they were made to do something great. The couple struggles to accept the truth that they may not be any more special than their neighbors— with tragic results. (2008)

    Download to buy

    Download to rent

Titanic

This 1997 blockbuster disaster movie is less the true story of the ill-fated ocean liner *Titanic* than a 194-minute love story. Rose (Kate Winslet), a wealthy but unhappy bride-to-be, falls for Jack (DiCaprio), a poor artist who gives her life meaning. The scenes of the sinking of the magnificent *Titanic* are truly frightening. A romantic epic! (1997)

    Download to buy

    Download to rent

More DiCaprio clips

BY GENRE		BY TITLE		
comedy	crime	The Man in the Iron Mask (1998)	The Departed (2006)	Brave New World (2011)
drama	romance	The Beach (2000)	Body of Lies (2008)	The Rise of Theodore
action	disaster	Gangs of New York (2002)	Shutter Island (2010)	Roosevelt (2011)
		The Aviator (2004)	The Wolf of Wall Street (2010)	

A Pair work Look at all the Leonardo DiCaprio movies on the website. Talk about the movies you've seen and choose the ones you'd like to see.

B Discussion Where do you like to see movies: at home or in a movie theater? Explain your reasons.

C 🔊 **Photo story** Read and listen to a conversation at a movie theater.

Anna: So, what are you in the mood for? They've got a bunch of great classic movies tonight.

Peter: They sure do. Hey, you're a big DiCaprio fan. I missed *Gangs of New York* when it was playing. Have you ever seen it?

Anna: Nope, I haven't. I've heard it's pretty violent. Frankly, I just can't take all that fighting.

Peter: Yeah. It *is* supposed to be pretty bloody. ...What else?

Anna: Well, there's *Wall-E*. They say it's spectacular. What do you think?

Peter: Hmm. To tell you the truth, I can't stand animated films. Sorry. I don't think I could handle a picture with two hours of a machine talking. I think I'd rather see something...

Peter: Hey! What about *Casablanca*?

Anna: *Casablanca*? Now you're talking! And by the way, it's my treat. You paid last time. What do you say?

Peter: It's a deal! I'll get the popcorn.

D Focus on language Find an underlined word or expression in the Photo Story that has a similar meaning to each of the following words and phrases.

1 "I'll pay."

2 "really don't like"

3 "To tell you the truth..."

4 "a lot of"

5 "didn't see"

6 "They say..."

E Infer meaning With a partner, discuss and find...

1 two different nouns that have the same meaning as "movie."

2 two different adjectives that are related to "fighting" or "killing."

3 an adjective that means "really great."

F Think and explain Answer each question. Then explain your answer with a sentence from the Photo Story.

1 What actor does Anna like? ....
How do you know?
Peter says, " *Hey, you're a big DiCaprio fan* ."

2 Did Anna see *Gangs of New York*? ....
How do you know?
She says, " ...."

3 What movie does Anna suggest? ....
How do you know?
She says, " ...."

4 Who is going to pay for the popcorn? ....
How do you know?
Peter says, " ...."

G Pair work Make a list of movies playing in your town. Which movies would you like to see? Which movies would you not like to see? Explain why or why not.

GOAL   Apologize for being late

GRAMMAR BOOSTER ▸ p. 123

GRAMMAR   *The present perfect: for and since; Other uses*

Use <u>since</u> with a specific time or date in the past. Use <u>for</u> to describe a period of time.

How long have you been here?
  { I've been here **since eight o'clock**. (a time in the past)
    I've been here **for ten minutes**. (a period of time)

Other uses:

• with <u>always</u>: I've **always** wanted to see *Car Planet*.

• with ordinals, superlatives, <u>only</u>:
  This is **the third time** I've seen *Ping Pong*.
  It's **the best** movie I've ever seen.
  My husband has **only** seen it once.

• with <u>lately, recently, just</u>:
  Have you seen a good movie **recently**?
  I've **just** seen *The Beach*—what a great movie!

• with <u>still, so far</u>: You **still** haven't seen *Tomato Babies*? I've seen it three times **so far**!

• The present perfect continuous: unfinished actions
• Spelling rules for the present participle: review, common errors

A Grammar practice Choose the correct words to complete the paragraph.

I've been a big fan of Penélope Cruz (1 for / since) more than five years. I've followed her career (2 since / so far) I was in high school. That means I've watched every movie she's made (3 for / since) 1988, except for *Volver*. I (4 yet / still) haven't seen that one, but I plan to see it soon. I've (5 still / always) loved Penélope's work. I've (6 since / always) been the first person in line at the theater when her movies open. Of the movies Penélope has made (7 lately / always), the most interesting to me is *Nine*. I think it's the (8 best / still) movie she's made (9 so far / still). I've (10 always / already) seen it five times!

B Pair work Take turns asking and answering the following questions. Use the present perfect in all your answers.

1 Is there a movie you've always wanted to see?
2 Have you seen any good movies recently?
3 What's the best movie you've ever seen?

4 What's the worst movie you've ever seen?
5 How many movies have you seen so far this month?
6 Have you ever seen a movie more than once?

VOCABULARY   *Explanations for being late*

1:18
A 🔊)) Read and listen. Then listen again and repeat.

I overslept.   I missed the bus.   I couldn't get a taxi.   I couldn't find a   I got stuck in traffic.
                                                                           parking space.

B Pair work Think of two other explanations for being late.

C 🔊 **Listening comprehension** Listen to the conversations. Complete the sentences, using the Vocabulary.

1 Ted's late because he ....

3 They're going to be late because they ....

2 Maude probably ....

4 First they .... Then they probably ....

PRONUNCIATION   *Reduction of h*

🔊 Notice how the sound /h/ often disappears in present perfect questions. Read and listen. Then listen again and repeat.

1 How long have you waited?

4 When did he buy the tickets?

2 Where have you been?

5 What's her favorite movie?

3 What has he heard about the film?

6 Who's his favorite star?

CONVERSATION MODEL

A 🔊 Read and listen to someone apologize for being late.

A: Have you been here long?

B: For about ten minutes.

A: Sorry I'm late. I got stuck in traffic. Did you get tickets?

B: Yes. But the 8:00 show for *The Love Boat* is sold out. I got tickets for *Paradise Island*. I hope that's OK.

A: That's fine. How much do I owe?

B: Nothing. It's on me.

A: Well, thanks! Next time it's my treat.

B 🔊 **Rhythm and intonation** Listen again and repeat. Then practice the Conversation Model with a partner.

NOW YOU CAN   Apologize for being late

A Add four more movies to the showtimes.

B **Pair work** Personalize the Conversation Model with your movies and explanations. Then change roles.

A: Have you been here long?

B: For ....

A: Sorry I'm late. I .... Did you get tickets?

B: Yes. But .... I hope that's OK.

A: ....

The Sun King	7:00	9:00	11:00
	7:30	9:35	[7:30 sold out]
	7:45	10:20	midnight
	8:00	11:00	[8:00 sold out]
	7:50	10:10	

♻ **Be sure to recycle this language.**

Don't stop!
Say more about the movie.
Offer to pay.
Discuss what to do after the show.

___ is sold out.
We missed ___ .
It started ___ minutes ago.
I've already seen ___ .
That's past my bedtime!
I can't stand ___ .
I'm not a(n) ___ fan.

I've heard it's ___ .
It's supposed to be ___ .
How much do I owe?
It's on me.
It's my treat.
What do you say?

C **Change partners** Practice the conversation again, making other changes.

17

GOAL | **Discuss preferences for movie genres**

VOCABULARY Movie genres

A ◀») Read and listen. Then listen again and repeat.

1:23

an action film

a horror film

a science-fiction film

an animated film

a comedy

a drama

a documentary

a musical

B Pair work Compare your favorite movies for each genre.

> 66 My favorite animated film is *Shrek*.99

C ◀») **Listening comprehension** Listen to the conversations about movies. Write the genre for each movie. Then circle the movie if the people decided to see it.

1:24

Movie	Genre
1 *The Bottom of the Sea*	
2 *Tango in Tap Shoes*	
3 *The Ant Who Wouldn't Die*	
4 *Chickens Never Wear Shoes*	
5 *Goldilocks Grows Up*	
6 *The Equalizer*	
7 *Twelve Angry Women*	
8 *City Under the Sea*	

D Discussion Which movies sound good to you? Listen again if necessary. Explain your choices.

GRAMMAR *Would rather* + base form

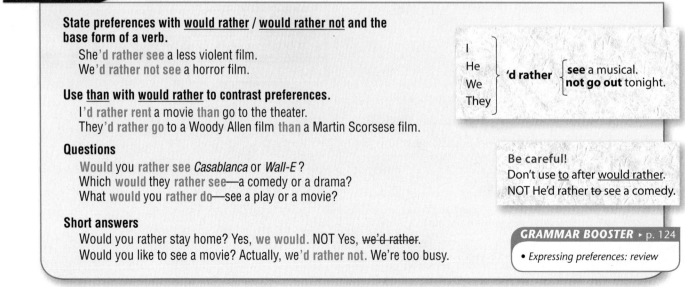

State preferences with <u>would rather</u> / <u>would rather not</u> and the base form of a verb.
   She'd rather see a less violent film.
   We'd rather not see a horror film.

Use <u>than</u> with <u>would rather</u> to contrast preferences.
   I'd rather rent a movie than go to the theater.
   They'd rather go to a Woody Allen film than a Martin Scorsese film.

Questions
   Would you rather see *Casablanca* or *Wall-E*?
   Which would they rather see—a comedy or a drama?
   What would you rather do—see a play or a movie?

Short answers
   Would you rather stay home? Yes, we would. NOT Yes, we'd rather.
   Would you like to see a movie? Actually, we'd rather not. We're too busy.

I		
He	'd rather	see a musical.
We		not go out tonight.
They		

Be careful!
Don't use <u>to</u> after <u>would rather</u>.
NOT He'd rather to see a comedy.

GRAMMAR BOOSTER ▸ p. 124
• Expressing preferences: review

A Grammar practice Complete each response, using 'd rather or 'd rather not and expressing a different preference.

1 "I'd love to see a drama tonight."   (YOU) Actually, ...

2 "I'm in the mood for a horror film."   (YOU) Actually, ...

3 "Let's get tickets for the late show."   (YOU) Actually, ...

4 "Ben told me you wanted to rent a movie."   (YOU) Actually, ...

5 "Would you like to see a comedy?"   (YOU) Actually, ...

6 "How about some dinner after the film?"   (YOU) Actually, ...

B Pair work Practice the conversations in Exercise A. Take turns reading the items.

CONVERSATION MODEL

A 🔊 1:25 Read and listen to people discuss their movie preferences.

A: What would you rather see—a classic or a new release?

B: It doesn't matter to me. You choose.

A: Well, what would you say to a documentary?

B: Hmm. To tell you the truth, I'm not that big on documentaries.

A: What about a comedy?

B: That works for me.

Describing preferences

🙂 I love ___s. ___s are great. ___s are my favorite.	😐 I can take them or leave them. ___s are OK.	☹ I'm not that big on ___s. I don't like ___s. I can't stand ___s.

B 🔊 1:26 **Rhythm and intonation** Listen again and repeat. Then practice the Conversation Model with a partner.

NOW YOU CAN   Discuss preferences for movie genres

A Pair work Personalize the Conversation Model, expressing your own preferences in movie genres. Then change roles.

A: What would you rather see—........ or ....?

B: It doesn't matter to me. You choose.

A: Well, what would you say to ....?

B: Hmm. To tell you the truth, I ....

A: What about ....?

B: ....

B Change partners Change the conversation from a video store to in front of a movie theater. Talk about specific movies.

♻ **Be sure to recycle this language.**

It's on me.	Actually, ___ .
It's my treat.	Frankly, ___ .
I'm sorry I'm late.	I'm not that big on ___ s.
Have you been here long?	I can't stand ___ s.
Have you ever seen ___ ?	
I missed it.	

BEFORE YOU LISTEN

A 🔊 **1.27** **Vocabulary • *Adjectives to describe movies*** Read and listen. Then listen again and repeat.

funny something that makes you laugh

hilarious very, very funny

silly not serious; almost stupid

boring not interesting

romantic about love

weird very strange or unusual, in a negative way

unforgettable something you are going to remember

thought-provoking something that makes you think

violent bloody; with a lot of fighting and killing

B **Pair work** Write the title of a movie for each adjective. Then compare choices.

a funny movie	
a hilarious movie	
a silly movie	
a boring movie	
a romantic movie	
a weird movie	
an unforgettable movie	
a thought-provoking movie	
a violent movie	

LISTENING COMPREHENSION

A 🔊 **1:28** **Listen for main ideas** Listen to the movie reviewer. Write a check next to the movies he recommends and write an <u>X</u> next to the ones he doesn't.

1 ☐ *Popcorn*   **2** ☐ *The Vacation*   **3** ☐ *Aquamundo*   **4** ☐ *Wolf Babies*

B 🔊 **1:29** **Infer meaning** Listen carefully to each movie review again. Based on the reviewer's opinion, circle one or more adjectives to describe each movie.

1 *Popcorn*   (weird / funny / boring)   **3** *Aquamundo*   (boring / violent / thought-provoking)

2 *The Vacation*   (romantic / violent / unforgettable)   **4** *Wolf Babies*   (violent / boring / hilarious)

C 🔊 **1:30** **Dictation** Listen to the following excerpts from the reviews. Complete each statement, based on what you hear.

POPCORN ★

① First up is *Popcorn*, a new .... starring David Bodine and Judy Crabbe. ② Unfortunately, *Popcorn* is a complete waste of ....

THE VACATION ★ ★ ★ ★ ★

③ Our next film, *The Vacation*, is a well-acted and .... ④ I highly .... wonderful ....

AQUAMUNDO ★ ★ ★

⑤ *Aquamundo* is no .... film; it's based on real scientific research. ⑥ A .... film. Don't ....

WOLF BABIES ★ ★ ★

⑦ Adults will find the story .... , but children won't forget these .... , scary scenes for a long time.

NOW YOU CAN · Describe and recommend movies

A Pair work Read the short movie reviews and choose the movie you think sounds the most interesting. Then compare movie choices. Explain your reasons.

WHAT'S YOUR ALL-TIME FAVORITE MOVIE?

Rebecca Lane
Miami, USA

I've just seen *Casablanca* for the hundredth time, at least. It's the most romantic movie in the world, and there's no movie I would rather see. Humphrey Bogart and Ingrid Bergman star as former lovers who meet after many years. They're still in love and have to make some difficult choices. The ending is unforgettable and always makes me cry. This movie was made in 1942, but it's always "new." I guess that's what makes it a classic.

Winston Cornish
Kingston, JAMAICA

The Hunt for Red October, starring Alec Baldwin and Sean Connery, is one of my all-time favorites. It was made in 1990, so it's a little dated now, but it's still one of the most exciting action movies ever made. This fast-paced thriller kept me on the edge of my seat from beginning to end. I hope you go to see this movie, so I don't want to give away the plot, but the movie is about a Soviet nuclear submarine that comes very close to American waters. The crew of an American submarine must decide: Is the submarine trying to escape the Soviet Union—or start a nuclear war?

Diana Bedell
Calgary, CANADA

Wow! I've just seen *Phantom of the Opera*. I once saw the musical on stage, but it really comes alive on screen. The Andrew Lloyd Webber music is stunningly beautiful, and the tragic love story is always unforgettable. This musical isn't for everybody. Some people find the story kind of weird, but I love it.

Omar Gebert
Temuco, CHILE

I've just seen *Tootsie*. What a great movie—perhaps one of the most hilarious romantic comedies of all time. Dustin Hoffman stars as out-of-work actor Michael Dorsey, who dresses as a woman to get a part on a TV soap opera. But complications arise when he falls in love with his co-star, Jessica Lange, who doesn't know Michael is a man. If you want a good laugh, be sure to see this film!

B Notepadding Write notes about a movie you've seen recently. (It's OK if you don't have all the information.)

Title of film:
Genre:
Stars:
Director or producer:
Adjectives that describe the movie:
What the movie is about:

C Group work Describe and recommend the movies on your notepads.

Don't stop!
Ask questions.

♻ **Be sure to recycle this language.**

Questions	More adjectives	
Was it (funny)?	thrilling	exciting
Who was in it?	fascinating	great
What kind of movie was it?	frightening	interesting
Do you recommend it?	disgusting	bloody
What was it about?		

Text-mining (optional)
Underline language in the reviews in Exercise A to use in Group Work.
For example:
"— stars as a / an ___."

GOAL | **Discuss effects of violence on viewers**

Warm-up At what age do you think it's safe to permit children to see violent movies and TV shows? Explain.

READING 🔊))) 1:31

Can Violent Movies or TV Programs Harm Children?

A number of scientific studies have reported that watching violence can make children more aggressive. According to the research, two kinds of programs and movies encourage aggressive behavior in young children more than others: (1) realistic violent action programs and movies and (2) violent cartoons.

One disturbing conclusion is that the effects of violent viewing last for many years. One study showed that children who watched violent TV programs when they were 8 years old were more likely to behave aggressively at age 18. Furthermore, as adults they were more likely to be convicted of violent crimes, such as child abuse and murder.

Studies have also demonstrated that watching violent movies and TV shows can affect children's attitudes towards violence in the world around them. Children who watch a lot of violence become less sensitive to it in the real world. If children find violence normal, they may accept more violence in society or even commit violent acts themselves.

Very often, characters in movies and on television who commit violent crimes are not sorry for their actions and don't face consequences or punishment. When children see fictional characters like these, they learn that doing bad things is OK. For children, who are growing and developing, this is a bad message.

So what can we do? With young children, we have the power to control the TV programs and movies they watch, so we can protect them from seeing any violence at all. However, with older children it's impossible to completely prevent their exposure to violence. But we can try to limit the number of hours they spend watching it. And when children have seen a violent film or TV show, it's important to discuss it with them, to help them understand that violence is not a normal part of life.

Information source: education.pitt.edu

A Confirm content Discuss the following questions, using the information in the article. Then share your answers with the class.

1 Research has found that TV and movie violence can hurt children. What are some ways that viewing violence can affect children?

2 What kinds of programs and movies are most harmful?

3 Some studies show that viewing violence can have long-term effects, lasting for many years. What are some of the effects that studies have shown?

4 What bad "message" can come from violent programs and movies?

5 What suggestions does the article make to help parents prevent the bad effects of violent TV programs and movies in very young children? In older children?

B Evaluate ideas Do you agree with the article that "violence is not a normal part of life"? Explain your answer.

On your *ActiveBook* Self-Study Disc:
Extra Reading Comprehension Questions

NOW YOU CAN   Discuss effects of violence on viewers

A Complete the chart with three films or television shows you know. Rate the level of violence from 0 to 3, with 3 being the most violent.

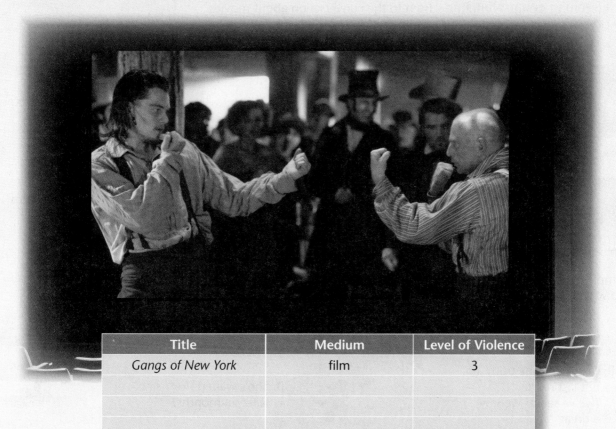

Title	Medium	Level of Violence
Gangs of New York	film	3

0 = not violent, 1 = somewhat violent, 2 = violent, 3 = ultra violent

B Notepadding Write notes about the most violent film or TV show on your chart.

Should children see it? Why? / Why not?
Is it OK for adults to see it? Why? / Why not?

Text-mining (optional)
Underline language in the Reading on page 22 to use on your notepad. For example:
"According to (the research), ..."

C Discussion Discuss the effects of violence on viewers. Use the information from your notepad to help you express your ideas. Here are some questions to consider in your discussion:

• In your opinion, are there some people who should not see violent movies? If so, who?

• Is the effect of viewing violence the same in children and adults?

• Does violence encourage adults to behave aggressively?

❝ **I think** violent movies can make people violent. They see violence and they go out and do the same thing they see in the movie. ❞

❝ **I disagree. I feel** ... ❞

❝ **I agree** ... ❞

Review

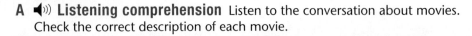
A 🔊 **Listening comprehension** Listen to the conversation about movies.
Check the correct description of each movie.

1

- ☐ a romantic film
- ☐ a documentary about Brazil
- ☐ a horror movie

2

- ☐ an animated police story
- ☐ a weird love story
- ☐ an unforgettable comedy

3

- ☐ an unforgettable movie
- ☐ a weird police story
- ☐ an animated children's film

4

- ☐ a documentary about cooking ham
- ☐ a musical tragedy
- ☐ a silly comedy

5

- ☐ a documentary
- ☐ a movie only for adults
- ☐ an animated musical

6

- ☐ a comedy
- ☐ an animated film
- ☐ a drama

B Complete the conversations. Choose the correct verbs and adverbial expressions,
and write the movie genres.

1 A: (Have you seen / Did you see)
a good .... (just / lately)?

B: To tell you the truth, no.
But last night
(we've seen / we saw)
a great ....

2 A: How many times (have they seen /
did they see) *War of the Worlds*?

B: That remake of the old
.... movie? I think
(they saw it / they've seen it)
twice (still / so far).

3 A: Sally is such a .... fan.
How long (has she waited /
did she wait) for this film to
come out on DVD?

B: She's waited (for / since) at
least six months.

4 A: I (didn't see / haven't seen)
a .... as good as *Twelve
Angry Men*.

B: Really? I (lately / still)
(didn't see / haven't seen) it.

C Complete each statement or question with <u>for</u> or <u>since</u>.

1 That film has played at the Metroplex .... two weeks.

2 *The Talking Parrot* has been available on DVD .... last Tuesday.

3 I've loved animated movies .... I was a child.

4 Have you been here .... more than an hour?

5 I've been a fan of science fiction movies .... over thirty years.

6 I've been in the ticket line .... 6:30!

🎵 1:33/1:34
Top Notch Pop
"Better Late Than Never"
Lyrics p.149

D Writing Write two paragraphs about violence in movies and
on TV. Explain why some people think it's harmful and why
others think it isn't.

WRITING BOOSTER ▶ p. 140

- *Paragraphs*
- *Topic sentences*
- *Preparation for Exercise D*

ORAL REVIEW

Pair work

1 With a partner, guess the genre of the three movies. Imagine what the movies are about and choose actors to star in the movies. Present your ideas to the class. Use the following as a model.

"Love in Paradise" is a romantic film. We think the movie is about a man and a woman who meet on vacation in Hawaii. They fall in love. We chose Brad Pitt and Angelina Jolie to star in the film.

2 Create a conversation for one of the couples. Say as much as you can. For example:

It's 7:30. Did we miss "Love in Paradise"?

SOLD OUT

Cult of Blood
7:20 9:00 Midnight

Love in Paradise
7:15 9:45

Ticket to the Moon
8:00 10:00

Ticket to the Moon

Love in Paradise

Cult of Blood

7:30

NOW I CAN... ✓

- ☐ Apologize for being late.
- ☐ Discuss preferences for movie genres.
- ☐ Describe and recommend movies.
- ☐ Discuss effects of violence on viewers.

Staying in Hotels

GOALS After Unit 3, you will be able to:
1 Check into a hotel.
2 Leave and take a message.
3 Request housekeeping services.
4 Choose a hotel.

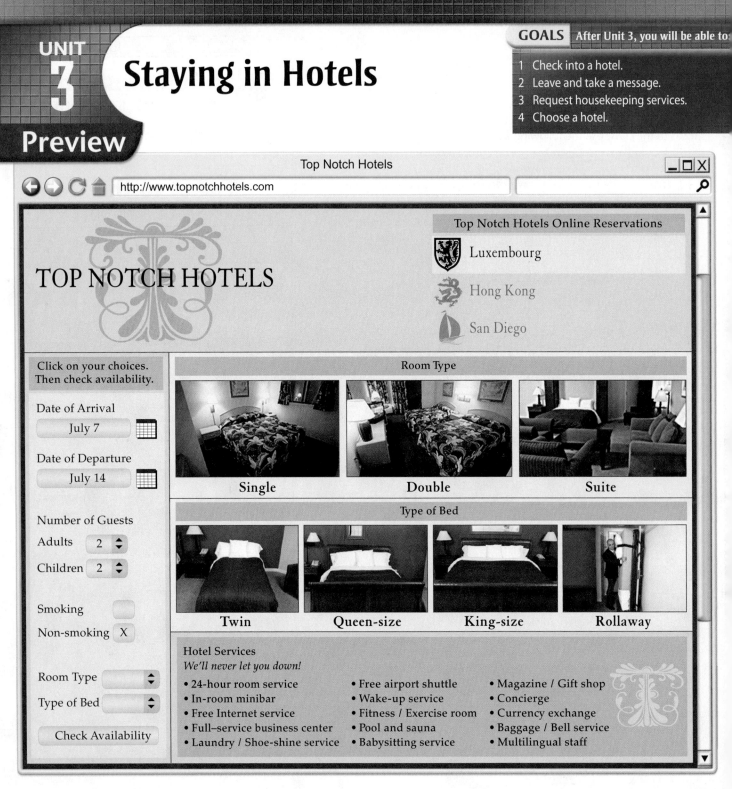

Top Notch Hotels

http://www.topnotchhotels.com

TOP NOTCH HOTELS

Top Notch Hotels Online Reservations

Luxembourg

Hong Kong

San Diego

Click on your choices.
Then check availability.

Date of Arrival
July 7

Date of Departure
July 14

Number of Guests
Adults   2
Children   2

Smoking
Non-smoking   X

Room Type
Type of Bed

Check Availability

Room Type

Single   Double   Suite

Type of Bed

Twin   Queen-size   King-size   Rollaway

Hotel Services
We'll never let you down!

• 24-hour room service
• In-room minibar
• Free Internet service
• Full–service business center
• Laundry / Shoe-shine service

• Free airport shuttle
• Wake-up service
• Fitness / Exercise room
• Pool and sauna
• Babysitting service

• Magazine / Gift shop
• Concierge
• Currency exchange
• Baggage / Bell service
• Multilingual staff

A ◀)) **Vocabulary** • *Hotel room types and features* Read and listen.
Then listen again and repeat.

2:02

1 smoking
2 non-smoking
3 a single room

4 a double room
5 a suite
6 a twin bed

7 a queen-size bed
8 a king-size bed
9 a rollaway bed

B Pair work Have you—or has someone you know—ever stayed at a hotel?
Tell your partner about the hotel features and services.

C ◀⁰)) **Photo story** Read and listen to someone checking out of a hotel.

Guest: Good morning. I'm checking out of Room 604.

Clerk: I'll be happy to help you with that. Was your stay satisfactory?

Guest: Yes. Very nice. Thanks.

Clerk: Did you have anything from the minibar last night?

Guest: Just a bottle of spring water.

Clerk: OK. Let me add that to your bill.

Clerk: And would you like to put this on your Vista card?

Guest: Yes, I would, please.

Clerk: Here you go, ma'am. Thank you for staying at the Top Notch Hotel. Will you be taking the shuttle to the airport?

Guest: Yes, I will.

Clerk: Well, the next shuttle will be arriving shortly. I'd better ask the bellman to give you a hand with your luggage.

Guest: Thanks. Actually, I'd like to pick up a paper at the newsstand. I'll just be a minute.

Clerk: No problem. The bellman will let you know when the shuttle's here.

Guest: Korean speaker

D **Focus on language** Find an underlined word or expression in the Photo Story with the same meaning as each of the following.

1 pay with   2 help   3 leaving   4 OK   5 only   6 soon

E **Think and explain** All the following statements are false. Explain how you know they are false.

1 The guest is staying for a few more days.

2 The guest has complaints about the hotel.

3 The guest pays the bill in cash.

4 The shuttle is arriving in an hour.

❝ The guest says, 'I'm checking out.' ❞

F **Pair work** Match each picture with a hotel service from the website on page 26. Then explain which services are important and which are not.

❝ Wake-up service is important. If you oversleep, you can miss a meeting or a tour. ❞

1 ....   2 ....   3 ....   4 ....   5 ....

6 ....   7 ....   8 ....   9 ....

GOAL **Check into a hotel**

GRAMMAR *had better*

Use <u>had better</u> and the base form of a verb to warn of a possible negative result. It is a stronger form of advice than <u>should</u>.

> They'**d better make** a reservation right away. (The hotel is almost full.)
> You'**d better not check out** late. (There is a late-checkout fee.)

Remember: To give a suggestion or advice, use <u>should</u> and the base form of a verb.

> You **should make** reservations right away.
> She **shouldn't forget** her passport.

The negative form <u>shouldn't</u> is more common in questions than <u>had better</u>.

> **Shouldn't** we **call** the airline first?
> We'**d better**. There could be delays.
> We'**d better not**. There's no time.

Contractions
had better = 'd better
had better not = 'd better not

Note: In spoken English, <u>had better</u> is almost always contracted.

GRAMMAR BOOSTER ▸ p. 125

- *Obligation:* <u>have to</u> / <u>must</u>, common errors
- *Suggestions and advice:* <u>could</u> / <u>should</u> / <u>ought to</u> / <u>had better</u>
- *Expectation:* <u>be supposed to</u>

A Grammar practice Complete the conversations. Use a verb from the box and a contraction of <u>had better</u> or <u>had better not</u>, depending on the meaning.

arrive	ask	be	call	hurry	walk

1 A: Is the gift shop still open?

   B: Yes, it is. But you .... It closes in five minutes.

2 A: When does the sales meeting begin?

   B: At 2:00 sharp. We .... late.

3 A: Do you think I could walk to the museum from here?

   B: Well, it looks like rain. You ....
   You should take a taxi instead.

4 A: Do you think we could get a table at Carlo's for dinner on Friday?

   B: Well, it gets pretty busy. You .... the concierge to make a reservation for you.

5 A: Hello, front desk? I'm trying to connect to the Internet but I can't seem to get online.

   B: I'm so sorry. I .... the business center for you. They can send someone up to check it.

6 A: Is the fitness center open early tomorrow?

   B: Yes. It opens at 7:00. But you .... early. It gets very crowded after 7:30.

B Find the grammar Look at the Photo Story on page 27 again. Circle one use of <u>had better</u>. Explain the possible negative result, using <u>could</u>.

CONVERSATION MODEL

A 🔊 2:04 Read and listen to someone checking into a hotel.

A: Hi. I'm checking in. The name's Baker.

B: Let's see. That's a double for two nights. Non-smoking?

A: That's right.

B: May I have your credit card?

A: Here you go. By the way, is the restaurant still open?

B: It is. But you'd better hurry. It closes at 9:00.

B 🔊 2:05 **Rhythm and intonation** Listen again and repeat. Then practice the Conversation Model with a partner.

C 🔊 2:06 **Listening comprehension** Listen to guests checking into a hotel. Complete the information about what each guest needs.

	Type of bed(s)	Non-smoking?	Bell service?
1		☐	☐
2		☐	☐
3		☐	☐
4		☐	☐

NOW YOU CAN   Check into a hotel

A **Pair work** Change the Conversation Model to role-play checking into a hotel. Discuss room and bed types and ask about hotel facilities. Imagine the time is now 8:30 P.M. Use the pictures or your own ideas. Then change roles.

A: Hi, I'm checking in. The name's ....

B: Let's see. That's a .... for .... night(s). Non-smoking?

A: ....

B: May I have your credit card?

A: .... By the way, is the .... still open?

B: ....

Business Center Hours
9 AM to 5 PM

Pool Hours
6 AM to 10 PM

Gift Shop Hours
8 AM to 9 PM

Fitness Center Hours
6 AM to 9 PM

Sauna Hours
11 AM to 8 PM

B **Change partners** Practice the conversation again. Discuss other room and bed types and hotel facilities.

GOAL **Leave and take a message**

CONVERSATION MODEL

A 🔊))) **2:07** Read and listen to someone leave a message.

A: Hello? I'd like to speak to Anne Smith. She's a guest.

B: I'll ring that room for you . . .
I'm sorry. She's not answering. Would you
like to leave a message?

A: Yes. Please tell her Tim Klein called.
I'll meet her at the hotel at three this afternoon.

B: Is that all?

A: Yes, thanks.

B 🔊))) **2:08** **Rhythm and intonation** Listen again and repeat.
Then practice the Conversation Model with a partner.

GRAMMAR   *The future with will*

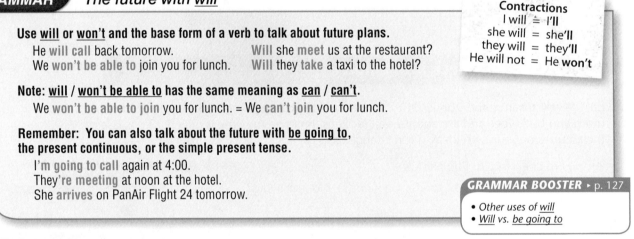

Contractions
I will = I'll
she will = she'll
they will = they'll
He will not = He **won't**

Use will or won't and the base form of a verb to talk about future plans.
He **will call** back tomorrow.   **Will** she **meet** us at the restaurant?
We **won't be able to** join you for lunch.   **Will** they **take** a taxi to the hotel?

Note: will / won't be able to has the same meaning as can / can't.
We **won't be able to join** you for lunch. = We **can't join** you for lunch.

Remember: You can also talk about the future with be going to,
the present continuous, or the simple present tense.
I**'m going to call** again at 4:00.
They**'re meeting** at noon at the hotel.
She **arrives** on PanAir Flight 24 tomorrow.

GRAMMAR BOOSTER ▸ p. 127

• Other uses of *will*
• *Will* vs. *be going to*

A Find the grammar Look at the Conversation Model again. Circle two uses
of will.

B Grammar practice Complete the messages, using will or won't and the base form
of the verb. Use a contraction when possible.

1 Please tell Ms. Yalmaz .... back later.
    I / call

2 Please give Mr. Ballinger this message:

    .... at the Clayton Hotel until after 5:00.
    We / not / be

3 Could you please tell the concierge ....
    I / need
    a dinner reservation for four at the Three Seasons
    tonight at 7:00?

4 Tell Ms. Harris ....
    her brother / not / be able to
    pick her up at the airport before 6:00, please.

5 Tell everyone ....
    the conference call / start
    at 3:00 tomorrow, London time.

6 Could you please tell Mrs. Park ....
    she / have to
    come in early tomorrow?

C 🔊 **Listening comprehension** Listen to the phone messages. Then listen again and complete each message slip, according to the information you hear. Use the future with <u>will</u> in each message.

1 ☎ *PHONE MESSAGE*
FOR: *Judy Diller*
FROM: ☑ Mr. ☐ Ms.
       ☐ Mrs. ☐ Miss *Pearl*
☐ Please call   ☐ Will call again
☐ Wants to see you   ☐ Returned your call
Message: *He'll be . . .*

2 ☎ *PHONE MESSAGE*
FOR: *HANK PITT*
FROM: ☐ Mr. ☐ Ms.
       ☐ Mrs. ☐ Miss
☐ Please call   ☐ Will call again
☐ Wants to see you   ☐ Returned your call
Message:

3 ☎ *PHONE MESSAGE*
FOR: *Collin Mack*
FROM: ☐ Mr. ☐ Ms.
       ☐ Mrs. ☐ Miss
☐ Please call   ☐ Will call again
☐ Wants to see you   ☐ Returned your call
Message:

4 ☎ *PHONE MESSAGE*
FOR: *Patricia Carlton*
FROM: ☐ Mr. ☐ Ms.
       ☐ Mrs. ☐ Miss
☐ Please call   ☐ Will call again
☐ Wants to see you   ☐ Returned your call
Message:

PRONUNCIATION   *Contractions with <u>will</u>*

A 🔊 Notice that each contraction is one syllable. Read and listen. Then listen again and repeat.

1 I'll call back later.
2 She'll be at the Frank Hotel.
3 He'll bring his laptop to the meeting.
4 We'll need a taxi.
5 You'll have to leave at 6:30.
6 They'll meet you in twenty minutes.

B Look at the message slips you wrote in Exercise C above. Read each message aloud, using the correct pronunciation of the contracted form of <u>will</u>.

NOW YOU CAN   **Leave and take a message**

A **Frame your ideas** On a separate sheet of paper, write four messages you could leave someone.

B **Pair work** Change the Conversation Model, using your own messages. Your partner completes the message slip. Then change roles.

A: Hello? I'd like to speak to ....
B: I'm sorry. .... Would you like to leave a message?
A: Yes. Please tell ....
B: Is that all?
A: ....

Don't stop!
• Leave another message.
• Confirm that you've understood the message correctly.
• Ask for more information.

|||||||||||||||||||||||||||||||||||||||||||||||||||||||||
WHILE YOU WERE OUT …
FOR:
☐ Mr. ☐ Ms. ☐ Mrs. ☐ Miss _____ called.
Phone:
☐ Please call back
☐ Will call again
Message:

♻ **Be sure to recycle this language.**

How do you spell your last name?
Could you please spell that for me?
Could you please repeat that?
What's your ___ ?

C **Change partners** Leave other messages.

31

GOAL | **Request housekeeping services**

BEFORE YOU LISTEN

A 🔊 2:11 **Vocabulary • *Hotel room amenities and services*** Read and listen. Then listen again and repeat.

┌─ **We need...** ───

 extra towels.

extra hangers.

skirt hangers.

an iron.

a hair dryer.

┌─ **Could someone...** ──

make up the room?

turn down the beds?

pick up the laundry?

bring up a newspaper?

take away the dishes?

B **Expand the vocabulary** Complete the statements with other items you know. Then compare items with a partner.

1 We need extra ..*glasses and coffee cups*.......... .

2 We also need ....

3 Could someone pick up my ....?

4 Could someone bring up
....?

5 Could someone take away
the ....?

Ideas
- dirty towels
- breakfast / lunch / dinner
- bags / luggage
- a coffee maker
- a rollaway bed
- laundry bags
- (your own idea) ___

LISTENING COMPREHENSION

A 🔊 2:12 **Listen for main ideas** Decide if the guests are satisfied or not. Then explain your answers.

Room 586
☐ Satisfied
☐ Not satisfied

Room 587
☐ Satisfied
☐ Not satisfied

B 🔊 2:13 **Listen for details** Listen again and complete each statement.

Room 586
The guest wants someone to take away ...., bring up .... and ...., and pick up ....

Room 587
The guest wants someone to .... the ...., bring up ...., and .... the ....

A Pair work Look at the pictures. With a partner, discuss what you think each guest is saying.

B Pair work Role-play a telephone conversation between one of the guests and hotel staff. Use your ideas from Exercise A. Then change roles. Start like this:

A: Hello. Room service. How can I help you?
B: Hi, I'd like to order...

Don't stop!
- Complain about other problems.
- Ask for a wake-up call.
- Ask about hotel services.
- Leave a message for another hotel guest.

♻ **Be sure to recycle this language.**

Hotel staff	Hotel guest
Hello, (business center).	Is the ___ still open?
Is everything OK?	What time does the ___ close / open?
What's the problem?	Could someone ___ ?
I'm sorry to hear that.	Can I make a reservation for ___ ?
Let me check.	
Certainly.	The ___ isn't / aren't working.
You'd better hurry.	The ___ won't turn on.
Hotel services	I need ___ .
Internet service	I'd like to order ___ .
business center	I'd like to leave a message for ___ .
wake-up service	
bell service	That would be great.

GOAL   Choose a hotel

BEFORE YOU READ

Explore your ideas What do you think is the best way to get information about a hotel?

☐ by word of mouth   ☐ from a travel guide book   ☐ other ....

☐ from an online hotel booking service   ☐ from a travel agency

READING 2:14 🔊

WHERE TO STAY IN NEW YORK

New York City has some of the best hotels in the world—and, believe it or not, some are not too expensive. Here are our picks for "the best of the best."

| $$$$ VERY EXPENSIVE | $$$ EXPENSIVE | $$ MODERATELY PRICED | $ BUDGET |

Most Famous Hotel

The Plaza Hotel $$$

Located at the southeast corner of New York's fabulous Central Park, The Plaza is as near as it gets to the best shopping along New York's famous Fifth Avenue. This 1907 hotel, with its beautiful fountain, is a famous location in many popular movies and books. Long the choice of the rich and famous.

4 restaurants, full-service spa and health club, concierge, car-rental desk, business center, 24-hour room service

Most Interesting Hotel

Hotel Chelsea $$

If you're looking for the usual, go elsewhere. But if you're looking for atmosphere—the New York of artists, actors, and writers—this is the place. Artists and writers live here, even today. The rooms in this 1884 Victorian hotel are simple but generally large. Everything is clean, but don't expect new.

Note: Not all rooms have air-conditioning. No laundry or room service, but the staff will take your clothes to the cleaners for you or help you order out for food.

Restaurant, bell service

Best Service at a Low Price

The Broadway Inn $$

Impeccably clean and very comfortable, this hotel is a real winner. Suites can be a great deal—with sofa, microwave, mini-fridge, and lots of closet space. Located in noisy Broadway's Theater District, the hotel is peaceful and quiet inside. Best of all are the attentive staff who work hard to make their guests happy.

Note: This hotel has no elevators.

2 restaurants next door, concierge, fax, copy service

Best Health Club

The Peninsula-New York $$$$

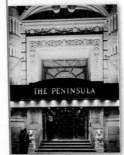

This is really a place to see. High-tech rooms with remote-control lighting, music, TV, and air-conditioning—even in the bathrooms! As a matter of fact, these are the most beautiful hotel bathrooms in New York City. Wonderful food and a very helpful concierge desk. ("We'll do anything guests ask, as long as it's legal!") And on the roof you'll find one of the biggest and best spa and health clubs anywhere.

Valet parking, 2 restaurants, business center, 24-hour room service, in-room massage

For the Budget-Minded

Hotel Pennsylvania $
A huge hotel and a great value. Only ten blocks south of Times Square. Traveling with your dog or cat? Pets are welcome.

The Habitat Hotel $
Built in 1999, offers inexpensive—but small—rooms with style. Near shopping.

The Hotel Newton $
Even though it's located on the Upper West Side, far from many of New York's most popular attractions, this inexpensive hotel features large clean rooms and firm beds for a good night's sleep. No pets.

The Lucerne $
Comfort and service but without the high prices. Large rooms. Great for kids.

Casablanca Hotel $
Free breakfast, coffee, tea, and cookies all day. Free passes to a nearby health club. Small rooms. Unusual Moroccan theme.

Source: Adapted from *Frommer's New York City*

A Draw conclusions Write statements with <u>'d better</u> or <u>'d better not</u> and the name of a hotel from the Reading. You may include more than one hotel.

1 Stella Myer likes to travel, but she is 70 years old. She has some difficulty with stairs.
   She'd better not stay at the ....

2 On his vacations, Carl Ryan likes to stay near the Theater District.
   ....

3 Mark and Nancy Birdsall are traveling with their kids. ....

4 Lucy Lee loves a hotel that is very comfortable and offers a lot of services.
   ....

5 At home, Burt and Susan Rey are very active and they go to a gym every day. They like to continue exercising when they're on vacation. ....

6 James Kay always travels with his dog, Louie. ....

B Identify supporting details Compare responses in Exercise A with a partner. If you disagree, explain why you chose a particular hotel.

On your *ActiveBook* Self-Study Disc:
Extra Reading Comprehension Questions

NOW YOU CAN Choose a hotel

A Frame your ideas What's important to you in choosing a hotel? Rate the following factors on a scale of 1 to 5.

not important ←→ very important

price	1	– 2	– 3	– 4	– 5
room size	1	– 2	– 3	– 4	– 5
cleanliness	1	– 2	– 3	– 4	– 5
location	1	– 2	– 3	– 4	– 5
service	1	– 2	– 3	– 4	– 5
amenities	1	– 2	– 3	– 4	– 5
atmosphere	1	– 2	– 3	– 4	– 5

B Pair work Find each of the hotels from the Reading on the map. Discuss the advantages and disadvantages of each. Then choose a hotel.

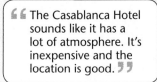
"The Casablanca Hotel sounds like it has a lot of atmosphere. It's inexpensive and the location is good."

Text-mining (optional) Underline language in the Reading on page 34 to use in the Pair Work. For example: "If you're looking for..."

C Survey and discussion Take a survey of how many classmates chose each hotel. Discuss and explain your choices.

"Most of us chose the Hotel Newton because..."

More Practice

ActiveBook *Self-Study Disc*

grammar · vocabulary · listening
reading · speaking · pronunciation

A 🔊 **Listening comprehension** Listen to the phone conversations in a hotel.
Then listen again and complete each statement, using words from the box.

2:15

babysitting	bell	box	dinner	hangers	make up the room
laundry	room	shoeshine	towels	wake-up	turn down the beds

1 She wants someone to bring up .... She also needs .... service.

2 He needs .... service. And he wants someone to bring up extra ....

3 She wants someone to .... , and she wants someone to bring up extra ....

4 He needs .... service and .... service.

B What hotel room type or feature should each guest ask for?
Explain your answers.

2:16/2:17

🎵 *Top Notch Pop*
"Checking Out"
Lyrics p. 149

1 Ms. Gleason is traveling alone. She doesn't need much
space. …*a single room*………

2 Mr. and Mrs. Vanite and their twelve-year-old son Boris are checking
into a room with one king-sized bed. ....

3 Mike Krause plans to use his room for business meetings with important
customers. ....

4 George Nack is a big man and he's very tall. He needs a good night's
sleep for an important meeting tomorrow. ....

5 Paul Krohn's company wants him to save some money by sharing a
room with a colleague. ....

C Read each situation and write your own strong advice, using contractions of <u>had better</u> or <u>had better not</u>.

1 It's raining. Mona is going outside.
YOU *She'd better take a raincoat because she…*

2 It takes Ms. Grant 30 minutes to walk to work. She has to be there in 15 minutes.
YOU ....

3 Mr. Wang is going to take an English test tomorrow. If he does well, he can get a better job.
YOU ....

4 Karl works really hard. He hasn't had a vacation in three years.
YOU ....

5 Marie and Paul Handel like quiet hotels. The World Hotel is very noisy.
YOU ....

D **Writing** Write a paragraph about the hotel you chose in Lesson 4. Explain why you would like
to stay there. What are its advantages and disadvantages?

> I would like to stay at the Hotel Casablanca.
>
> Atmosphere is very important to me and …

WRITING BOOSTER ▶ p. 141

• *Avoiding sentence fragments
with <u>because</u> or <u>since</u>*
• *Guidance for Exercise D*

Pair work

1 Create a conversation between the hotel guest in Room 816 and the woman at the front desk. Ask for hotel services or complain about a problem. Start like this:

Hello? Is this the front desk?

2 Create a conversation between the man at the front desk and the caller. Use <u>will</u>. Complete the message slip. Start like this:

A: *Front desk. Can I help you?*
B: *Yes, thanks. I'd like to leave a message for . . .*

3 Create a conversation between the two men at the front desk. Check into or check out of the hotel. Discuss hotel amenities, services, and schedules. Start like this:

Hi. I'm checking in. The name's . . . .

☎ **PHONE MESSAGE**

FOR: _____
FROM: ☐ Mr. ☐ Ms.
      ☐ Mrs. ☐ Miss
☐ Please call
☐ Wants to see you   ☐ Will call again
                        ☐ Returned your call
Message: _____
_____

THE BELMAR

DIRECTORY

Business Center	2
9:00 AM – 4:00 PM	
Gift Shop	Lobby
9:00 AM – 9:00 PM	
Fitness Center	3
6:00 AM – 10:00 PM	
Spa	5
10:00 AM – 3:00 PM	
Belmar Café	12
8:00 AM – 11:00 PM	

NOW I CAN... ✓

- Check into a hotel.
- Leave and take a message.
- Request housekeeping services.
- Choose a hotel.

Cars and Driving

GOALS   After Unit 4, you will be able to

1 Describe a car accident.
2 Report a problem with a car.
3 Rent a car.
4 Discuss good and bad driving.

Serving Europe and the world . . .

Maxi **CARS** RENTALS

Choose from the following car types:

Name: *Daniela Chaves*
Pick up: *Frankfurt*
Pick up date: *8 May*
Drop off: *Frankfurt*
Drop off date: *10 May*

Full-size Sedan
Daily Rate €45

Convertible
Daily Rate €70

Compact Car
Daily Rate €30

SUV
Daily Rate €65

Wagon
Daily Rate €45

Sports Car
Daily Rate €70

Minivan / Van
Daily Rate €55

Luxury Car
Daily Rate €80

A ◀)) 2:18 **Vocabulary • *Car types*** Read and listen. Then listen again and repeat.

1 a full-size sedan
2 a compact car
3 a wagon
4 a minivan / a van
5 a convertible
6 an SUV
7 a sports car
8 a luxury car

B **Discussion** What factors would influence your choice of a rental car from Maxi Cars Rentals? Explain the importance of each factor.

Factors:
• daily rate
• type of car
• size of car
• pickup locations

❝ To me, the location of the rental office is the most important factor. If I need to rent a car, I can't get to an office that's far away! ❞

C 🔊 2:19 **Photo story** Read and listen to a conversation in a car rental agency.

ENGLISH FOR TODAY'S WORLD
connecting people from different cultures
and language backgrounds

Renter: Good morning. The name is Kenji Kijima. I have a reservation.

Agent: Certainly, sir. Just a moment… Oh, yes. We were expecting you. A full-size sedan with GPS.

Renter: That's right.

Agent: And was that with automatic transmission or manual?

Renter: Either way.

Agent: OK, I've got a nice automatic that's all ready to go. I'll need to see your driver's license and a major credit card.

Renter: Here you go.

Agent: Thanks.

Agent: I have you returning the car on August 14th here at the airport.

Renter: Yes. That's correct.

Agent: Well, you're all set. Here are your keys and documents. The car's right outside.

Renter: Japanese speaker

D **Think and explain** All the following statements are false. Explain how you know they are false, using a quotation from the Photo Story.

1 The agent was surprised to see Mr. Kijima.

It's false because she says, "We were expecting you."

2 Mr. Kijima has to wait for the agency to get his car.

....

3 A passport is required at this rental agency to rent a car.

....

4 Mr. Kijima didn't choose the kind of car he wanted when he made his reservation.

....

5 Mr. Kijima can't drive a car with a manual transmission.

....

6 Mr. Kijima doesn't have his driver's license with him.

....

E **Pair work** Write a check mark for the situations in which it's good to rent a car. Discuss the reasons with your partner.

☐ for a shopping trip nearby

☐ for travel someplace where you don't speak the language

> ❝ It's too expensive to rent a car for a shopping trip. It's better to ask a friend to take you. ❞

☐ for a business trip with a lot of driving

☐ for a vacation with a large family

☐ for normal use when your car is in the service garage

☐ for another situation: ....

GOAL | **Describe a car accident**

VOCABULARY | *Car parts*

A 🔊 2:20 Read and listen. Then listen again and repeat.

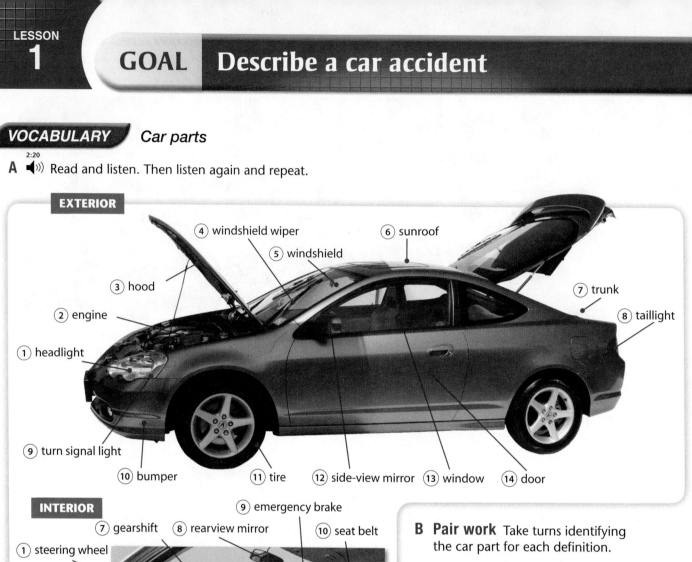

EXTERIOR

④ windshield wiper
⑤ windshield
⑥ sunroof
③ hood
② engine
⑦ trunk
① headlight
⑧ taillight
⑨ turn signal light
⑩ bumper
⑪ tire
⑫ side-view mirror
⑬ window
⑭ door

INTERIOR

⑨ emergency brake
⑦ gearshift   ⑧ rearview mirror   ⑩ seat belt
① steering wheel
② horn
③ dashboard
④ gas pedal
⑤ brake pedal
⑥ clutch

B Pair work Take turns identifying the car part for each definition.

1 a light at the back of the car
2 a light that indicates a turn
3 a part the driver uses to turn the car
4 a part that cleans the front window
5 a part that makes the car go faster
6 a part that keeps passengers safe during an accident
7 a light that helps the driver see the road
8 a place in the back for carrying things

GRAMMAR | *The past continuous*

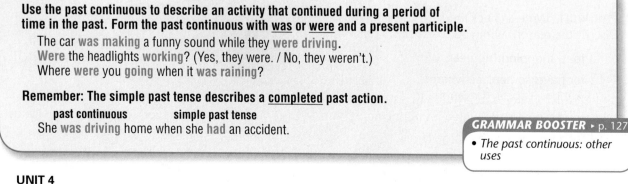

Use the past continuous to describe an activity that continued during a period of time in the past. Form the past continuous with <u>was</u> or <u>were</u> and a present participle.

The car **was making** a funny sound while they **were driving**.
Were the headlights **working**? (Yes, they were. / No, they weren't.)
Where **were** you **going** when it **was raining**?

Remember: The simple past tense describes a <u>completed</u> past action.

past continuous   simple past tense
She **was driving** home when she **had** an accident.

GRAMMAR BOOSTER ▸ p. 127

• *The past continuous: other uses*

A Grammar practice Complete the paragraph with the past continuous or the simple past tense.

I .... an accident yesterday. I .... slowly and I was
     1 have   2 drive
sure I .... attention. But I .... for a phone call. When
       3 pay   4 wait
the phone .... , I .... it. Suddenly, the car in front of me
              5 ring   6 answer
.... , and I .... it. I certainly ....
        7 stop   8 hit   9 learn
my lesson! Luckily, I .... a seat belt when I .... the accident.
                        10 wear   11 have

2:21
B 🔊 **Listening comprehension** Listen to the conversations about accidents.
Write the number of each conversation in the box under the picture.

□ □ □ □

CONVERSATION MODEL

2:22
A 🔊 Read and listen to a conversation about a car accident.

A: I had an accident.

B: I'm so sorry. Are you OK?

A: I'm fine. No one was hurt.

B: Thank goodness. How did it
happen?

A: Well, the other driver was tailgating,
and he hit my car.

B: Oh, no! Was there much damage?

A: No. I'll only have to replace a taillight.

2:24
🔊 **Ways to show concern**
I'm so sorry.
Oh, no!
How awful!
I'm sorry to hear that.
That's terrible.

2:23
B 🔊 **Rhythm and intonation** Listen again and repeat.
Then practice the Conversation Model with a partner.

NOW YOU CAN Describe a car accident

Pair work Change the Conversation Model
to role-play a new conversation. Describe
a car accident. Use the pictures, the past
continuous, and the simple past tense.

A: I had an accident.

B: .... Are you OK?

A: ....

B: .... How did it happen?

A: Well, ... , and ....

B: .... Was there much damage?

A: ....

Don't stop!
Ask about the location
of the accident and
other damage.

speeding

not paying attention

tailgating

talking on a cell phone

41

GOAL Report a problem with a car

VOCABULARY *Phrasal verbs for talking about cars*

A 🔊 2:25 Read and listen. Then listen again and repeat.

| turn on | turn off | pick up | fill up | drop off |

B Complete the sentences with the two parts of each phrasal verb.

1 The car's almost out of gas. Let's go in here so I can .... it ....

2 It's raining and I can't .... the windshield wipers .... They aren't working.

3 Do you have a van for this afternoon? I can .... it .... at 3:30.

4 We need to return the car before 6:00. Let's .... it .... early at the airport and get something to eat, OK?

5 I can't .... the air conditioning .... It's freezing in here!

GRAMMAR *Direct object placement with phrasal verbs*

Phrasal verbs contain a verb and a particle that together have their own meaning.

| main verb | particle | | |
| turn | + | on | = | start (a machine) |

Many phrasal verbs are separable. This means that a direct object noun can come before or after the particle. <u>Turn on</u>, <u>turn off</u>, <u>pick up</u>, <u>drop off</u>, and <u>fill up</u> are separable.

      direct object   direct object
I'll drop off the car. OR I'll drop the car off.

Be careful! If the direct object is a pronoun, it must come before the particle.
I'll drop **it** off. (NOT I'll ~~drop off it~~.)
Did you fill **them** up? (NOT Did you ~~fill up them~~?)
Where will they pick **us** up? (NOT Where will they ~~pick up us~~?)

> **GRAMMAR BOOSTER** ▸ p. 128
> • *Nouns and pronouns: review*

PRONUNCIATION *Stress of particles in phrasal verbs*

A 🔊 2:26 Stress changes when an object pronoun comes before the particle. Read and listen. Then listen again and repeat.

1 A: I'd like to pick up my car.
   B: OK. What time can you pick it up?

2 A: They need to drop off the keys.
   B: Great. When do they want to drop them off?

B Integrated practice Write statements or questions, placing the direct objects correctly. Then practice reading the sentences aloud with a partner. Use correct stress.

1 The taillights aren't working. (can't / I / on / them / turn) ....

2 They're expecting the car at 10:00. (off / drop / 10:00 / at / I'll / it) ....

3 It's too cold for air conditioning. (button / which / off / it / turns) .... ?

4 Thanks for fixing the car. (it / pick / what time / I / can / up) .... ?

5 The car is almost out of gas. (up / please / fill / it) ....

CONVERSATION MODEL

A 🔊 2:27 Read and listen to a conversation about car problems.

A: I'm dropping off my car.

B: Was everything OK?

A: Well, actually, the windshield wipers aren't working.

B: I'm sorry to hear that. Any other problems?

A: No. That's it.

B: Is the gas tank full?

A: Yes. I just filled it up.

B 🔊 2:28 **Rhythm and intonation** Listen again and repeat. Then practice the Conversation Model with a partner.

C Find the grammar Find and circle two direct objects in the Conversation Model.

NOW YOU CAN Report a problem with a car

A Notepadding Write one or more car parts for each possible car problem.

won't open / close: *the sunroof*
won't turn on / off:
(is / are) making a funny sound:
(isn't / aren't) working:

B Pair work Change the Conversation Model to role-play a new conversation. Report a problem with a car. Use your notepad for ideas. Then change partners, problems, and roles.

A: I'm dropping off my car.

B: Was everything OK?

A: Well, actually, ...

B: .... Any other problems?

A: ....

C Option Role-play a conversation in which you report an accident when you drop off the car. Describe the accident. Say what you were doing when you had the accident. Use the past continuous. Then change roles. Start like this:

A: I'm dropping off my car. I had an accident …

> ♻ **Be sure to recycle this language.**
>
> Oh, no!
> I'm so sorry.
> How awful!
> I'm sorry to hear that.
> Are you OK?
> Is the car OK?
> Thank goodness.
> How did it happen?
> Was there much damage?

GOAL   Rent a car

A Discussion Review the car types on page 38. For what kind of situations would someone rent each type of car? Explain your answers.

> " A compact car is good for driving in a big city. It is easier to park in a small parking space. "

B Pair work Read about each customer at a car rental agency. Choose the best type of car for each person. Discuss reasons with your partner.

1
Mr. Taylor is a businessman from Geneva, Switzerland, attending a business meeting in Kota Kinabalu, Malaysia. He doesn't have a lot of luggage. He only needs the car for local travel.

car type: ....
reason: ....

4
Ms. Móntez is a tourist from Veracruz, Mexico, visiting national parks and cities in the U.S. with her husband and their five children. They plan to do a lot of shopping.

car type: ....
reason: ....

2
Ms. Peres is a banker from Porto Alegre, Brazil. Her daughter is getting married in Puebla, Mexico. She wants to drive to Puebla from Mexico City with her husband and two other children for the wedding. They have a lot of clothes and presents for the wedding.

car type: ....
reason: ....

5
Dr. Sato is from Osaka, Japan. He's traveling to an international medical meeting in Buenos Aires, Argentina. He has to invite three doctors to dinner and after-dinner entertainment. He likes to drive.

car type: ....
reason: ....

3
Mr. Soo is a tourist from Seoul, Korea, visiting western Australia with his brother. They enjoy hiking and fishing, and they're planning a road trip through the Lake District. They plan to drive on some rough roads, so they want a car with four-wheel drive.

car type: ....
reason: ....

2:29

🔊 **Listen to summarize** Listen to the four phone conversations. Write a check if the caller rented a car. Then listen again. Write the reasons the other callers <u>didn't</u> rent a car.

☐ **1** ....

☐ **2** ....

☐ **3** ....

☐ **4** ....

A Notepadding Plan a trip for which you need a rental car.

Destination	Pickup date	Drop off date	Number of companions	Activities

B Pair work Role-play a phone call to a car rental agency. Rent a car for the trip you planned on your notepad. Choose one of the cars from Wheels Around the World rental agency. Ask about the rate. Discuss the trip and your needs. Then change roles.

♻ **Be sure to recycle this language.**

Agent	Caller
Hello. ___ Rental Agency. How can I help you?	I'd like to make a reservation.
When will you pick up / drop off the car?	I'm traveling with ___ .
Where will you drop off the car?	It's a business trip / vacation.
Please bring your (driver's license / credit card).	I have / don't have a lot of luggage.
	I'd like a (compact car).
	I'd rather have a (van).
	I need a car with (automatic / manual) transmission.

Wheels Around the World

Invocation SL
Daily Rate: US $60

Turbo
Daily Rate: US $90

Lexor 320i
Daily Rate: Inquire about price

Micro 220
Daily Rate: US $45

Sea Breeze
Daily Rate: US $75

Amigo
Daily Rate: US $70

Outing
Daily Rate: US $68

Overland
Daily Rate: US $80

GOAL Discuss good and bad driving

BEFORE YOU READ

A 🔊 2:30 **Vocabulary** • *Aggressive driving behavior* Read and listen. Then listen again and repeat.

stare   gesture   honk

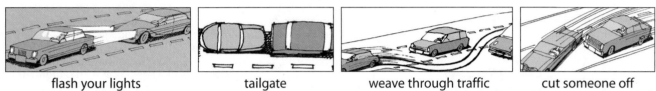

flash your lights   tailgate   weave through traffic   cut someone off

B **Warm-up** Which of the aggressive driving behaviors bother you the most? Which behaviors are the most dangerous? Why?

READING 🔊 2:31

FEATURE ARTICLE

Six Tips for Defensive Driving

We all know that not everyone drives well. Some people tailgate, gesture, weave through traffic, and honk— classic signs of the aggressive driving that causes one third of all car crashes. But more and more people are now talking on the phone, eating, and even watching TV as they drive— examples of the multitasking and inattentive driving that is a growing cause of accidents. Although we can't control the actions of other drivers, the following defensive driving tips can help us reduce the risks caused by our own driving and the bad driving of others.

1 **Slow down.** Driving too fast for weather or road conditions gives you less time to react to dangers on the road ahead of you. Also, as you increase your speed, your car becomes harder to control and takes longer to come to a stop.

2 **Follow the "3-second rule."** The greatest chance of a collision is in front of you. Maintaining a safe following distance of three seconds behind the car in front of you will give you enough time to react if that car slows or stops suddenly.

3 **Pay attention to your surroundings.** Be aware of where other vehicles are and what is happening on the road. Check your rearview and side-view mirrors frequently. Before changing lanes, always look over your shoulder to check your "blind spots"—areas to the side and rear of your car that aren't visible in your mirrors.

4 **Signal your intentions early.** Use turn signals to let other drivers know what you're going to do before you do it. This helps other drivers understand your plans, so they can make their own defensive driving decisions.

5 **Expect the unexpected.** Assume that other drivers will make mistakes. Plan ahead what you will do if another driver breaks a traffic law or cuts you off. For example, don't assume that a vehicle coming to a stop sign or a red light is going to stop. Be prepared to stop your own car if necessary.

6 **Don't take others' aggressive driving personally.** Other people will drive badly. They're not thinking about you. If you permit them to make you angry, it can affect your own driving and lead to an accident. When other drivers show signs of aggressive driving, just slow down or pull over to let them pass.

A Understand from context Circle the correct word or phrase to complete each statement.

1 A person who is doing more than one activity at the same time is (multitasking / driving defensively).

2 Following the "3-second rule" means maintaining a safe (road condition / following distance).

3 Tailgating, gesturing, and honking are three examples of (inattentive / aggressive) driving.

4 Not paying attention is an example of (inattentive / aggressive) driving.

5 *Collision* and *crash* are two words that mean (danger / accident).

6 A part of the road that you can't see in your mirrors is called a (blind spot / lane).

B Critical thinking How can defensive driving help drivers avoid accidents? Explain your opinion, using the Vocabulary and examples from the Reading or from your own experience.

> On your *ActiveBook* Self-Study Disc:
> **Extra Reading Comprehension Questions**

NOW YOU CAN | **Discuss good and bad driving**

A Pair work Complete the survey and then compare surveys with a partner. Do the same things bother you?

How does the driving behavior of others affect you?

Rate each behavior on a scale of 1 to 3.

- [ ] Tailgating to make others go faster or get out of the way
- [ ] Making rude gestures at others
- [ ] Honking excessively
- [ ] Staring angrily at other drivers
- [ ] Flashing lights to signal others to move to another lane
- [ ] Weaving in and out of traffic
- [ ] Driving too slowly
- [ ] Cutting other drivers off

1 = Doesn't bother me
2 = Annoys me
3 = Makes me very angry

Total your score.

If your score is...

▶ **20-24** Calm down. Don't take other people's bad driving personally. They're not thinking about you.

▶ **13-19** Stay focused. Don't allow bad drivers to distract you. Pay attention to your own driving instead.

▶ **8-12** Congratulations! You're as cool as a cucumber.

B Notepadding Make a list of good and bad driving behaviors.

Good drivers	Bad drivers
pay attention	flash their lights at others

C Discussion Discuss good and bad driving. Do you think most people are good drivers? Use your notepad for support.

> **Text-mining** (optional)
> Underline language in the Reading on page 46 to use in the Discussion. For example:
> "If the driver of another vehicle is ..."

Review

More Practice
ActiveBook *Self-Study Disc*

grammar · vocabulary · listening
reading · speaking · pronunciation

A 2:32 🔊 **Listening comprehension** Listen to the conversations. Then complete the statements with aggressive driving behavior vocabulary from page 46.

1 The other driver just .... them ....

2 Jim's mother says he's ....

3 The driver behind them is .... at them.

4 The driver opened his window and .... at them.

5 The driver is .... because he wants to pass.

6 The driver is ....

7 The driver is .... at them.

2:33/2:34
🎵 **Top Notch Pop**
"Wheels around the World"
Lyrics p. 149

B Read the definition. Write the name of the car part.

1 a window on the top of the car:
....

2 a part that stops the car: ....

3 a window the driver looks through to see the cars in front: ....

4 a place where the driver can find information about speed and amount of gas: ....

5 a part that people wear to avoid injuries in an accident: ....

6 a part that prevents the car from moving when it's parked: ....

C Complete each statement or question about driving. Use the past continuous or the simple past tense.

1 I ...., and I .... an accident.
        not pay attention   *have*

2 The other driver .... at the stop sign, and she .... a seat belt.
         not stop   *not wear*

3 He .... on a cell phone and his car .... my trunk.
      talk   *damage*

4 Who .... when the accident ....?
      drive   *occur*

5 Where .... they .... when they .... the accident?
           stand   *see*

D Complete each conversation, putting the phrasal verbs and objects in order.

1 A: Won't the car start?

   B: No, I / it / can't / turn / on ....

2 A: Do you need gas, sir?

   B: Yes. Please / up / fill / it ....

3 A: Hey, you haven't turned on your headlights.

   B: Oops. Thanks. I can't believe / I / forgot / turn / on / to / them ....

   ....

4 A: Can All Star Limo drive us to the airport?

   B: Yes. They / us / pick / will / up / at 5:30 ....

E Writing On a separate sheet of paper, write a short paragraph about the differences between good and bad drivers.

WRITING BOOSTER ▶ p. 142

• *Connecting words and sentences:* And, In addition, Furthermore, *and* Therefore
• *Guidance for Exercise E*

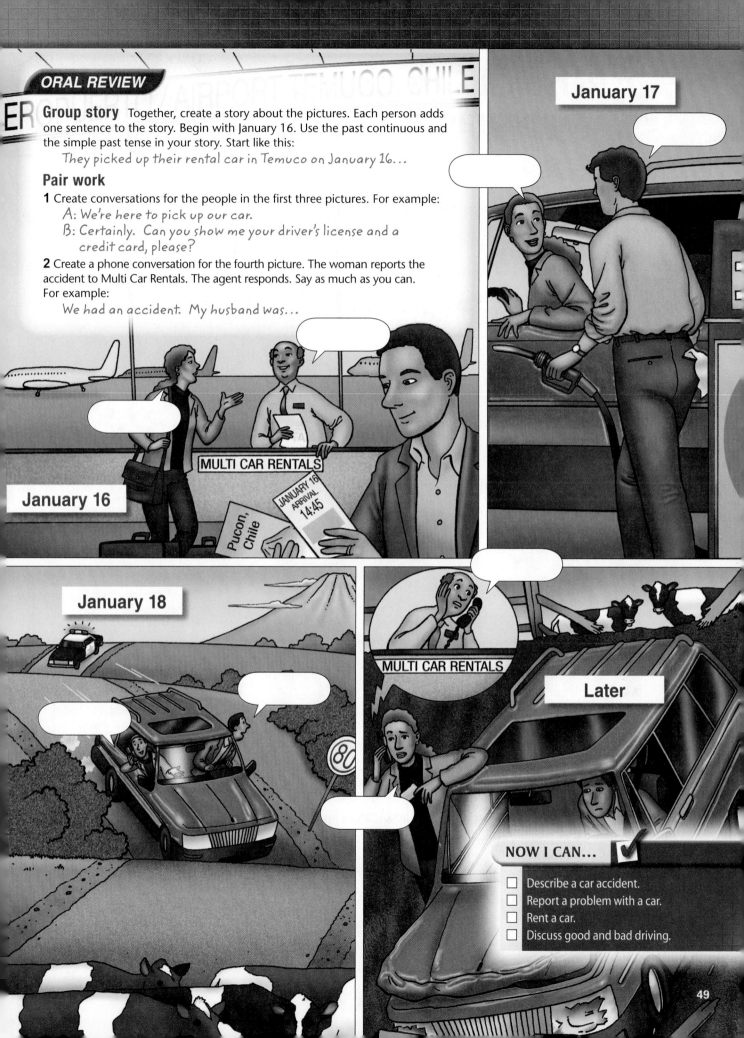

Group story Together, create a story about the pictures. Each person adds one sentence to the story. Begin with January 16. Use the past continuous and the simple past tense in your story. Start like this:

They picked up their rental car in Temuco on January 16...

Pair work

1 Create conversations for the people in the first three pictures. For example:

A: We're here to pick up our car.
B: Certainly. Can you show me your driver's license and a credit card, please?

2 Create a phone conversation for the fourth picture. The woman reports the accident to Multi Car Rentals. The agent responds. Say as much as you can. For example:

We had an accident. My husband was...

January 17

MULTI CAR RENTALS

JANUARY 16
ARRIVAL
14:45

Pucon, Chile

January 16

January 18

80

MULTI CAR RENTALS

Later

NOW I CAN... ✓

☐ Describe a car accident.
☐ Report a problem with a car.
☐ Rent a car.
☐ Discuss good and bad driving.

49

Personal Care and Appearance

GOALS | After Unit 5, you will be able to

1 Ask for something in a store.
2 Request salon services.
3 Discuss ways to improve appearance.
4 Define the meaning of beauty.

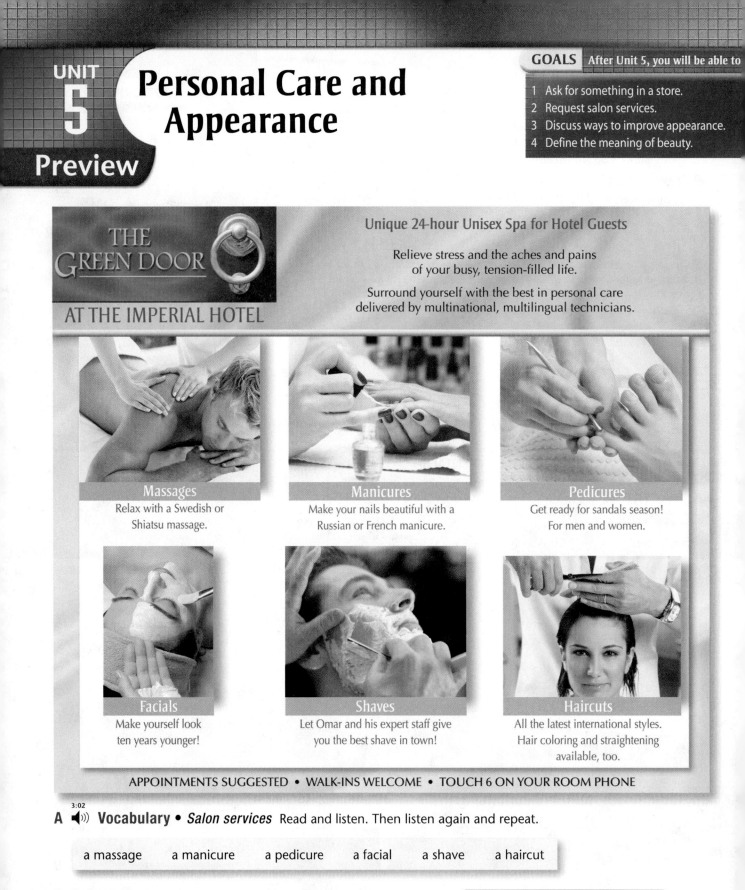

THE GREEN DOOR

AT THE IMPERIAL HOTEL

Unique 24-hour Unisex Spa for Hotel Guests

Relieve stress and the aches and pains of your busy, tension-filled life.

Surround yourself with the best in personal care delivered by multinational, multilingual technicians.

Massages
Relax with a Swedish or Shiatsu massage.

Manicures
Make your nails beautiful with a Russian or French manicure.

Pedicures
Get ready for sandals season! For men and women.

Facials
Make yourself look ten years younger!

Shaves
Let Omar and his expert staff give you the best shave in town!

Haircuts
All the latest international styles. Hair coloring and straightening available, too.

APPOINTMENTS SUGGESTED • WALK-INS WELCOME • TOUCH 6 ON YOUR ROOM PHONE

A ◀))) **Vocabulary • *Salon services*** Read and listen. Then listen again and repeat.
3:02

| a massage | a manicure | a pedicure | a facial | a shave | a haircut |

B Pair work Take turns asking questions about the salon services.

" What salon service should you get when your hair is too long? "

C 🔊 **Photo story** Read and listen to a conversation at a hotel salon.

ENGLISH FOR TODAY'S WORLD
connecting people from different cultures
and language backgrounds

Receptionist: Can I help you, sir?

Client: Would it be possible to get a massage? I don't have an appointment.

Receptionist: Well, actually, you're in luck. Our eleven o'clock just called to cancel his appointment.

Client: Terrific.

Receptionist: Let me show you to the dressing area.

Client: Thanks. Oh, while I'm at it, do you think I could get a haircut, too?

Receptionist: Yes. But you might have to wait a bit. We don't have anything until 12:00.

Client: Not a problem. By the way, how much will the massage and haircut come to? I don't have much cash on me.

Receptionist: Let's see, it will be 110 euros in all. But you can charge it to your room.

Client: Great. One more question. Is it customary to tip the staff?

Receptionist: Well, that's up to you. But most clients give the stylist and the masseuse a euro or two each.

Receptionist: French speaker

D **Focus on language** Answer the following questions, using language from the Photo Story.

1 How does the client ask for a massage?

2 How does the receptionist indicate that the client can have a massage without an appointment?

3 How does the client say "That's OK"?

4 How does the client ask about the price of a massage and a haircut?

5 What phrase does the receptionist use to tell the client the total cost of the salon services?

6 How does the receptionist tell the client that he doesn't have to pay until he checks out of the hotel?

7 What expression does the receptionist use to tell the client that the amount to tip is <u>his</u> decision?

E **Personalize** Check the word or phrase that best describes how often you get these salon services. Then compare charts with a partner.

	never	once in a while	monthly	weekly	too often to count
shampoo	☐	☐	☐	☐	☐
haircut	☐	☐	☐	☐	☐
facial	☐	☐	☐	☐	☐
shave	☐	☐	☐	☐	☐
manicure	☐	☐	☐	☐	☐
pedicure	☐	☐	☐	☐	☐
massage	☐	☐	☐	☐	☐

F **Pair work** In your opinion, what is the value of each of these services? Compare opinions with a partner.

❝ I think massages are great for backaches. A massage helps me feel better. ❞

❝ A shave? Are you kidding? I do that myself. I don't go to salons! ❞

GOAL   Ask for something in a store

VOCABULARY   Personal care products

A 🔊 3:04 Read and listen. Then listen again and repeat.

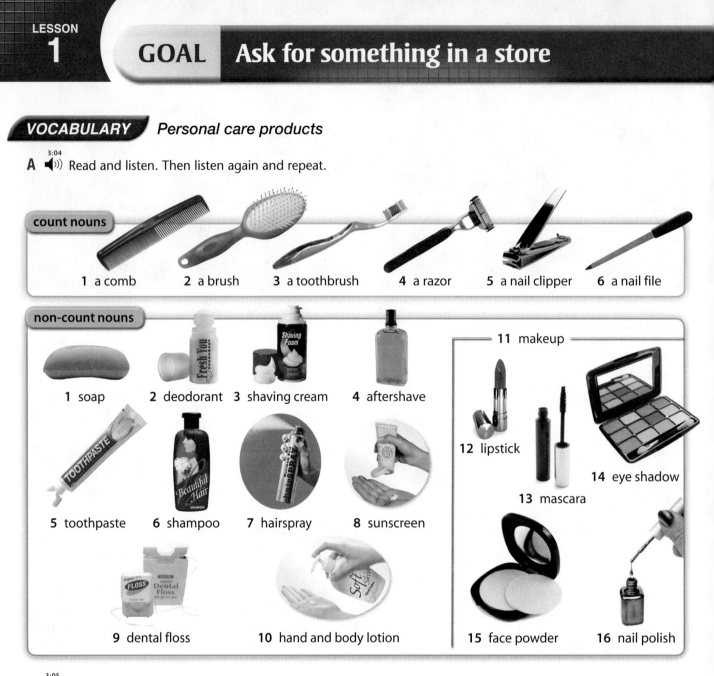

count nouns

1 a comb   2 a brush   3 a toothbrush   4 a razor   5 a nail clipper   6 a nail file

non-count nouns

1 soap   2 deodorant   3 shaving cream   4 aftershave

5 toothpaste   6 shampoo   7 hairspray   8 sunscreen

11 makeup
12 lipstick   13 mascara   14 eye shadow

9 dental floss   10 hand and body lotion   15 face powder   16 nail polish

B 🔊 3:05 **Listening comprehension** Listen and circle the kind of product each ad describes.

1 Spring Rain (shampoo / deodorant)
2 Rose (soap / nail polish)
3 Pro-Tect (sunscreen / hand and body lotion)
4 All Over (face powder / hand and body lotion)
5 Scrubbie (toothpaste / shaving cream)
6 Maximum Hold (hairspray / shampoo)

GRAMMAR   Quantifiers for indefinite quantities and amounts

Use some and any with both plural count nouns and non-count nouns.

some: affirmative statements
We bought some combs. Now we have some.
They need some soap. We have some.

any: negative statements
I don't have any razors. I don't want any.
We don't want any makeup. We don't need any.

some or any: questions
Do you want any aftershave? OR Do you want some aftershave?
Does she have any nail files? OR Does she have some nail files?

Use <u>a lot of</u> with both plural count nouns and non-count nouns in statements and questions.
That store has **a lot of** razors. / They don't have **a lot of** sunscreen. / Do they have **a lot of** makeup?

Use <u>many</u> and <u>much</u> in negative statements.

<u>many</u>: with plural count nouns
They don't have **many** brands of makeup.

<u>much</u>: with non-count nouns
The store doesn't have **much** toothpaste.

GRAMMAR BOOSTER ▸ p. 128
- *Some* and *any*: indefiniteness
- *Too many, too much,* and *enough*
- Comparative quantifiers *fewer* and *less*

Grammar practice Complete the conversation between a husband and wife packing for a trip.

Dana: Do we have (1 any / many) shampoo?

Neil: Yes. We have (2 many / a lot of) shampoo.

Dana: And Maggie uses (3 much / a lot of) sunscreen. Is there (4 many / any)?

Neil: No, there isn't (5 some / any). And we don't have (6 much / many) toothpaste, either. I can pick (7 some / any) up on my way back from work.

Dana: Hey, Adam's shaving now. Does he need (8 any / much) shaving cream?

Neil: He doesn't shave every day. He can use mine!

CONVERSATION MODEL

3:06

A 🔊)) Read and listen to someone looking for personal care products in a store.

A: Excuse me. Where would I find sunscreen?

B: Sunscreen? Have a look in the cosmetics section, in aisle 2.

A: Actually, I did and there wasn't any.

B: I'm sorry. Let me get you some from the back. Anything else?

A: Yes. I couldn't find any razors either.

B: No problem. There are some over there. I'll show you.

3:07

B 🔊)) **Rhythm and intonation** Listen again and repeat. Then practice the Conversation Model with a partner.

C **Find the grammar** Find and circle all the quantifiers in the Conversation Model.

NOW YOU CAN | Ask for something in a store

A Pair work Use the store directory to role-play a conversation. Change the Conversation Model, using other products and quantifiers. Then change roles.

A: Excuse me. Where would I find .... ?

B: .... ? Have a look in ....

A: Actually, I did and there .... any.

B: I'm sorry. Let me get you .... from the back. Anything else?

A: ....

B Change partners Change the kind of store and ask for other kinds of products.

Other products
- clothes
- food
- electronics

Cosmetics Plus

DIRECTORY

	Aisle
Hair Care	3
Tooth Care	4
Skin Care	2
Nail Care	2
Makeup	2
Shaving Supplies	1

GOAL   Request salon services

CONVERSATION MODEL

3:08

A 🔊 Read and listen to someone request salon services.

A: I'm Linda Court. I have a two o'clock appointment for a haircut with Sean.

B: Hello, Ms. Court. Sean's running a little late. Do you mind waiting?

A: Not at all. Can I get a manicure in the meantime?

B: Yes, but it'll be a few minutes. There's someone ahead of you.

3:09

B 🔊 **Rhythm and intonation** Listen again and repeat. Then practice the Conversation Model with a partner.

GRAMMAR   *Indefinite pronouns: someone / no one / anyone*

Someone, no one, and anyone are indefinite pronouns. Each refers to an unnamed person. Use indefinite pronouns when the identity of the person is unknown or unimportant.

Affirmative statements

There's { someone / no one } ahead of you.

{ Someone / No one } is waiting for the manicurist.

I saw **someone** at the front desk.

Negative statements

There isn't **anyone** waiting.
I didn't see **anyone** at the salon.

Questions

Can { anyone / someone } wash my hair?

Is there { anyone / someone } at the front desk?

Did you see { anyone / someone } waiting for a shave?

Be careful!
Use <u>anyone</u>, not <u>no one</u>, with the negative form of a verb.
DON'T SAY I didn't speak to ~~no one~~.

GRAMMAR BOOSTER ▸ p. 130

• *Indefinite pronouns: something, anything, and nothing*

3:10

A 🔊 **Listening comprehension** Listen to the conversations. Complete each statement with <u>someone</u> or <u>anyone</u> and the salon service(s).

1 They can't find .... to give her a .... this afternoon.

2 .... can give him a .... and a .... at 4:00.

3 There is .... who can give her a .... and a .... at 6:30.

4 There isn't .... who can give him a .... today.

B Grammar practice Complete each statement or question with <u>someone</u>, <u>no one</u>, or <u>anyone</u>. In some cases, more than one answer is correct.

1 There's *someone* (or *no one*) at the front desk.

2 They didn't tell .... it would be a long wait.

3 Did you see .... giving a manicure?

4 I don't have the nail file. I gave it to ....

5 There will be .... here to give you a pedicure in a few minutes.

6 .... can cut your hair at 12:30 if you can wait.

7 Please don't tell .... the price. It was very expensive!

8 .... called and left you this message while you were getting your shampoo.

9 Please give this list of services to .... to read.

10 There wasn't .... there when she called for an appointment.

11 I didn't speak to .... about the bad haircut.

12 .... told me the salon offers Shiatsu massage now.

13 I didn't ask .... about the price.

PRONUNCIATION *Pronunciation of unstressed vowels*

3:11

A 🔊 The vowel in an unstressed syllable is often pronounced /ə/. Read and listen, paying attention to the syllable or syllables marked with /ə/. Then listen again and repeat.

1 ma ssage
/ə/

2 fa cial
/ə/

3 ma ni cure
/ə/

4 pe di cure
/ə/

5 de o do rant
/ə/ /ə/

B Now practice saying the words on your own.

NOW YOU CAN **Request salon services**

A Pair work Create a conversation requesting salon services. Change the Conversation Model, using the services and staff at the Unisex Salon. Then change roles.

A: I'm .... I have .... appointment for .... with ....

B: Hello, ... running a little late. Do you mind waiting?

A: Not at all. Can I get a .... in the meantime?

B: ....

♻ **Be sure to recycle this language.**

Don't stop!
• Make an appointment for your next visit.
• Make an appointment for someone else.
• Change the ending.

I'd like to make an appointment for a — on — .
Is someone available on ___ ?
How much do you charge for a ___ ?

UNISEX SALON

Services   *Staff*

shampoo   *Lisa / Choi*

haircut   *Judy / Jun / Bruce*

manicure   *Sonia / Natasha*

pedicure   *Karin*

shave   *Nick*

facial   *Svetlana / Ella*

massage   *Vladimir / Edouard*

B Change partners Make appointments for other services.

GOAL | Discuss ways to improve appearance

BEFORE YOU READ

Predict Look at the photos and title of the article. What questions do you think the people will ask Dr. Weiss?

READING 3:12

Write a letter to Dr. Weiss:
The Daily Mail
1601 Carroll Mews
Munyville, NY 10544

Cosmetic surgery— for everyone?

Some people consider cosmetic surgery no more serious than visiting a spa or a salon. But others say, "I think I'll pass." They're aware that cosmetic surgery is, in fact, surgery, and surgery should never be taken lightly. Cosmetic surgeons have made great progress in repairing injuries and damage from burns. But more and more, people with the necessary financial resources have chosen cosmetic surgery to improve appearance. Fitness editor Dr. Gail Weiss answers readers' questions about cosmetic surgery.

BEFORE cosmetic surgery   **AFTER** cosmetic surgery

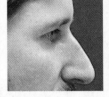

Dear Dr. Weiss:

When I was young, I was a chocoholic. I ate a lot of chocolate, but I never gained any weight. Now that I'm older, I can't eat anything without gaining weight! I've heard that liposuction is the answer to an overweight person's dreams. What's up with that?

Dawson

Dear Dawson:

It's true that liposuction can remove fat deposits that don't respond to dieting and exercise, but it's expensive and can be dangerous. It would be a good idea to ask your doctor for some help in dieting first. Then, if you are unsuccessful, be sure to find a surgeon with a lot of experience before deciding on liposuction.

Gail Weiss, M.D.

. . . .

Dear Dr. Weiss:

I'm a 24-year-old man who is already losing his hair. Dr. Weiss, I'm looking for a wife and I'm afraid no woman will want to marry a 25-year-old baldie! I need some advice.

Calvin

Dear Calvin:

There are several surgical procedures which a cosmetic surgeon can perform to help treat hair loss and restore hair for both men and women. But if that's not practical, remember that some of the world's most attractive men are bald!

Gail Weiss, M.D.

. . . .

Dear Dr. Weiss:

Can anyone help me with my problem? I have too much hair on my body and I'm sick and tired of shaving. It's so embarrassing!

Cassandra

Dear Cassandra:

Before you call a cosmetic surgeon for hair removal, try a depilatory cream. Depilatories are available in any drugstore, and they remove hair easily and safely in your own home. Why don't you give that a try first?

Gail Weiss, M.D.

. . . .

Dear Dr. Weiss:

I'm at my wits' end with my face. I have wrinkles and sun damage. I'm only 30 but I look 50. Do you think a face-lift is an option for me?

Josephine

Dear Josephine:

Both men and women of all ages request this popular and effective surgery. It lifts the face and the neck in one operation and has excellent results. But this is surgery, and afterwards you will have to stay home for a number of days. It takes time to recover. And you may have to do it again after a number of years. Before you decide to have a face-lift, ask your dermatologist or a cosmetic surgeon about a chemical peel. A chemical peel removes the top layer of skin and can improve the appearance of the skin without surgery. Compared to surgery, a half-hour visit to your dermatologist would be a piece of cake! Good luck!

Gail Weiss, M.D.

. . . .

Information Source: cosmeticsurgery.org

Confirm content and apply information Complete the chart with information from the article. Then, with a partner, give your own advice for each person.

On your *ActiveBook* Self-Study Disc:
Extra Reading Comprehension Questions

	Problem	Dr. Weiss's advice	Your advice
Dawson			
Calvin			
Cassandra			
Josephine			

NOW YOU CAN | Discuss ways to improve appearance

A Frame your ideas Take the opinion survey about ways to improve appearance.

How far would you go to improve your appearance?

Would you try...	definitely	maybe	probably not	absolutely not!
diet?	○	○	○	○
exercise?	○	○	○	○
massage?	○	○	○	○
creams and lotions?	○	○	○	○
hair removal?	○	○	○	○
hair restoration?	○	○	○	○
makeup?	○	○	○	○
facials?	○	○	○	○
face-lifts?	○	○	○	○
liposuction?	○	○	○	○
chemical peels?	○	○	○	○

B Notepadding Choose one method you would try and one method you would not try. On the notepad, write advantages and disadvantages.

Method	Advantage(s)	Disadvantage(s)
I would try diet.	free, safe	It's hard to do!

Method	Advantage(s)	Disadvantage(s)

Text-mining (optional)
Underline language in the Reading on page 56 to use in the Discussion. For example: "— has excellent results."

C Discussion What's the best way to improve your appearance? What ways would you NOT try? Explain. Use your notepad for support.

GOAL Define the meaning of beauty

A 🔊 3:13 **Vocabulary •** *Discussing beauty* Read and listen. Then listen again and repeat.

physical features: skin, hair, body shape and size, eyes, nose, mouth, etc.

beauty: having physical features most people of a particular culture consider good-looking

attractive: having a beautiful or pleasing physical or facial appearance

unattractive: the opposite of *attractive*

youth: the quality of being young; the opposite of *old age*

health: the general condition of one's body and how healthy one is

B **Explore your ideas** On a separate sheet of paper, describe the characteristics of an attractive woman and an attractive man:

> *An attractive woman has long hair and dark eyes.*

C **Pair work** Talk about the physical features you consider attractive for men and women. Use the Vocabulary and your ideas from exercise B.

> ❝In my opinion, an attractive woman has... ❞

A 🔊 3:14 **Listen to summarize** Listen to the interview. Check all of the statements that summarize Maya Prasad's and Ricardo Figueroa's ideas about beauty.

Maya Prasad

☐ I'm very lucky to be so beautiful.

☐ All the contestants were beautiful. I was just lucky.

☐ Physical beauty only lasts a short time.

☐ Love makes people beautiful.

Ricardo Figueroa

☐ Physical beauty is not important at all.

☐ Both physical beauty and inner beauty are important.

☐ Only inner beauty is important.

☐ Prasad represents an almost perfect combination of inner and outer beauty.

B 🔊 3:15 **Listen to take notes** Listen and take notes about what Figueroa says about each of the qualities below. Then compare your notes with the class.

warmth:	
patience:	
goodness and kindness:	

C Discussion Talk about one or more of the following questions.

1 In what ways do you agree or disagree with Prasad's and Figueroa's ideas about beauty?

2 Do you think the Miss World contest sounds better than the usual beauty contest? Why or why not?

3 Do you think there should be beauty contests for men as well as for women? Why or why not? What in your opinion is the difference between a woman's beauty and a man's beauty?

4 How do you explain these words in the song Prasad talks about: "Do you love me because I'm beautiful, or am I beautiful because you love me"?

NOW YOU CAN   Define the meaning of beauty

A Notepadding Look at the four photos. What qualities of beauty do you find in each person? Write notes.

1	Outer beauty	Inner beauty
	She has beautiful skin.	She looks warm and friendly.

1 Outer beauty

Inner beauty

2 Outer beauty

Inner beauty

3 Outer beauty

Inner beauty

4 Outer beauty

Inner beauty

B Pair work Discuss the qualities of beauty you found in the people in the pictures. Compare your opinions. Use your notepads for support.

C Discussion Define the meaning of beauty.

> ❝I think beauty is hard to describe. It's a combination of things. I consider my grandmother really beautiful because...❞

Review

More Practice
ActiveBook *Self-Study Disc*

grammar · vocabulary · listening
reading · speaking · pronunciation

A 3:16 ◄)) **Listening comprehension** Listen to the conversations. Infer what kind of product the people are discussing. Complete each statement.

1 Hawaii Bronzer is a brand of ....
2 Swan is a brand of ....
3 Truly You is a brand of ....
4 Mountain Fresh is a brand of ....
5 Silk 'n Satin is a brand of ....
6 Fresh as a Flower is a brand of ....

B Complete each statement or question.

1 There aren't (many / much) customers in the store right now.
2 Do they sell (any / many) sunscreen at the hotel gift shop? I forgot to pack some.
3 Your sister doesn't want (some / any) body lotion.
4 She doesn't wear (much / some) makeup. She doesn't need to—she has beautiful skin.
5 My son uses (any / a lot of) shaving cream.
6 There's (anyone / someone) on the phone for you. Do you want me to take a message?
7 There are (any / a lot of) salons in this neighborhood.

C Complete each statement about salon services.

1 There's nothing like a professional .... when you're sick and tired of your beard.
2 If your hair is too long, get a ....
3 If the skin on your face looks tired and dry, get a ....
4 In the summer, before you wear sandals for the first time, your feet will look great if you get a ....
5 When your hands are a mess, you can get a ....
6 When your muscles are sore from too much work or exercise, a .... can help.

D Complete each conversation in your own way.

1 A: Is it ....?
   B: That's up to you. Most people give about 10 percent of the bill to the hair stylist.

2 A: Would you ....?
   B: I think I'll pass. I don't have much cash on me.

3 A: How ....?
   B: The two together will come to about US $60. But you can charge it to your room.

4 A: Can I ....?
   B: Actually, you're in luck. We've just had a cancellation.

5 A: I have ....
   B: Oh, yes. Welcome. Olga can see you right away.

3:17/3:18
Top Notch Pop
"Piece of Cake"
Lyrics p. 149

E **Writing** Re-read the letters on page 56. Choose one letter and write a response, using your own opinion and making your own suggestions. Explain what you think is OK or appropriate for men and women.

WRITING BOOSTER ▸ p. 143
• Writing a formal letter
• Guidance for Exercise E

Contest Look at the picture for a minute, and then close your books. With a partner, try to remember all the products and services in the picture. The pair who remembers the most products and services wins.

Pair work

1 Create a conversation between the client and the clerk at the front desk of the hotel salon. Start like this:

Hi. I have a 2:30 appointment for ...

2 Create a conversation for the man and woman waiting for salon services. For example:

What are you here for?

NOW I CAN... ✔

☐ Ask for something in a store.
☐ Request salon services.
☐ Discuss ways to improve appearance.
☐ Define the meaning of beauty.

Eating Well

GOALS After Unit 6, you will be able to
1 Talk about food passions.
2 Make an excuse to decline food.
3 Discuss lifestyle changes.
4 Describe local dishes.

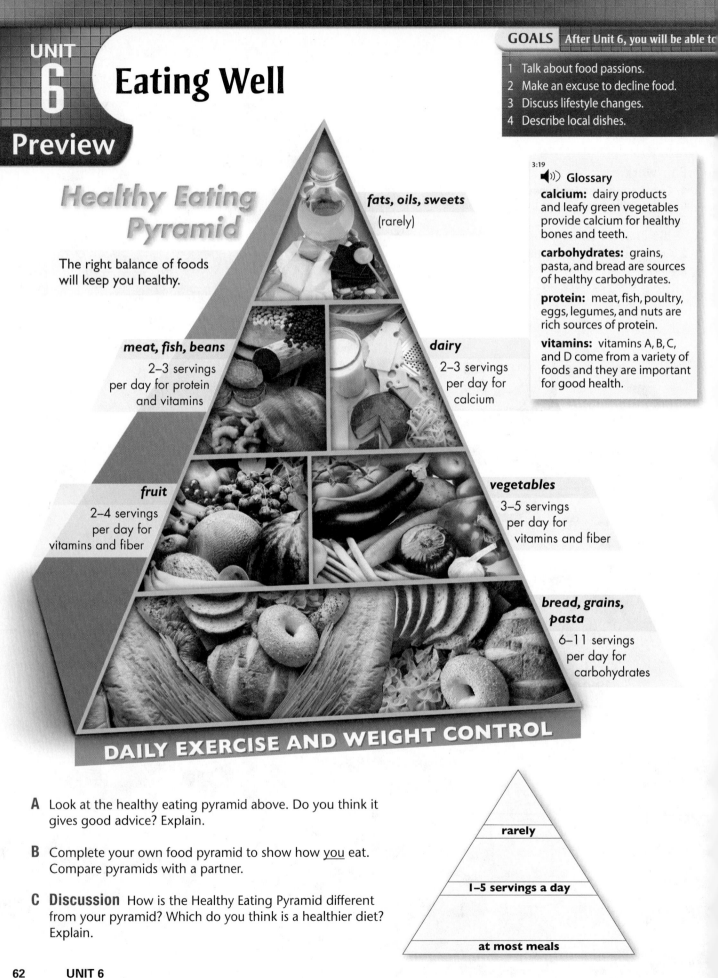

Healthy Eating Pyramid

The right balance of foods will keep you healthy.

fats, oils, sweets
(rarely)

meat, fish, beans
2–3 servings per day for protein and vitamins

dairy
2–3 servings per day for calcium

fruit
2–4 servings per day for vitamins and fiber

vegetables
3–5 servings per day for vitamins and fiber

bread, grains, pasta
6–11 servings per day for carbohydrates

DAILY EXERCISE AND WEIGHT CONTROL

3:19
🔊 **Glossary**

calcium: dairy products and leafy green vegetables provide calcium for healthy bones and teeth.

carbohydrates: grains, pasta, and bread are sources of healthy carbohydrates.

protein: meat, fish, poultry, eggs, legumes, and nuts are rich sources of protein.

vitamins: vitamins A, B, C, and D come from a variety of foods and they are important for good health.

A Look at the healthy eating pyramid above. Do you think it gives good advice? Explain.

B Complete your own food pyramid to show how you eat. Compare pyramids with a partner.

C **Discussion** How is the Healthy Eating Pyramid different from your pyramid? Which do you think is a healthier diet? Explain.

rarely

1–5 servings a day

at most meals

D 🔊 **Photo story** Read and listen to people talking about food choices.

Rita: Didn't you tell me you were avoiding sweets?

Joy: I couldn't resist! I had a craving for chocolate.

Rita: Well, I have to admit it looks pretty good. How many calories are in that thing anyway?

Joy: I have no idea. Want to try some?

Rita: Thanks. But I think I'd better pass. I'm avoiding carbs.*

Joy: You? I don't believe it. You never used to turn down chocolate!

Rita: I know. But I'm watching my weight now.

Joy: Come on! It's really good.

Rita: OK. Maybe just a bite.

Joy: Hey, you only live once!

*carbs (informal) = carbohydrates

E **Focus on language** Find an underlined sentence or phrase in the Photo Story with the same meaning as each of the following.

1 I don't know. ....
2 I should say no. ....
3 I couldn't stop myself. ....
4 I'm trying not to get heavier. ....

5 I really wanted . . . .
6 I agree. ....
7 say no to ....
8 I'll try a little. ....

F **Discussion** Read the descriptions of the diets. Would you ever try any of them? Why or why not?

The High-Fiber Diet

For maintaining better health, preventing disease, and watching weight. Eat anything you want. Be sure to consume 25 to 40 grams of fiber per day from grains, fruits, beans, and vegetables.

The Vegan Diet

For better health and prevention of disease. Avoid all animal products, including dairy and eggs. Eat lots of grains, beans, vegetables, and fruits.

The Atkins Diet

A high-protein, low-carbohydrate weight-loss diet. Eat foods such as meat, eggs, and cheese that are high in protein and fat. Avoid foods that are high in carbohydrates, such as starchy vegetables, bread, grains, sugar, and dairy products (except cheese, cream, and butter).

The Low-Fat Diet

For weight loss and the prevention of disease. Cut back fat to 20 to 30 percent of daily calories. Limit cholesterol in food to less than 300 mg per day (about the amount in one large egg).

I don't believe in the Atkins Diet. It has too much fat for me.

GOAL Talk about food passions

A 🔊 3:21 Read and listen. Then listen again and repeat.

I'm **crazy about** seafood.
I'm **a big** meat **eater**.
I'm **a big** coffee **drinker**.
I'm **a chocolate addict**.
I'm **a pizza lover**.

I **can't stand** fish.
I'm **not crazy about** chocolate.
I **don't care for** steak.
I'm **not much of a** pizza **eater**.
I'm **not much of a** coffee **drinker**.

B 🔊 3:22 **Listening comprehension** Circle the correct words to complete each statement about the speakers' food passions.

1 She (is crazy about / doesn't care for) sushi.

2 He (loves / can't stand) asparagus.

3 She (is a mango lover / doesn't care for mangoes).

4 He (is a big pasta eater / isn't crazy about pasta).

5 She (is an ice cream addict / can't stand ice cream).

sushi

mangoes

pasta

ice cream

asparagus

C Pair work Tell your partner about some of your food passions.

❝ I'm really a seafood lover, but I'm not crazy about clams. ❞

GRAMMAR _Use to / used to_

Be careful!
They **used** to … BUT ⎰ They didn't **use** to …
⎱ Did they **use** to …

Use <u>use to</u> and <u>used to</u> and the base form of a verb for habitual actions in the past that no longer occur.

I **used to be** crazy about candy, but now I don't care for it.
She **didn't use to eat** cheese, but now she has it all the time.

Did you **use to eat** a lot of fatty foods?   Yes, I did.   OR   Yes, I used to.
No, I didn't.   No, I didn't use to.

What **did** you **use to have** for breakfast? Eggs and sausage. But not anymore.
Why **did** you **use to eat** so much? Because I didn't use to worry about my health.

GRAMMAR BOOSTER ▸ p. 130

• _Use to / used to_: use and form, common errors
• _Be used to vs. get used to_
• Repeated actions in the past: _would_ + base form, common errors

Grammar practice Use the context to help you complete each sentence with <u>used to</u> or <u>didn't use to</u>. Then write two sentences about yourself.

1 Gary .... go out to eat a lot. But now he eats at home more often.

2 Nina .... eat a lot of pasta. But now she does.

3 Vinnie .... drink a lot of coffee. But now he's a coffee addict.

4 Anton .... eat a lot of vegetables. But now he doesn't.

5 Cate .... hate seafood. But now she's crazy about fish.

6 Ted .... eat a lot of fatty foods. But now he avoids them.

7 Burt .... drink a lot of water. But now he has several glasses a day.

8 May .... like salads. But now she has salads several times a week.

9 (used to) I ....
....

10 (didn't use to) I ....
....

PRONUNCIATION   *Sound reduction: <u>used to</u>*

3:23

🔊 Notice how the pronunciation of <u>to</u> in <u>used to</u> changes to /tə/. Read and listen. Then listen again and repeat. Then practice the sentences on your own.

1 I used to be a big meat eater.

2 Jack used to like sweets.

3 Sally used to be crazy about fries.

4 They didn't use to like seafood.

CONVERSATION MODEL

3:24

A 🔊 Read and listen to two people talk about their food passions.

A: Are you a big coffee drinker?

B: Definitely. I'm crazy about coffee. What about you?

A: I used to have it a lot. But I've been cutting back.

B: Well, I couldn't live without it.

3:25

B 🔊 **Rhythm and intonation** Listen again and repeat. Then practice the Conversation Model with a partner.

NOW YOU CAN   Talk about food passions

A **Notepadding** Complete the notepad with foods you like and dislike.

B **Pair work** Change the Conversation Model to role-play a conversation about food passions. Talk about foods and drinks you like and dislike. Talk about what you used to and didn't use to eat or drink. Start like this:

A: Are you a big ....?

B: .... What about you?

A: ....

C **Change partners** Change the Conversation Model again. Talk about other foods and drinks.

Foods I'm crazy about	Foods I can't stand

65

GOAL   **Make an excuse to decline food**

CONVERSATION MODEL

A 🔊 3:26 Read and listen to a dinner guest making an excuse to decline food.

A: Please help yourself.

B: Everything looks great! But I'll pass on the chicken.

A: Don't you eat chicken?

B: Actually, no. I'm a vegetarian.

A: I'm sorry. I didn't know that.

B: It's not a problem. I'll have something else.

B 🔊 3:27 **Rhythm and intonation** Listen again and repeat. Then practice the Conversation Model with a partner.

🔊 3:28 **Variations**
It's not a problem.
Don't worry.
I'm fine.

VOCABULARY   *Excuses for not eating something*

A 🔊 3:29 Read and listen. Then listen again and repeat.

Coffee **doesn't agree with me**.

I'm **on a diet**. /
I'm **trying to lose weight**.

I don't eat beef.
It's **against my religion**.

I'm **allergic to** chocolate.

I'm **avoiding** sugar.

I **don't care for** broccoli.

B 🔊 3:30 **Listening comprehension** Listen to each conversation. Write the letter to complete each statement. Then listen again to check your work.

.... **1** Cindy...   **a** is a vegetarian.

.... **2** Frankie...   **b** is avoiding fatty, salty foods.

.... **3** Marie...   **c** is trying to lose weight.

.... **4** Susan...   **d** is allergic to something.

.... **5** George...   **e** doesn't care for seafood.

C **Pair work** Talk about foods or drinks you avoid. Explain why.

> ❝ I usually don't eat fried foods. I'm trying to lose weight. ❞

Use negative <u>yes</u> / <u>no</u> questions ...

- **to confirm information you think is true.**
  Isn't Jane a vegetarian? (Yes, she is.)
  Didn't he go on a diet last week? (Yes, but he changed his mind.)

- **when you want someone to agree with you.**
  Don't you love Italian food? (Yes, it's delicious!)
  Wasn't that a terrible dinner? (Actually, no. I thought it was good.)

- **to express surprise.**
  Aren't you going to have cake? (I'm sorry. I'm on a diet.)
  Hasn't he tried the chicken? (No. He's a vegetarian.)

Use <u>Why don't</u> ...? to make an offer or a suggestion.
<u>Why don't we</u> ...? has the same meaning as <u>Let's</u>.
Why don't you have some more tea? (Thanks.)
Why don't we sit down? (Great idea.)

> **GRAMMAR BOOSTER** ▶ p. 132
> - *Negative <u>yes</u> / <u>no</u> questions: short answers*
> - *Suggestions with <u>Why don't</u> ... ?: expansion*

Grammar practice Complete each negative <u>yes</u> / <u>no</u> question.

1 A: .... you allergic to tomatoes?
   B: Me? No. You're thinking of my brother.

2 A: .... that lunch yesterday delicious?
   B: It was fantastic!

3 A: .... we already have steak this week?
   B: Yes, we did.

4 A: .... your husband been on a diet?
   B: Yes. But it's been driving him crazy.

5 A: .... asparagus disgusting?
   B: Actually, I like it.

6 A: .... you like your pasta?
   B: Actually, it was a little too spicy for me.

NOW YOU CAN **Make an excuse to decline food**

A Notepadding Look at the photos. On a separate sheet of paper, use the Vocabulary to write an excuse to decline each food.

B Pair work Change the Conversation Model to role-play a dinner conversation. Use the pictures and your notepads. Offer foods. Make excuses to decline the foods. Then change roles.

A: Please help yourself.

B: Everything looks .... ! But I'll pass on the ....

A: Don't you ....?

B: Actually, ...

A: I'm sorry. I didn't know that.

B: .... I'll have ....

> **Don't stop!**
> Offer other foods. Talk about food passions.

♻ **Be sure to recycle this language.**

be crazy about ___	can't stand ___
be a big ___ eater / drinker	be not crazy about ___
be a(n) ___ addict / lover	not care for ___

C Change partners Practice the conversation again.

shellfish

chocolate

tofu

steak

fries

noodles

sardines

BEFORE YOU READ

Explore your ideas Do you think people's eating habits are better or worse than they used to be? Explain with examples.

READING 3:31

How Can It Be? Americans Gain Weight, While the French Stay Thin

Have you ever wondered why Americans struggle with watching their weight, while the French, who consume all that rich food—the bread, the cheese, the wine, and the heavy sauces—continue to stay thin? Now a report from Cornell University suggests a possible answer. A study of almost 300 participants from France and the U.S. provides clues about how lifestyle and decisions about eating may affect weight. Researchers concluded that the French tend to stop eating when they feel full. However, Americans tend to stop when their plate is completely empty or they have reached the end of their favorite TV show. As a matter of fact, Americans are taught from an early age to "clean their plates" because children in poorer countries "are going hungry."

According to Dr. Joseph Mercola, who writes extensively about health issues, the French see eating as an important part of their lifestyle. They enjoy food and therefore spend a fairly long time at the table. In contrast, Americans see eating as something to do quickly as they squeeze meals between the other activities of the day. Mercola believes Americans have lost the ability to sense when they are actually full. So they keep eating long after the French would have stopped. In addition, he points out that Americans drive their cars to huge supermarkets to buy canned and frozen foods for the week, while the French tend to shop daily, walking to small shops and farmers' markets where they have a choice of fresh fruits, vegetables, and eggs as well as high-quality meats and cheeses for each meal.

Mireille Guiliano, author of *French Women Don't Get Fat*, decided to write about the subject after discovering she had gained weight after a visit to the U.S. Rather than suggesting how to avoid food, she writes about the importance of "restraint"—knowing when to stop. Today she continues to stay slim. And she rarely goes to the gym.

Despite all these differences, new reports show that recent lifestyle changes may be affecting French eating habits. Today the rate of obesity—or extreme overweight—among adults is only 6%. However, as American fast-food restaurants gain acceptance and the young turn their backs on older traditions, the obesity rate among French children has reached 17%—and is growing.

Sources: sciencedaily.com and mercola.com

A **Understand from context** With a partner, use the context of the article to help you define each of the following underlined words or phrases.

1 Why do Americans <u>struggle with</u> watching their weight?

2 The French <u>consume</u> all that rich food.

3 The French see eating as an important part of their <u>lifestyle</u>.

4 Americans are taught from an early age to "<u>clean their plates</u>."

5 Americans have lost the ability to <u>sense</u> when they are actually full.

6 Guliano writes about the importance of <u>restraint</u>.

7 Today she continues to stay <u>slim</u>.

8 The rate of <u>obesity</u> among French children has reached 17 percent.

B Summarize According to the article, why do the French stay slim while Americans gain weight? On a separate sheet of paper, write a four-sentence summary of the Reading. Then share your summary with your class.

> Compared to Americans, the French stay slim because …

C Compare and contrast In your country, do people generally stay slim easily or do they struggle with watching their weight? Are lifestyles in your country closer to those of France or the U.S., as described in the article?

> **"** I think people here are more like people in France. They like to eat, but they don't gain weight easily. **"**

On your *ActiveBook* Self-Study Disc:
Extra Reading Comprehension Questions

NOW YOU CAN Discuss lifestyle changes

A Frame your ideas Complete the lifestyle self-assessment.

1 Have you ever changed the way you eat in order to lose weight? ● yes ● no

If so, what have you done?
- ○ ate less food
- ○ cut back on desserts
- ○ avoided fatty foods
- ○ other (explain) _____

Were you successful? ○ yes ○ no
Why or why not? Explain _____
_____

2 Have you ever changed the way you eat in order to avoid illness? ● yes ● no

If so, what changes have you made?
- ○ stopped eating fast foods
- ○ started eating whole grains
- ○ started eating more vegetables
- ○ other (explain) _____

Were you successful? ○ yes ○ no
Why or why not? Explain _____
_____

3 Have you ever tried to lead a more active lifestyle? ● yes ● no

If so, what have you done?
- ○ started working out in a gym
- ○ started running or walking
- ○ started playing sports
- ○ other (explain) _____

Were you successful? ○ yes ○ no
Why or why not? Explain _____
_____

B Class survey On the board, summarize your class's lifestyles.

How many students …
- are there in the class?
- want to make some lifestyle changes?
- have gone on a diet to lose weight?
- have changed their diet to avoid illness?
- have been successful with a diet?
- lead an active lifestyle?

C Discussion How do you think your classmates compare to most people in your country? Are they generally healthier or less healthy? What do you think people need to do to have a healthy lifestyle?

> **"** I think my classmates are healthier than most people in this country. I think people eat too many fast foods, but most of us try not to. **"**

Text-mining (optional)
Underline language in the Reading on page 68 to use in the Discussion. For example:
"(The French) tend to …"

GOAL **Describe local dishes**

BEFORE YOU LISTEN

A 🔊 3:32 **Vocabulary • *Food descriptions*** Read and listen. Then listen again and repeat.

It **looks** terrific.

It **smells** terrible.

It tastes
- sweet.
- spicy.
- salty.
- sour.

It **smells like**
It **tastes like** } chicken.
It **looks like**

It's { soft.
hard.

It's { chewy.
crunchy.

B **Pair work** Use the Vocabulary to describe foods you know.

❝ Apples are crunchy. ❞

LISTENING COMPREHENSION

kim chee / Korea

cabbage

A 🔊 3:33 **Listen for details** First, listen to the descriptions of foods from around the world and write the letter of each food. Then listen again and choose the Vocabulary that completes each description.

...*a*... **1** They're (crunchy / chewy / hard) and they taste (salty / sweet / spicy).

.... **2** It tastes (salty / sweet / spicy) and it's (soft / hard / crunchy).

.... **3** It's (soft / chewy / crunchy) and it tastes (salty / sweet / spicy).

.... **4** It tastes (salty / sweet / spicy). Some think it (tastes / smells / looks) awful.

.... **5** It (smells / tastes / looks) great and it (smells / tastes / looks) awful.

.... **6** It's (crunchy / chewy / hard) and it tastes (salty / sweet / sour).

Vegemite / Australia

chapulines / Mexico

grasshopper

cho dofu / China

mochi / Japan

Jell-O / United States

B 🔊 3:34 **Listen to personalize** Listen again. After each food, discuss with a partner whether you would like to try that food. Explain why or why not.

NOW YOU CAN   Describe local dishes

A Frame your ideas Choose three local dishes that you would recommend to a visitor to your country. Write notes about each.

Name of dish:
fried cheese balls

Description:
salty, chewy

What's in it?
cheese, flour, oil

Name of dish:

Description:

What's in it?

Name of dish:

Description:

What's in it?

Name of dish:

Description:

What's in it?

B Pair work Role-play a conversation in which one of you is a visitor to your country. Ask questions and describe dishes. For example:

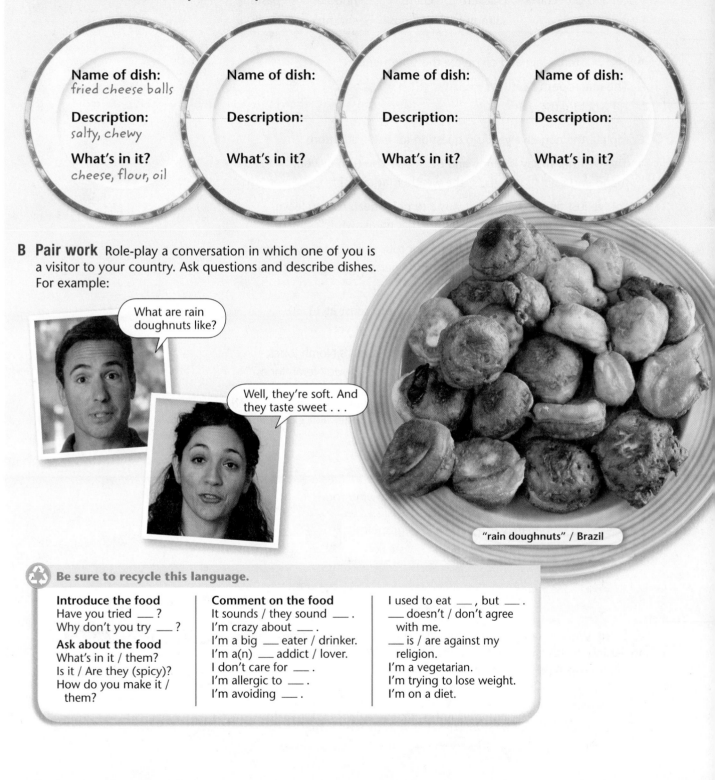

What are rain doughnuts like?

Well, they're soft. And they taste sweet . . .

"rain doughnuts" / Brazil

♻ **Be sure to recycle this language.**

Introduce the food
Have you tried ___ ?
Why don't you try ___ ?

Ask about the food
What's in it / them?
Is it / Are they (spicy)?
How do you make it / them?

Comment on the food
It sounds / they sound ___ .
I'm crazy about ___ .
I'm a big ___ eater / drinker.
I'm a(n) ___ addict / lover.
I don't care for ___ .
I'm allergic to ___ .
I'm avoiding ___ .

I used to eat ___ , but ___ .
___ doesn't / don't agree with me.
___ is / are against my religion.
I'm a vegetarian.
I'm trying to lose weight.
I'm on a diet.

More Practice

ActiveBook *Self-Study Disc*

grammar · vocabulary · listening
reading · speaking · pronunciation

3:35

A ◀))) **Listening comprehension** Listen to the conversation in a restaurant. Cross out the foods that the speakers don't mention.

beef and broccoli	chicken	clams	noodles	pasta
pizza	salmon	scallops	shrimp	steak

3:36

B ◀))) Now listen again and complete the statements.

The man doesn't care for ....

He would rather eat ....

C Complete the negative <u>yes</u> / <u>no</u> question for each situation.

1 The weather today is sunny and beautiful. You turn to your friend and say: "............... the weather fantastic?"

2 You've just finished dinner. It was a terrible meal. As you leave, you say to your friend: "............... that meal awful?"

3 You're sightseeing in China. From your tour bus window you see a long wall in the distance. You say to the person sitting next to you: "............... that the Great Wall?"

4 You're surprised to see your friend eating breakfast at 11:30. You say: "............... you .... breakfast yet?"

5 You see a woman on the street. You're pretty sure it's Norah Jones, the singer. You go up to her and ask: "............... you Norah Jones?"

D On a separate sheet of paper, write five sentences about things you used to or didn't use to do or think when you were younger. For example:

> *I didn't use to like coffee when I was younger.*

3:37/3:38

Top Notch Pop
"A Perfect Dish"
Lyrics p. 150

E On a separate sheet of paper, describe the following foods.

apples	bananas	carrots	grapefruit
ice cream	onions	squid	steak

> *Carrots are orange and they're sweet and crunchy.*

F **Writing** Write a paragraph on the following topic: Do you think people are eating healthier or less healthy foods than they used to? Give examples to support your opinion.

> *I think people are eating a lot of unhealthy foods today.*
>
> *People used to eat a lot of fresh foods. However, lately…*

WRITING BOOSTER ► p. 144

• *Connecting ideas: subordinating conjunctions*
• *Guidance for Exercise F*

International Buffet

Today's Selections

PAD THAI • Thailand

Ingredients: rice noodles, tofu, peanuts, fish sauce, sugar, lime juice, vegetable oil, garlic, shrimp, eggs, hot peppers

BI BIM BOP • Korea

Ingredients: rice, beef, soy sauce, sesame oil, garlic, black pepper, salt, eggs, lettuce, rice wine, hot peppers

CHICKEN MOLE • Mexico

Ingredients: chicken, salt, vegetable oil, onions, garlic, tomatoes, chocolate, hot peppers

POTATO SOUP • Colombia

Ingredients: chicken, three kinds of potatoes, corn, avocados

TABOULEH SALAD • Lebanon

Ingredients: parsley, mint, onions, tomatoes, salt, black pepper, cracked wheat, lemon juice, olive oil

POT STICKERS • China

Ingredients: flour, cabbage, pork, green onions, sesame oil, salt

STUFFED ROCOTO PEPPERS • Peru

Ingredients: onions, garlic, ground beef, hard-boiled eggs, raisins, cheese, rocoto peppers, vegetable oil

ORAL REVIEW

Challenge Choose one dish and study the photo and the ingredients for one minute. Then close your book. Describe the dish.

Pair work

1 Create a conversation for the man and woman in which they look at the foods and talk about their food passions. For example:

Have you tried pad Thai? It's terrific!

2 Create a conversation in which the man or the woman suggests and offers foods. The other makes excuses. Start like this:

A: Would you like some ___ ?
B: Actually, ___ .

3 Choose a dish and create a conversation between someone from that country and a visitor. For example:

Have you ever tried ___ ?

NOW I CAN...

- [ ] Talk about food passions.
- [ ] Make an excuse to decline food.
- [ ] Discuss lifestyle changes.
- [ ] Describe local dishes.

73

About Personality

GOALS After Unit 7, you will be able to
1 Get to know what someone likes.
2 Cheer someone up.
3 Discuss personality and its origin.
4 Examine the impact of birth order.

The Psychology of Color

According to research, colors have a powerful effect on us. Take the test and then see if your answers are confirmed by the research. You may be surprised! (Check your answers below.)

1) What color is the most attention-getting?

● black   ○ yellow   ● red   ○ other

2) What color is most likely to make people feel angry?

● black   ○ yellow   ● pink   ○ other

3) What color is best for a hospital room?

○ pink   ○ white   ● green   ○ other

4) What color often makes people feel tired?

○ green   ● blue   ○ pink   ○ other

5) What is the least appealing color for food?

● black   ○ yellow   ● blue   ○ other

What are your color preferences?
Look at the colors below.

golden brown · dark blue · white
pink-orange · tomato red · emerald green · dark gray
light blue

Write the color you find the most appealing. [   ]

Write the color you would most associate with happiness. [   ]

Write the color you would most associate with being sad. [   ]

Answers

1) Experts say red attracts the most attention. Using red for traffic lights and warning lights makes them more noticeable.
2) Studies have shown that being in a yellow room makes it more likely for adults to lose their tempers and for babies to cry.
3) Green is the easiest color on the eye, and it causes people to relax. Painting a hospital room green helps patients get the rest they need.
4) Research has shown that looking at pink can cause people to feel tired. Some sports teams have painted the dressing room of the opposing team pink to reduce the players' energy.
5) Researchers in marketing have found that using blue in processed foods is unappealing. They believe that this is because blue is rare in nature. Painting a restaurant red, on the other hand, increases the appetite. Many restaurants are painted red.

A Class survey Which color was the most popular in your class? Which was the least popular?

B Discussion In your opinion, what makes people like some colors and dislike others?

❝ I think people like colors that remind them of things they like. ❞

❝ I agree. I love blue. It reminds me of the sky. I love being outdoors. ❞

C 🔊 **Photo story** Read and listen to a couple talking about what color to repaint their living room.

Later that day

Chelsea: You know what? I'm getting a little tired of looking at this wallpaper.

Chad: Well, maybe it's time for a change. What would you think about getting the room painted? I never loved that wallpaper, anyway.

Chelsea: Actually, I don't think either of us did. We only got it because we couldn't agree on a paint color.

Chad: Oh, yeah. Now I remember. You wanted pink and I said it was too feminine.

Chelsea: Actually, I never thought it was pink. To me it was a soft rose.

Chad: Well, what would you say to a nice blue?

Chelsea: Blue? *Way* too masculine.

Chad: *What?!*

Chelsea: I'm just pulling your leg, silly! Blue would be great.

Chad: This one's nice—very relaxing.

Chelsea: True, but I'm not sure the furniture would go with it.

Chad: Good point. I'd hate to have to get all new stuff ... You know, maybe we're on the wrong track.

Chelsea: What do you mean?

Chad: All of a sudden, I'm thinking white. It's classic, and ...

Chelsea: And it goes with everything!

D Paraphrase Restate the following expressions from the Photo Story in your own way.

1 "I'm just pulling your leg."

2 "I'm not sure the furniture would go with it."

3 "Good point."

4 "Maybe we're on the wrong track."

E Think and explain All the following statements are false. Explain how you know they are false.

1 Chelsea still likes the wallpaper.

> 66 Chelsea says, 'I'm getting a little tired of looking at this wallpaper.' 99

2 Chelsea didn't want a rose-colored living room.

3 Chelsea truly thinks that blue is too masculine.

4 Chelsea thinks the blue Chad likes would go nicely with the furniture.

5 Chad would like to buy new furniture.

6 It's Chelsea's idea to paint the living room white.

7 They agree the furniture wouldn't go with white.

F Pair work Choose colors for rooms in a house. Review the color test on page 74 and the Photo Story to prepare your ideas. Then compare charts with a partner. Do you have the same tastes?

Room	Color	Your reason
a bedroom for a married couple		
a bedroom for a teenaged girl		
a bedroom for a 10-year-old boy		
a kitchen		
a family living room		

GOAL	Get to know what someone likes

GRAMMAR *Gerunds and infinitives as direct objects*

> **Remember two other -ing forms:**
> She is **painting.** (present participle)
> The trip was **relaxing.** (participial adjective)

Gerunds and infinitives come from verb forms but function as nouns. A gerund or an infinitive can be a direct object of a verb.

> **Gerund = an -ing form of a verb**
> She enjoys **painting.**
>
> **Infinitive = to + a base form**
> He wants **to paint** the kitchen yellow.

Use a gerund after the following verbs: avoid, discuss, dislike, don't mind, enjoy, feel like, practice, quit, suggest

Use an infinitive after the following verbs: agree, be sure, choose, decide, expect, hope, learn, need, plan, seem, want, wish, would like

Other verbs can be followed by either a gerund or an infinitive: begin, can't stand, continue, hate, like, love, prefer, start

> **GRAMMAR BOOSTER** ▸ p. 133
> • *Gerunds and infinitives: other functions*

A Grammar practice Complete the advice about managing feelings, using the verbs plus gerund or infinitive direct objects.

Feeling blue? Then take care of yourself!

Everybody feels a little sad from time to time. If you _____
(1 not feel like / talk)
about what is making you unhappy and you _____ advice books,
(2 dislike / read)
here are some helpful hints. First of all, _____ your health.
(3 decide / take care of)
_____ coffee and alcohol. Coffee especially can make you feel nervous,
(4 Avoid / drink)
but exercise can reduce nervousness and calm you. If you _____,
(5 choose / exercise)
I _____ with a friend you _____ time with.
(6 suggest / go)   (7 enjoy / spend)
_____ right and, importantly, _____ lots of sleep. If
(8 Be sure / eat)   (9 be sure / get)
you _____ a day off from work and you _____ to the
(10 would like / take)   (11 want / go)
movies or _____ a walk in the park, just do it. Everybody needs to take
(12 plan / take)
a break sometimes. And when life gets too depressing, _____ yourself
(13 learn / cheer)
up. You can be your own best friend! Oh, and a final note: Everybody finds certain
colors "happy." Try to wear the colors *you* find most cheerful.

B Find the grammar Find all the gerunds and infinitives in the "Answers" box of the color test on page 74.

PRONUNCIATION *Reduction of to in infinitives*

4:03
🔊)) Notice how an unstressed **to** reduces to /tə/. Read and listen. Then listen again and repeat.

1 I decided to repaint the bedroom a happier color.

2 We plan to see the World Cup Finals.

3 She doesn't like to hear people talking on cell phones.

4 I know you'd like to choose a more cheerful color.

CONVERSATION MODEL

A 🔊 4:04 Read and listen to a conversation about likes and dislikes.

A: So tell me something about yourself.

B: What would you like to know?

A: Well, for example, what do you like doing in your free time?

B: Let's see. Most of all, I enjoy playing tennis. I find it relaxing. What about you?

A: Well, I find tennis a little boring. But I <u>do</u> love going to the movies.

B: So do I. We should go to the movies together sometime, then.

B 🔊 4:05 **Rhythm and intonation** Listen again and repeat. Then practice the Conversation Model with a partner.

🔊 4:06 **Positive adjectives**
relaxing
enjoyable
exciting

🔊 4:07 **Negative adjectives**
boring
depressing
annoying
scary

NOW YOU CAN Get to know what someone likes

A Notepadding List your likes and dislikes in gerund form. Write a statement with "It's..." to say why.

Likes	Dislikes
skiing: It's exciting.	not getting enough sleep: It's awful.

Likes	Dislikes

B Pair work Using your notepad, personalize the Conversation Model. Include gerund and infinitive direct objects. Ask about other times and occasions.

A: So tell me something about yourself.

B: What would you like to know?

A: Well, for example, what do you like doing ....?

B: Let's see. Most of all, I enjoy .... I find it .... What about you?

A: Well, I ....

B: ....

C Change partners Talk about other likes and dislikes.

Other times and occasions
• on weekends
• on vacations
• with your friends / family
• for lunch / dinner

Don't stop!
Ask about your partner's plans for this weekend. Use the following verbs with direct object infinitives:

need   want
plan   would like

For example:
"What do you **plan to do** this weekend?"

LESSON 2

GOAL **Cheer someone up**

CONVERSATION MODEL

A ◀))) 4:08 Read and listen to someone trying to cheer a friend up.

A: You look down. What's up?

B: Oh, nothing serious. I'm just tired of the same old grind. But thanks for asking.

A: I know what you mean. I'm tired of working, too. How about going to a movie?

B: Great idea. Let's go!

B ◀))) 4:09 **Rhythm and intonation** Listen again and repeat. Then practice the Conversation Model with a partner.

GRAMMAR *Gerunds as objects of prepositions*

A gerund (-ing form of a verb) can function as an object of a preposition.

	preposition	object
I'm afraid	of	flying.
She's bored	with	cooking.
She objects	to	discussing her feelings.

Be careful! Don't use an infinitive as the object of a preposition.
Don't say: Let's go to a movie instead ~~of to watch~~ TV.

Expressions followed by gerunds

Adjective + preposition

angry about	afraid of
excited about	sick / tired of
depressed about	bored with
happy / sad about	

Verb + preposition

complain about	apologize for
talk about	believe in
worry about	object to
think about	

GRAMMAR BOOSTER ▸ p. 133

• Negative gerunds

A Grammar Practice Complete the descriptions with prepositions and gerunds.

Ted

Ted is an extrovert. Like most extroverts, he's direct. And he's honest; he believes .... the truth to everyone.
1 tell

At his job, he works with other people and he never complains .... long hours. He works hard and doesn't worry .... work on weekends or holidays.
2 work
3 have to

He has a few fears, though. Most of all, he's afraid ....
4 fly

Nicole

Ted's wife, Nicole, on the other hand, is an introvert. But she doesn't object .... about herself from time to time.

5 talk

Right now, she's bored .... a student, and she's sick and tired

6 be

.... so many long reports and

7 write

.... exams every few weeks!

8 take

She's angry .... spend

9 have to

so much time in front of a computer.

However, unlike Ted, she's not at all afraid ....! She's

10 fly

excited .... on

11 go

vacation.

B Pair work Answer the questions about yourself, using gerunds. Then share the information with a partner.

> " Right now, I'm happy about getting engaged! "

Right now, what are you...	
happy about?	
excited about?	
bored with?	
sick and tired of?	

NOW YOU CAN   Cheer someone up

A Notepadding Make a list of things that you are tired of. Write them as gerunds.

What are you tired of?
studying so hard

B Pair work Role-play cheering someone up. Use your partner's list for ideas. Then change roles.

A: You look down. What's up?

B: Oh, nothing serious. I'm just tired of .... But thanks for asking.

A: I know what you mean. ....

B: ....

> **Don't stop!**
> Make more suggestions.
> Use gerunds and infinitives.

C Change partners Cheer your new partner up.

♻ **Be sure to recycle this language.**

Be sure to (get enough sleep).
You'd better start (eating healthier food).
You should think about (quitting your job).
What about (spending the weekend at a spa)?
How about (getting a pedicure)?

That always helps me.
That's a good idea.
I'll think about that.

79

GOAL **Discuss personality and its origin**

Explore your ideas In what way does a parent's behavior affect a child's development?

READING 4:10

Personality: from Nature or Nurture?

What is personality? Many people define personality as a person's usual manner or style of behavior. These patterns of behavior tend to be predictable throughout a person's lifetime. Some people are introverts; others are extroverts. Some people have easygoing personalities: they are usually cheerful and calm and able to cope with life's difficulties without much trouble. Their emotions are usually under control: they don't get extremely angry about little things. Others, at the other end of the personality spectrum, are more emotional, experiencing higher highs and lower lows. Most people's personalities, however, don't fall at the extreme ends but rather fall somewhere in-between.

Where do we get our personality? For hundreds of years, psychologists and ordinary people have never stopped debating this fascinating question. Some people think personality develops as a result of the environment—the combination of influences that we learn from, such as our families, our culture, our friends, and our education. The people who believe this theory believe that all babies are born without a personality and that it's the environment that determines, or forms, each child's personality. This school of thought is called the "nurture school."

At the other end of the continuum we find people who believe that personality is determined by "nature,"

or the characteristics we receive, or "inherit," from our parents biologically, through their genes. These people believe that our personality is not determined by the environment, but rather by genetics, and that each baby is born with a personality.

The "nature-nurture controversy" The nature-nurture controversy is very old. Experimental psychologists have tried to discover which of these two factors, genetics or the environment, is more important in forming our personality. However, it's very difficult, if not impossible, to conduct research on real people with real lives. There's just no way to put people in a laboratory and watch them develop. For this reason, there's no scientific way to settle the nature-nurture controversy. Recently, however, most researchers have come to believe that both the environment AND the genes—nurture and nature— work together and are both important.

Even though the experts have largely discarded the idea that personality development is so black and white, the nature-nurture controversy remains a popular discussion among friends. It seems that everyone has an opinion.

A Understand vocabulary from context Match the words and phrases in the two columns.

.... **1** genes

.... **2** environment

.... **3** emotions

.... **4** the "nature school" (of thought)

.... **5** the "nurture school" (of thought)

.... **6** personality

a a person's usual pattern of behavior

b what we feel, such as anger, love, and happiness

c the source of traits we inherit from our parents

d the world around us

e the belief that learning determines personality

f the belief that genetics determines personality

> On your *ActiveBook* Self-Study Disc:
> **Extra Reading Comprehension Questions**

B Make personal comparisons How is your personality similar to or different from those of your parents? If you have children, how are your children similar to or different from you? Use language from the Reading.

A Frame your ideas Complete the survey to find out if you are an introvert or an extrovert.

ARE YOU AN EXTROVERT OR AN INTROVERT?

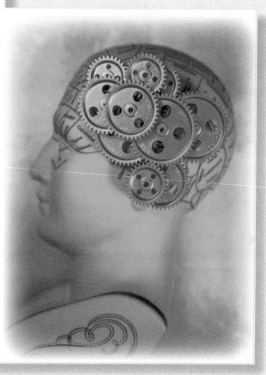

Instructions: From each pair of personality traits, check one that sounds like your personality. At the end, add up your selections for each column. Then decide for yourself: Are you an introvert or an extrovert?

Extroverts tend to:	Introverts tend to:
1. ○ enjoy being in a group.	○ enjoy being alone.
2. ○ need to interact with others.	○ avoid interacting unnecessarily.
3. ○ be active.	○ be quiet.
4. ○ be interested in events.	○ be interested in feelings.
5. ○ talk without thinking.	○ think without talking.
6. ○ be easy to understand.	○ be hard to understand.
7. ○ know many people a little.	○ know few people, but well.
8. ○ talk.	○ listen.
9. ○ seek excitement.	○ seek peace.
10. ○ express their opinions openly.	○ keep their ideas to themselves.

Total extrovert selections [   ]   Total introvert selections [   ]

○ I'm an extrovert.   ○ I'm an introvert.   ○ I'm a mixture of both!

B Pair work Discuss the personality traits you checked. For each, provide a real example from your life to explain your choices.

I'm pretty active. I like to go out almost every night, to the movies or to play sports.

I enjoy staying home most nights. It gives me time to think.

C Discussion Where do you think your personality came from, nurture or nature? Did your personality traits come from your parents' genes or did you <u>learn</u> to be the way you are? Explain with examples using gerunds and infinitives.

♺ **Be sure to recycle this language.**

be crazy about ___ .	(never) complain about ___ .
not care for ___ .	(sometimes) worry about ___ .
get angry / excited / happy / sad about ___ .	believe in ___ .
	(usually) apologize for ___ .
be sick and tired of ___ .	object to ___ .
be bored with ___ .	prefer ___ .
be afraid of ___ .	avoid ___ .

GOAL Examine the impact of birth order

Explore your ideas Do you think the first child in a family has different personality traits from those of siblings who are born later? Explain your answer.

A 🔊 **Listen for main ideas** Read the statements below. Then listen to all three parts of the discussion. Choose the statement that best expresses the main idea of the discussion.

4:11

☐ First-born children are often too critical of themselves.

☐ Children in the same family usually have personalities that are determined by order of birth.

☐ Children usually have personalities that are determined by genes.

B 🔊 **Listen for specific information** Read the exercise. Then listen to each part of the discussion again separately. Complete the exercise as you listen.

4:12

Part 1: Check <u>True</u> or <u>False</u> for each statement.

		True	**False**
1	Brian is usually dissatisfied with himself.	☐	☐
2	Brian obeys rules.	☐	☐
3	Brian does most things well.	☐	☐
4	Brian's mother thinks her husband pushed Brian to be successful.	☐	☐
5	Brian never liked being with adults when he was growing up.	☐	☐

Part 2: Complete each statement by circling the correct information.

1 Annie is (the middle child / the "baby").

2 Annie had (a lot of / only a little) time with her parents before her younger sister was born.

3 Annie is jealous of (Brian / Brian and Lucy).

4 Annie (breaks / obeys) rules.

5 Annie is (rebellious and / rebellious but not) popular.

Part 3: Circle the answer to each question.

1 How old was Annie when Lucy was born?
  a 13 years
  b 13 months

2 What does Lucy like most?
  a making other people laugh
  b laughing at other people

3 What did Lucy do to the dining room wall?
  a She painted it.
  b She washed it.

4 Why does Lucy drive her older siblings crazy?
  a She pays too much attention to them.
  b Others pay too much attention to her.

C Synthesize information Check the most common birth position for each personality, according to the discussion. Listen again if necessary.

Personality traits	First child	Middle child	Youngest child
Breaks rules	☐	☐	☐
Feels less important than siblings	☐	☐	☐
Grows up fast	☐	☐	☐
Grows up slowly	☐	☐	☐
Has a lot of friends	☐	☐	☐
Is creative	☐	☐	☐
Is rebellious	☐	☐	☐
Is self-critical	☐	☐	☐
Plays by the rules	☐	☐	☐
Shows off	☐	☐	☐

NOW YOU CAN Examine the impact of birth order

A Frame your ideas Complete the checklist for yourself.

1 What's your birth position in your family?
- ○ I'm the first child or the only child in the family.
- ○ I'm a middle child—neither the first nor the last.
- ○ I'm the "baby"—the youngest child in the family.

2 What are your personality traits? (Check all that are true.)
- ○ I'm self-critical. I always feel I should do better.
- ○ I'm a rebel.
- ○ I'm popular. I have a lot of friends.
- ○ I feel less important than my older or younger siblings.
- ○ I love to clown around and make people laugh.
- ○ I can be lovable one minute and a rebel the next.
- ○ I am creative.
- ○ I often feel jealous of my siblings.

B Group work Form three groups of students, according to your birth positions. Compare your checklists with other members of your group. Do you share the same personality traits? Report your findings to the class.

> ❝Almost everyone in our group checked 'I'm self-critical!'❞

Group 1: first or only children
Group 2: middle children
Group 3: youngest children

C Discussion Talk about how birth order can affect the development of a person's personality.

Ideas
- genetics / nature
- the environment / nurture
- introverts and extroverts
- parents' behavior

A 🔊 **Listening comprehension** Listen to the conversations. Then circle
a word or phrase to complete each statement.

4:13

  1 Andy is (feeling down / happy).

  2 Mollie is (an extrovert / an introvert).

  3 Greg is (an extrovert / an introvert).

  4 Millie thinks (genetics / the environment) is the most important
factor in personality development.

  5 Vera thinks (genetics / the environment) is the most important
factor in personality development.

4:14/4:15

🎵 **Top Notch Pop**
"The Colors of Love"
Lyrics p. 150

B Complete the paragraph with the correct prepositions.

    Extroverts don't worry .... talking in public. They believe .... being
honest, and they get bored .... being alone. They may talk .... staying
                           1   2
home and reading a book, but when they do, they complain .... having no one
                       3   4
to talk to. They object .... being by themselves.
                       6   5

C Complete each personal statement with a gerund or infinitive phrase.

  1 When I want to stay healthy, I avoid ....

  2 I really enjoy .... on Saturdays and Sundays.

  3 I wish other people would quit .... in the movies.

  4 Two things I can't stand are .... and ....

  5 On weekends, I dislike ....

  6 If the weather is bad, I don't mind ....

  7 Tomorrow I would really like ....

  8 If I want to do well in this class, I need ....

  9 Tomorrow I plan ....

  10 I think most people are afraid of ....

  11 I think people are usually excited about ....

  12 Too many people complain about ....

  13 My family worries most about ....

D Complete each statement. Circle the best answer.

  1 John is such an (extrovert / introvert). He doesn't like to talk about himself a lot.

  2 Our usual pattern of behavior is our (personality / environment).

  3 Another word for characteristics is (nurture / traits).

  4 Many people believe that (self-criticism / birth order) affects personality development.

  5 The nature-nurture controversy is an argument about the origin of the (environment / personality).

E **Writing** Write at least two paragraphs about the personality of someone
you know well. Use vocabulary and ideas from Lessons 3 and 4.

WRITING BOOSTER ▸ p. 145

• *Parallel structure*
• *Guidance for Exercise E*

Pair work

1 Create a conversation between the husband and wife in photo 1. Use gerunds and infinitives.

2 Create a discussion between the two women in the café in photo 2. They discuss the birth order of their siblings and their personalities.

Group work Choose one person to be the professor in photo 3. Help that person create a lecture about personality development. Then the other classmates listen to the lecture and ask questions.

1

What color would you like to paint the ___?

2

So, who is the youngest in your family?

3

Today we're discussing the nature-nurture controversy...

A-N

NOW I CAN... ✔

☐ Get to know what someone likes.
☐ Cheer someone up.
☐ Discuss personality and its origin.
☐ Examine the impact of birth order.

The Arts

GOALS | After Unit 8, you will be able to

1 Recommend a museum.
2 Ask about and describe objects.
3 Talk about artistic talent.
4 Discuss your favorite artists.

Drawing

Jewelry

Fashion

Sculpture

Pottery

Art Exhibit
Bank Street Gallery
Oct. 12–Nov. 24

Photography

Painting

A ◀)) **Vocabulary** • *Kinds of art* Read and listen. Then listen again and repeat.

4:16

B **Discussion** Which piece of art in the art show announcement do you find the most attractive? the most interesting? the least appealing? Why? Use some of the adjectives.

Adjectives to describe art

practical	feminine	awful
beautiful	masculine	boring
relaxing	depressing	weird
fascinating	unusual	silly

Lynn: Ted, this is just great. I had no idea you had so much talent!

Ted: Thank you!

Lynn: I mean it. Your work is very impressive.

Ted: It's so nice of you to say that. I don't think I'm particularly talented. I just love to paint.

Ted: Believe it or not, these were taken by Paul Johns.

Lynn: Your boss? How do you like that! They're really quite good.

Ted: I know. He doesn't look like the artistic type, does he?

Lynn: No. I had no idea he took photos. I guess you can't always judge a book by its cover.

Ted: Hey, this is an interesting piece. I kind of like it.

Lynn: You do? I find it a little weird, actually.

Ted: But that's what makes it so fascinating.

Lynn: Well, to each his own. I guess I'm just not really into abstract art.

D Focus on language Find an underlined expression in the Photo Story to match each of the following explanations.

1 I didn't know . . .

2 I don't really like . . .

3 Everyone has a different opinion.

4 I have some information that may surprise you.

5 I'm really surprised.

6 You can't really know someone just by looking at him or her.

7 In my opinion it's . . .

Dutch Interior I, by Joan Miró, an **abstract** painter from Spain

E Pair work What kinds of art do you prefer? Explain why.

❝ I prefer traditional painting. I'm just not into abstract art. ❞

❝ I'm really into fashion. I like clothes that are really modern. ❞

The Great Wave of Kanagawa, by Katsushika Hokusai, a **traditional** Japanese artist

GOAL   Recommend a museum

GRAMMAR   *The passive voice*

The active voice focuses on "the performer" of an action. The passive voice focuses on "the receiver" of the action.

Active voice: Picasso **painted** *Guernica* in 1937. (focus on the subject, Picasso—the performer)

Passive voice: *Guernica* **was painted by** Picasso in 1937. (focus on the object, *Guernica*—the receiver)

Form the passive voice with a form of <u>be</u> and the past participle of a verb.

Simple present tense:	These vases	**are**	**made**	in Korea.
Present perfect:	The *Mona Lisa*	**has been**	**kept**	at the Louvre Museum since 1797.

It is common to use the passive voice when the performer of the action is not known or not important.
Pottery **is made** in many parts of the world.

Use a <u>by</u> phrase in passive voice sentences when it is important to identify the performer of an action.
This dress was designed **by Donatella Versace**. (important)
This bowl was found ~~by someone~~ in Costa Rica. (not important)

GRAMMAR BOOSTER ▸ p. 133

• *Transitive and intransitive verbs*
• *The passive voice: form in all tenses*

A   Understand the grammar Read each passive voice sentence and decide
if the <u>by</u> phrase is necessary. If it isn't necessary, cross it out.

1 The Louvre Pyramids were added to the museum by workers in 1989.

2 The sculpture *The Thinker* was created by Auguste Rodin.

3 Antoni Gaudí designed and built some of the most famous buildings in Barcelona, Spain.
His plans for the Casa Mila were completed by him in 1912.

4 The melody of "Ode to Joy" is known all over the world. It was written by German
composer Ludwig van Beethoven.

5 China's famous Terracotta Army figures in Xi'an were discovered by people in 1974.

B   Grammar practice Change each sentence from the active to the passive voice.
Use a <u>by</u> phrase.

1 Leonardo da Vinci painted the *Mona Lisa* in the sixteenth century.

....

2 Brazilian photographer Sebastião Salgado took that photograph in 2007.

....

3 Mexican filmmaker Alejandro González directed *Babel* in 2006.

....

4 Japanese master printmaker Katsushika Hokusai made that print over a century ago.

....

5 Korean fashion designer Sang A Im-Propp created these beautiful handbags.

....

6 Middle Eastern weavers have produced beautiful Persian rugs for centuries.

....

CONVERSATION MODEL

A 🔊 4:18 Read and listen to someone recommend a museum.

A: Be sure not to miss the Prado Museum while you're in Madrid.

B: Really? Why's that?

A: Well, for one thing, *Las Meninas* is kept there.

B: No kidding! I've always wanted to see that.

A: They have a great collection of paintings. You'll love it.

B: Thanks for the suggestion!

B 🔊 4:19 **Rhythm and intonation** Listen again and repeat. Then practice the Conversation Model with a partner.

Las Meninas, painting by Diego Velázquez

PRONUNCIATION *Emphatic stress*

A 🔊 4:20 Notice how stress is emphasized to show enthusiasm. Read and listen. Then listen again and repeat.

1 No **KIDD**ing!   **2** That's fan**TA**stic!   **3** That's **PER**fect!   **4** How **IN**teresting!

B Now practice saying the following statements with emphatic stress.

1 That's terrific!   **2** That's wonderful!   **3** How exciting!   **4** How nice!

NOW YOU CAN Recommend a museum

Change the Conversation Model to recommend a museum, using the information in the pictures or museums you know. Use the passive voice and emphatic stress. Then changes roles.

A: Be sure not to miss .... while you're in ....

B: Really? Why's that?

A: Well, for one thing, ... is kept there.

B: ....! I've always wanted to see that.

A: They have a great collection of .... You'll love it.

B: ....!

Don't stop!
Recommend other things to see or do.

♻ **Be sure to recycle this language.**

Have you ever . . .
  tried ___ ?
  climbed ___ ?
  gone to the top of ___ ?
  gone sightseeing in ___ ?
  taken a tour of ___ ?
  taken pictures of ___ ?

The Accademia Gallery
Florence, Italy

Famous for its collection of sculptures by Michelangelo

David, sculpture by Michelangelo

The National Palace Museum
Taipei, Taiwan

Known for its huge collection of Chinese painting, pottery, and sculpture

Travelers Among Mountains and Streams, painting by Fan K'uan

The Palace of Fine Arts
Mexico City, Mexico

Known for its collection of murals by some of Mexico's most famous artists

The Grinder, painting by Diego Rivera

GOAL   **Ask about and describe objects**

CONVERSATION MODEL

A ◀)) 4:21 Read and listen to someone asking about an object.

A: Excuse me. What's this figure made of?

B: Wood. It's handmade.

A: Really? Where was it made?

B: Mexico. What do you think of it?

A: It's fantastic!

◀)) 4:23 **Positive adjectives**

fantastic
wonderful
terrific
cool (very informal)

B ◀)) 4:22 **Rhythm and intonation** Listen again and repeat.
Then practice the Conversation Model with a partner.

VOCABULARY *Materials and objects*

A ◀)) 4:24 Read and listen. Then listen again and repeat.

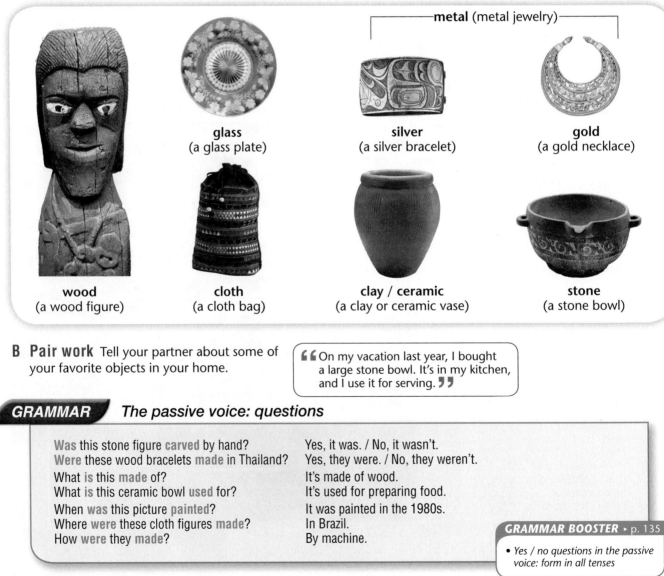

─── **metal** (metal jewelry) ───

glass
(a glass plate)

silver
(a silver bracelet)

gold
(a gold necklace)

wood
(a wood figure)

cloth
(a cloth bag)

clay / ceramic
(a clay or ceramic vase)

stone
(a stone bowl)

B **Pair work** Tell your partner about some of
your favorite objects in your home.

❝On my vacation last year, I bought
a large stone bowl. It's in my kitchen,
and I use it for serving.❞

GRAMMAR *The passive voice: questions*

Was this stone figure **carved** by hand?	Yes, it was. / No, it wasn't.
Were these wood bracelets **made** in Thailand?	Yes, they were. / No, they weren't.
What **is** this **made** of?	It's made of wood.
What **is** this ceramic bowl **used** for?	It's used for preparing food.
When **was** this picture **painted**?	It was painted in the 1980s.
Where **were** these cloth figures **made**?	In Brazil.
How **were** they **made**?	By machine.

GRAMMAR BOOSTER ▶ p. 135

• *Yes / no questions in the passive
voice: form in all tenses*

A Grammar practice Complete the questions in the interview. Use a question word and the passive voice.

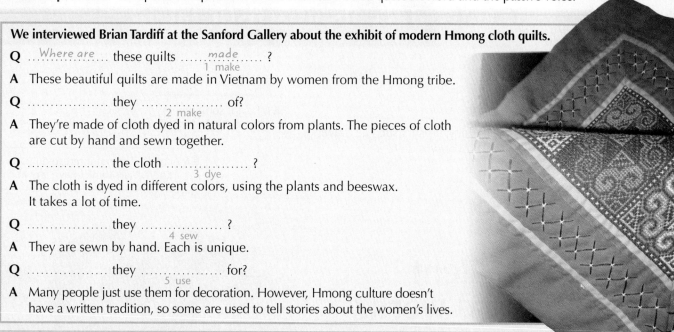

> **We interviewed Brian Tardiff at the Sanford Gallery about the exhibit of modern Hmong cloth quilts.**
>
> **Q** ...*Where are*... these quilts ......*made*...... ?
> 1 make
> **A** These beautiful quilts are made in Vietnam by women from the Hmong tribe.
>
> **Q** .... they .... of?
> 2 make
> **A** They're made of cloth dyed in natural colors from plants. The pieces of cloth are cut by hand and sewn together.
>
> **Q** .... the cloth .... ?
> 3 dye
> **A** The cloth is dyed in different colors, using the plants and beeswax. It takes a lot of time.
>
> **Q** .... they .... ?
> 4 sew
> **A** They are sewn by hand. Each is unique.
>
> **Q** .... they .... for?
> 5 use
> **A** Many people just use them for decoration. However, Hmong culture doesn't have a written tradition, so some are used to tell stories about the women's lives.

B Complete the conversations. Write information questions, using the passive voice.

1 A: .... ?
B: The glass cups? They were made by hand.

2 A: .... ?
B: That silver bowl? It's used for serving sugar.

3 A: .... ?
B: This beautiful figure? It's made of gold.

4 A: .... ?
B: These wood chairs? They were made in Venezuela.

5 A: .... ?
B: That Chinese bag? It was made by machine.

6 A: .... ?
B: This cup? It's made of ceramic.

NOW YOU CAN   Ask about and describe objects

A Pair work Change the Conversation Model to ask about and describe one of the objects. Use the Vocabulary. Then change roles.

A: Excuse me. What .... made of?
B: ....
A: .... Where .... made?
B: .... What do you think of .... ?
A: ....

> **Don't stop!**
> Ask other passive voice questions.

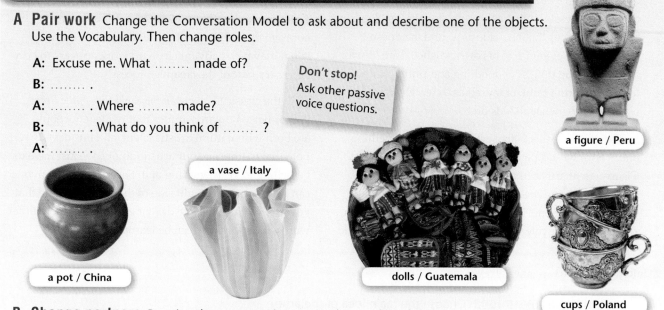

a figure / Peru

a vase / Italy

a pot / China

dolls / Guatemala

cups / Poland

B Change partners Practice the conversation again about other objects.

C Discussion Describe an object in your own home. Ask your classmates questions about the objects they describe.

> "In my living room, I have a small figure. It's made of wood. It's a piece of traditional art. I bought it on my vacation last year."

GOAL Talk about artistic talent

Warm-up Do you do anything artistic, such as drawing, painting, or handicrafts? Why or why not?

> I paint sometimes. I find it relaxing.

> Actually, I'm not interested in art. I don't really think I have any ability.

READING 4:25

Is it talent or hard work?

All young children scribble, doodle, and draw stick figures.

When children are asked to draw or paint a picture, they are happy to oblige. And they are willing to talk about and show their creation to anyone they meet. But when adults are asked to do the same thing, they typically get nervous and refuse to even try, claiming that they have no talent.

Most adults see themselves as lacking the "artistic gene." However, when you look at drawings made by artists when they were children, their work doesn't differ much from the scribbles and stick figures all children draw when they are young. When Don Lipski, who makes a successful living as a professional artist, looks back at drawings that he made as a child, he doesn't find any early evidence of his own artistic talent. "I was always making things . . . doodling and putting things together. I didn't think of myself as a creative person. I was just doing what all kids do."

The general belief is that artistic talent is something one is born with: a person either has talent or does not. Clearly, great artists like Michelangelo or Picasso had natural talent and possessed more artistic ability than the average person. However, one factor that isn't often considered is the role that years of training, practice, and hard work have played in the creation of great pieces of art. In addition, most artists are successful because they are passionate about their art—they love what they do. Their passion motivates them to continue to create—and improve their ability—day after day. While natural talent may be an advantage, hard work appears to be a necessary part of the creative process.

In the classic *Drawing on the Right Side of the Brain*, author Betty Edwards argues that while few people are born with natural artistic talent, all of us have the potential to improve our artistic ability. We just have to be willing to keep working at it. She claims that anyone can learn to use the right side of the brain, the side that governs visual skills like drawing and painting. In other words, artistic ability can be learned.

Information source: www.emptyeasel.com

A Recognize the main idea Choose the main idea of the article.

a Artistic skill can be taught.

b Children are better artists than adults.

c To draw well, you have to be born with artistic talent.

d Few people are born with artistic talent.

B **Identify supporting details** Read each statement. Check <u>True</u> or <u>False</u>, according to the article. Support your choice with details from the Reading.

	True	False
1 Young children generally don't worry if they are talented or not.	☐	☐
2 Most adults think they are not talented.	☐	☐
3 It's easy to see which children are going to be artists when you look at their drawings.	☐	☐
4 There isn't much difference between famous artists and other people.	☐	☐
5 Talent is all one needs to create great artistic work.	☐	☐
6 People who don't have natural talent can improve their artistic skill.	☐	☐

C **Paraphrase** Read the paragraph in the Reading about *Drawing on the Right Side of the Brain* again. In your own words, restate Betty Edwards's theory about artistic ability.

According to Betty Edwards, ...

On your *ActiveBook* Self-Study Disc:
Extra Reading Comprehension Questions

NOW YOU CAN Talk about artistic talent

A **Frame your ideas** Complete the survey. Then compare responses with a partner.

Who's Got Talent?

1 a. Do any of your family members or friends have artistic ability? ○ yes ○ no

Relationship to you: _____

Which of the arts? _____
_____

1 b. Where do you think this ability comes from?
_____

2 Do you think you have natural artistic talent?
○ yes ○ no ○ not sure

3 Do other people think you're talented?
○ yes ○ no ○ not sure

4 How would you rate your own artistic ability on a scale of 1 to 5?

1	2	3	4	5
POOR		AVERAGE		EXCELLENT

5 In which of the arts do you think you may have ability? Explain.

example ✔ **music** *I sing and play several musical instruments.*

○ music _____

○ drawing/painting _____

○ handicrafts _____

○ acting _____

○ dancing _____

○ taking photographs _____

○ other _____

B **Discussion** Do you think people are born with artistic talent? Or is it developed through years of training, practice, and hard work?

Text-mining (optional)
Underline language in the Reading on page 92 to use in the Discussion. For example:

"Most adults see themselves as ___ ..."

GOAL | Discuss your favorite artists

4:26

A **Vocabulary** • *Passive participial phrases* Read and listen.
Then listen again and repeat.

be inspired by	He **is inspired by** nature. He tries to capture nature's beauty in his photographs.
be influenced by	She **was influenced by** Georgia O'Keeffe's work. You can see similarities between O'Keeffe's paintings and her own.
be fascinated by	He's always **been fascinated by** the life of Vincent van Gogh. He loves to read about how it influenced his paintings.
be moved by	You **will be moved by** Charlie Chaplin's films. Even though they are funny, their themes of life and love really touch your heart.

White Flower on Red Earth, #1
Georgia O'Keeffe

Vase with Fourteen Sunflowers
Vincent van Gogh

B Pair work Tell your partner what inspires, influences, interests,
fascinates, and moves you. Use passive participial phrases.

LISTENING COMPREHENSION

4:27

A **Understand from context** Listen to the interviews.
Complete each statement with the name of the artist.

1 Burt Hildegard is fascinated by the work of ....

2 Susan Wallach is influenced by the work of ....

3 Katherine Wolf is inspired by the work of ....

4 Nick Jenkins is moved by the work of ....

Ang Lee

Frida Kahlo

Henri Cartier-Bresson

Valentino

B 🔊 **Listen to take notes** Listen again to each interview and write some of the details you hear about each artist. Compare notes with a partner.

1 Ang Lee	2 Henri Cartier-Bresson	3 Valentino	4 Frida Kahlo
explores culture	black and white	Italian	was sick as a child

C **Discussion** Which of the artists described in the Listening do you find the most fascinating? Use your notes to explain why.

NOW YOU CAN | **Discuss your favorite artists**

A **Frame your ideas** Complete the questionnaire. Then compare answers with a partner.

Check which qualities attract you to an artist.

His or her work...
- ○ is traditional.
- ○ is abstract.
- ○ is easy to understand.
- ○ makes you think.
- ○ touches your heart.
- ○ makes you laugh.
- ○ other: _____

He or she...
- ○ is a rebel.
- ○ is creative.
- ○ tries new things.
- ○ has his or her own style.
- ○ inspires people.
- ○ other: _____

Types of artists
painter
writer
sculptor
filmmaker / director
fashion designer
architect
photographer
actor
singer
dancer

Types of art
drawing
painting
sculpture
photography
jewelry
pottery
fashion

B **Notepadding** On your notepad, write about some of your favorite artists.

	Artist's name	Type of artist	Why I like this artist
1			
2			
3			

C **Group work** Discuss your favorite artists. Tell your class why you like them. Ask your classmates questions about the artists they describe.

❝I'm a real fan of Frida Kahlo and Diego Rivera. I'm fascinated by their lives.❞

❝Donatella Versace is my favorite designer. Her fashions are so creative!❞

❝One of my favorite artists is Naoki Urasawa. His drawings in the comic book *Yawara!* are really exciting.❞

Review

4:29

A ◀))) **Listening comprehension** Listen and write the letter of the piece of art each person is talking about. Then listen again and circle the best way to complete each statement.

a  b  c  d  e

.... **1** She thinks it's (beautiful / ugly / abstract).

.... **2** He thinks it's (traditional / ugly / fascinating). She thinks it's (fantastic / OK / abstract).

.... **3** She thinks it's (OK / awful / great). He thinks it's too (abstract / dark / traditional).

B Change each sentence from active to passive voice.

4:30/4:31

🎵 *Top Notch Pop*
"To Each His Own"
Lyrics p. 150

1 César Pelli designed the Petronas Twin Towers in Kuala Lumpur.

....

2 Guillermo del Toro directed *Pan's Labyrinth* in 2006.

....

3 Henri Matisse made the print *Icarus* in 1947.

....

4 Annie Leibovitz took that photograph of John Lennon in 1980.

....

5 Hokusai produced *The Great Wave of Kanagawa* in the early 1830s.

....

C List materials under each category. Answers may vary.

Materials that are expensive	Materials that weigh a lot	Materials that break easily
gold		

D Complete the statements.

1 The art of designing clothes is called ....

2 One type of .... is a figure carved from wood or stone.

3 Two types of metal often used to make jewelry are .... and ....

4 Art in a conservative style from the past is called .... art.

5 A piece of art made with a pen or pencil is called a ....

E Writing Choose a favorite object that decorates your home. Describe it in a paragraph.

Ideas
• a painting or drawing
• a photo or poster
• a piece of furniture
• a figure or sculpture
• a dish or vase
• (your own idea) ____

WRITING BOOSTER ▸ p. 146

• *Providing supporting details*
• *Guidance for Exercise E*

Contest Look at the page for one minute and close your books. Who can describe the most objects and art, using the passive voice?

The vase is made of ___ . The Mona Lisa is kept in the ___ .

Pair work

1 Create a conversation for the man and woman. Recommend a museum. Start like this:

Be sure not to miss the ___ while you're in ___ .

2 Create a conversation for the customer and the store clerk. Ask about the objects. Start like this:

Excuse me. What's this ___ made of?

Discussion Talk about the pieces of art in the photos. Say what you like or don't like about each one.

The Great Museums of EUROPE

The Louvre Museum (Paris, France)

The world's largest art museum—and some of the world's greatest art!

Mona Lisa, by Leonardo da Vinci (1519)

Tate Modern (London, U.K.)

Mustard on White, by Roy Lichtenstein (1963)

Open since 2000, the best international modern art from 1900 to the present day

Mexico

Japan

Peru

France

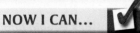

NOW I CAN...

- ☐ Recommend a museum.
- ☐ Ask about and describe objects.
- ☐ Talk about artistic talent.
- ☐ Discuss my favorite artists.

Living with Computers

GOALS After Unit 9, you will be able to
1 Troubleshoot a problem.
2 Recommend a better deal.
3 Describe how you use computers.
4 Discuss the impact of the Internet.

http://www.troubleshooter.com

TROUBLESHOOTER.COM

Your online technical support specialists

Click below
if your computer . . .

won't start

is slowing down

**freezes and won't
do anything**

Click below
if you want to . . .

recover lost files

get rid of a virus

Customer support

**Speak with an
expert by phone**

Send an e-mail

**Connect to an expert
by instant message**

Got a problem with . . .

a monitor?

a keyboard?

a mouse?

a touchpad?

Live Support: Hi, this is Ankush. How can I help you?

MParker: I'm having a problem. Can you tell me why my keyboard freezes when I try to install XP Pro? No matter how many times I hit the keys, nothing happens. Help!!!

Live Support: Sorry to hear that. I'm sure we can resolve this problem. Have you tried restarting your computer?

Send

Live Support

A ◄») **Vocabulary • *Computer parts*** Read and listen. Then listen again and repeat.

• a monitor
• a keyboard
• a mouse
• a touchpad

B Pair work Look at the technical support website. Have you ever had a problem with a computer part? Tell your partner.

C Discussion What do you think is the best way to get technical support: by instant message, by e-mail, by phone, or in person? Why?

D 🔊 **Photo story** Read and listen to a conversation about a computer problem.

Amy: What are you doing here at this hour?

Dee: Fooling around on my new laptop.

Amy: Am I interrupting you?

Dee: Not at all. Paul and I are just instant messaging. What's up?

Amy: Well, I was wondering if you could help me with something.

Dee: Of course.

Amy: When I try to log on to my e-mail, nothing happens.

Dee: Are you sure you used the right password?

Amy: Absolutely. And I've never had a problem before.

Dee: Maybe you should try rebooting. Sometimes that takes care of it.

Amy: You mean just shutting down and restarting?

Dee: Right.

Amy: You think that would do it?

Dee: It couldn't hurt. Listen, Paul's still there. Let me send a quick response, OK? I'll just be a second.

Amy: I'm sorry. I'll go and try rebooting to see if that does the trick.

E **Focus on language** Look at the six underlined expressions in the Photo Story. Write each expression next to its meaning. (Two expressions have the same meaning.)

1 won't take a long time ....

2 not doing anything serious ....

3 It doesn't work. ....

4 It's worth trying. ....

5 fixes the problem ....

6 fixes the problem ....

F **Pair work** Do you know how to solve computer problems? Answer the questions by checking <u>Yes</u>, <u>No</u>, or <u>Not sure</u>. Then compare your answers and discuss some possible solutions.

Do you know what to do if...	Yes	No	Not sure
1 you get a virus?	☐	☐	☐
2 your printer won't print?	☐	☐	☐
3 you can't log on to a website?	☐	☐	☐
4 your computer is really slow?	☐	☐	☐

Computer solutions
• run anti-virus software
• try rebooting
• contact a technical support expert
• check if it's turned on
• buy a new computer
• (your own idea) ___

GOAL   Troubleshoot a problem

CONVERSATION MODEL

A 🔊 5:04 Read and listen to people troubleshoot a computer problem.

A: Eugene, could you take a look at this?

B: Sure. What's the problem?

A: Well, I clicked on the toolbar to save a file and the computer crashed.

B: Why don't you try restarting? That sometimes works.

A: OK. I'll give that a try.

B 🔊 5:05 **Rhythm and intonation** Listen again and repeat. Then practice the Conversation Model with a partner.

🔊 5:06 **Ways to reassure someone**
That sometimes works.
That might help.
That may do the trick.

VOCABULARY   *Computer terms and commands*

A 🔊 5:07 Read and listen. Then listen again and repeat.

① **a pull-down menu** ② **the tool bar** ④ **the scroll bar**

File   Edit   View   Go   Window   Help

⑤ **open** a file   ⑧ **cut** text
⑥ **save** a file   ⑨ **copy** text
⑦ **print** a file   ⑩ **paste** text

③ **the cursor**

The meeting is tomorrow.

⑬ **scroll up**

mtg.doc

⑪ **click on** an icon   ⑫ **select / highlight** text   ⑭ **scroll down**

B 🔊 5:08 **Listening comprehension** Listen. Check the computer command each person needs.

	🗀	💾	🖨	✂	📄	📋	▲	▼
1 He needs to click on ...	☐	☐	☐	☐	☐	☐	☐	☐
2 She needs to click on ...	☐	☐	☐	☐	☐	☐	☐	☐
3 He needs to click on ...	☐	☐	☐	☐	☐	☐	☐	☐
4 She needs to click on ...	☐	☐	☐	☐	☐	☐	☐	☐
5 He needs to click on ...	☐	☐	☐	☐	☐	☐	☐	☐
6 She needs to click on ...	☐	☐	☐	☐	☐	☐	☐	☐

GRAMMAR BOOSTER ▸ p. 135

- Expressing purpose with *in order to*
- Expressing purpose with *for*, common errors

An infinitive can be used to express a purpose.
I scrolled down **to read** the text. (= because I wanted to read the text)
Put the cursor on the toolbar **to choose** a file. (= if you want to choose a file)

Answering a <u>Why</u> question with an infinitive of purpose is similar to answering with <u>Because</u>.
Why did you click on that icon?   **To save** the file before I close it. (= Because I want to save it.)
Why did you highlight that word?   **To select** it so I can copy it. (= Because I want to copy it.)

A Find the grammar Look at the Conversation Model on page 100. Find an infinitive of purpose. Restate the sentence, using <u>because</u>.

B Pair work Look at Cathy's to-do list. Ask and answer questions, using infinitives of purpose.

“ Why is Cathy going to go shopping? ”

“ To get something for … ”

C Grammar practice Complete each sentence in your own way. Use infinitives of purpose.

1 Don't forget to click on the save icon *to save your document* .
2 You can click on the print icon ....
3 Put the cursor on the pull-down menu ....
4 I bought a new scanner ....
5 I e-mailed my friend ....
6 I connected to the Internet ....

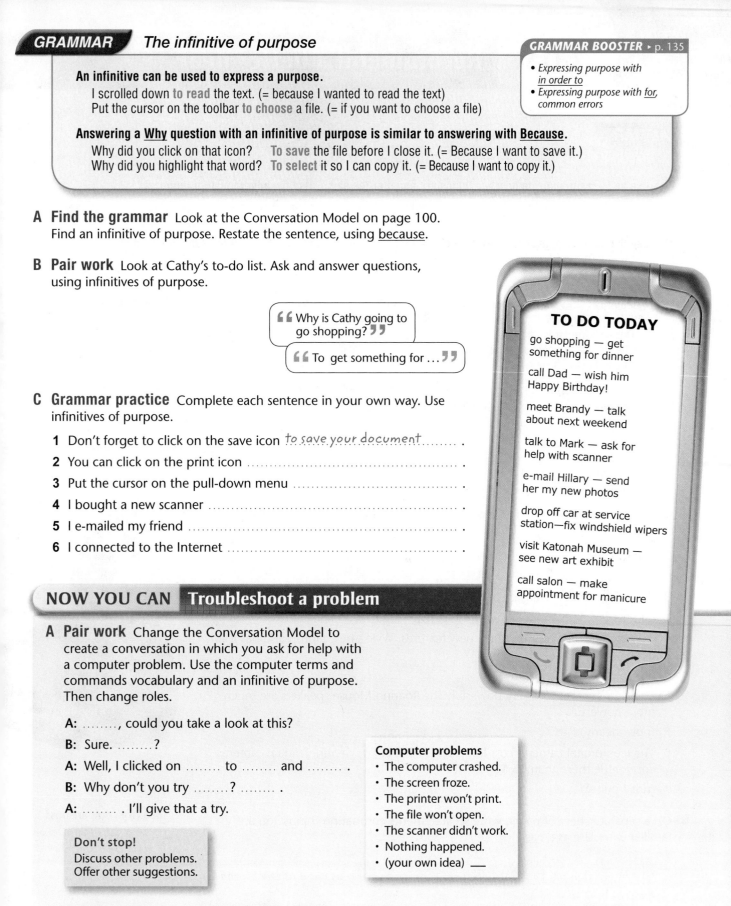

TO DO TODAY

go shopping — get something for dinner

call Dad — wish him Happy Birthday!

meet Brandy — talk about next weekend

talk to Mark — ask for help with scanner

e-mail Hillary — send her my new photos

drop off car at service station—fix windshield wipers

visit Katonah Museum — see new art exhibit

call salon — make appointment for manicure

NOW YOU CAN **Troubleshoot a problem**

A Pair work Change the Conversation Model to create a conversation in which you ask for help with a computer problem. Use the computer terms and commands vocabulary and an infinitive of purpose. Then change roles.

A: ...., could you take a look at this?
B: Sure. ....?
A: Well, I clicked on .... to .... and ....
B: Why don't you try ....? ....
A: .... I'll give that a try.

Computer problems
- The computer crashed.
- The screen froze.
- The printer won't print.
- The file won't open.
- The scanner didn't work.
- Nothing happened.
- (your own idea) —

Don't stop!
Discuss other problems.
Offer other suggestions.

B Change partners Practice the conversation again with other problems.

GOAL   Recommend a better deal

GRAMMAR   *Comparisons with as ... as*

> **To express similarity**
>
> Use **as** ... **as** to indicate how two things are equal or the same. Use the adverb **just** for emphasis.
>   The new speakers are **as good as** the old ones.
>   The iFriend has **just as many new features as** the F40.
>
> Use the adverbs **almost** or **nearly** to indicate that two things are very similar but not exactly the same.
>   The ZetaB has **almost as much memory as** the Panasox, but it's a lot cheaper.
>
> **To express difference**
>
> Use **not as** ... **as** to indicate how two things are different. Use the adverb **quite** when the difference is very small. Use the adverb **nearly** to indicate that there's a big difference.
>   Our new printer is**n't as noisy as** the old one.
>   The G4 does**n't** cost **quite as much as** the Z90.
>   And it does**n't** have **nearly as many problems as** the Z90.
>
> **You can use shortened statements with as when the meaning is clear.**
>   The old monitor was great. But the new one is **just as good**. (= as the old one)
>   Have you seen Carl's new laptop? Mine isn't **nearly as nice**. (= as his laptop)

GRAMMAR BOOSTER ▸ p. 136
- *As ... as to compare adverbs*
- *Comparatives and superlatives: review*
- *Comparison with adverbs*

A Grammar practice Read each statement about a product. Write a sentence with as ... as and the cue to compare the products.

1 The new Shine keyboard is popular. The one from Digitek is popular too.
   (just) ....

2 The XCue joystick is easy to use. The JRock joystick is also easy to use.
   (just) ....

3 The C50 monitor is large. The C30 monitor is a little larger than the C50.
   (almost) ....

4 Comtec's new laptop has many new features. Wyle's new laptop also has many new features.
   (just) ....

5 The CCV speakers are very powerful. The Roaring Mouse speakers are much more powerful.
   (not / nearly) ....

6 The Icon digital cameras cost less than US $300. The Sentinel digital cameras cost a little more than US $300.
   (not / quite) ....

a joystick

B On a separate sheet of paper, write six statements comparing things you are familiar with. Use as ... as.

In my opinion, the Mardino sports car isn't nearly as good as the Strega.

Ideas for comparisons
- cars
- electronic products
- stores
- restaurants
- (your own idea) ___

A 🔊 5:09 Read and listen. Then listen again and repeat.

1 The new printer is as slow as the old one.

2 My old smart phone is just as small as the new one.

3 The X12 mouse isn't nearly as nice as the X30.

4 My keyboard didn't cost quite as much as the Z6.

B Read the statements you wrote in Exercise B on page 102 aloud, paying attention to stress.

CONVERSATION MODEL

A 🔊 5:10 Listen to someone recommend a better deal.

A: I'm thinking about getting a new monitor.

B: Oh, yeah? What kind?

A: Everyone says I should get a Macro.

B: Well, I've heard that the Panatel is as good as the Macro, but it costs a lot less.

A: Really? I'll check it out.

B 🔊 5:11 **Rhythm and intonation** Listen again and repeat. Then practice the Conversation Model with a partner.

NOW YOU CAN Recommend a better deal

A Pair work Change the Conversation Model, using the magazine ratings to compare and recommend products. Use as ... as. Then change roles.

A: I'm thinking about getting a new ....

B: ....? What kind?

A: Everyone says I should get ....

B: Well, I've heard that ....

A: Really? ....

Don't stop!
Ask about other features.

♻ **Be sure to recycle this language.**

Which ...
is more popular?	is newer?
is easier / harder to use?	is quieter / noisier?
is lighter / heavier?	is slower / faster?
is larger / smaller?	has more features?
is less / more expensive?	looks nicer?
costs less / more?	got better reviews?

B Change partners Now practice the conversation again, using other products and features.

BUYER'S FRIEND *Magazine*

Our recommendations!

■ eMax Optical Mouse	very good	US $25
■ eMax X15 Keyboard	very comfortable	US $30
■ eMax Y80 Web Camera	easy to use	US $260
■ eMax Z40 Monitor	15 inches / 38 centimeters	US $250

The Electronics GUIDE *YOUR BEST BUYS!*

Klick Optical Mouse	very good	US $20
Klick P40 Keyboard	very comfortable	US $25
Klick Ultra Web Camera	easy to use	US $220
Klick P20 Monitor	19 inches / 48.3 centimeters	US $250

5:12

🔊 **Vocabulary** • *Internet activities* Read and listen. Then listen again and repeat.

attach (a file) place a document or photo into an e-mail

upload (a file) move a document, music file, or picture from a personal computer, phone, or MP3 player onto the Internet

download (a file) move a document, music file, or picture from the Internet onto a personal computer, phone, or MP3 player

surf the Internet visit a lot of different websites on the Internet for information that interests you

join (an online group) become a member of an Internet group to meet friends and share information about your hobbies and interests

post (a message) add your comments to an online discussion on a message board, a blog, or a social networking site

5:13

A 🔊 **Listen for the main idea** Listen to people describing how they use the Internet. Write a check in the box next to the person who seems to enjoy the Internet the least. Explain your answer.

 ☐ **1** George Thomas

 ☐ **2** Sonia Castro

 ☐ **3** Robert Kuan

 ☐ **4** Nadia Montasser

5:14

B 🔊 **Listen for details** Listen again and check the activities each person does.

	George Thomas	Sonia Castro	Robert Kuan	Nadia Montasser
buys products	☐	☐	☐	☐
downloads music	☐	☐	☐	☐
keeps up with the news	☐	☐	☐	☐
participates in online groups	☐	☐	☐	☐
plays online games	☐	☐	☐	☐
sends instant messages	☐	☐	☐	☐
surfs the Internet	☐	☐	☐	☐
uploads photos	☐	☐	☐	☐
uses a computer at work	☐	☐	☐	☐

Describe how you use computers

A Frame your ideas Complete the survey about your own computer use.

Computer User Survey

1. I use a computer ...

- ☐ for work
- ☐ for study
- ☐ for fun
- ☐ I never use a computer.

2. I usually spend ___ hours a week on a computer.

- ☐ 0 – 10
- ☐ 11 – 20
- ☐ 21 – 30
- ☐ 31 – 40
- ☐ 41 – 50
- ☐ over 50

3. I use the computer ...

- ☐ to surf the Internet
- ☐ to download pictures
- ☐ to design websites
- ☐ to write stories
- ☐ to create art
- ☐ to shop for things
- ☐ to take classes
- ☐ other:_____

- ☐ to send instant messages
- ☐ to keep in touch with people
- ☐ to send e-mail
- ☐ to watch movies
- ☐ to look at my bank accounts
- ☐ to sell things
- ☐ to practice English

- ☐ to download music
- ☐ to download videos
- ☐ to write reports
- ☐ to play games
- ☐ to pay bills
- ☐ to read the news
- ☐ to just fool around

4. Check the statements that are true about you.

- ☐ I'm actually a little afraid of computers. I never use them.
- ☐ I don't spend nearly as much time on a computer as most people.
- ☐ I spend just as much time on a computer as most people.
- ☐ Compared to most people, I spend WAY too much time on a computer.
- ☐ You could say I'm a computer addict.
- ☐ People consider me to be a computer expert. They come to me for help.

B Group work Walk around your classroom and ask your classmates about their computer use. Ask questions to get more information and take notes.

Ideas for questions
Why... When...
Where... How...

Find someone who...	Name	Notes
is a computer expert.		
is a computer addict.		
is afraid of computers.		
uses the Internet to meet people.		
uses the Internet to avoid people.		

C Discussion Tell your class what you found out about your classmates and how they use computers.

"May spends a lot of time on her computer. She uses it to meet new people and keep in touch with friends. But she doesn't use her computer as much as Paul does. He ..."

| GOAL | **Discuss the impact of the Internet** |

BEFORE YOU READ

Warm-up What kinds of problems have you had with the Internet? What kinds of Internet problems have you heard about on the news?

READING 5:15

Hackers Steal 40 Million Credit Card Numbers

Eleven hackers around the world were accused of stealing more than 40 million credit card numbers on the Internet. They included three people from the U.S. who are accused of hacking into the wireless networks of popular online stores.

Once inside these networks, they installed "sniffer" programs that search for customers' credit card numbers, passwords, and personal information. Credit card numbers were then sold on the Internet, allowing criminals to withdraw thousands of dollars at a time from ATMs.

Computer Virus Attacks Get Worse

"We're losing the battle against computer viruses," says David Farber, professor of computer science at Carnegie Mellon University. These viruses, which can enter computer systems through junk e-mail, have reached epidemic proportions, slowing down and sometimes shutting down computers in both large and small companies. In one year alone, they were reported to have caused $13 billion in damage.

Companies have been trying for years to protect themselves with anti-virus programs, but criminals are creating newer, improved viruses faster than these programs can keep up.

Cyberbullying Leads to Teenager's Death

Megan Taylor Meier, age 13, joined an online social networking group where she became online friends with a 16-year-old boy named Josh. Megan and Josh never communicated by phone or in person, but she enjoyed exchanging messages with him in the group.

Over time, Josh changed. He began to bully her daily—criticizing her personality and telling her what a bad person she was. Some of their communications were posted so everyone could see them. Josh's

last message to her said, "The world would be a better place without you." A short time later, Megan committed suicide by hanging herself in a closet.

After her death, it was discovered that there was no "Josh." The messages came from the mother of one of Megan's classmates. The mother had been angry with Megan because she believed Megan had said some untrue things about her daughter.

Information sources: disinfo.com, en.wikipedia.org, businessweek.com

A Understand from context Use the context of the articles to help you to complete each definition.

.... **1** A hacker is ...

.... **2** A computer virus is ...

.... **3** A criminal is ...

.... **4** Junk e-mail is ...

.... **5** An anti-virus program is ...

.... **6** A cyberbully is ...

a a software program that causes problems in computers.

b a software program that tries to stop the spread of viruses.

c a person who enters computer systems without an invitation.

d a person who sends cruel and negative messages to another person online.

e an unwanted message that tries to sell you something.

f a person who breaks the law; for example, by stealing money.

B Relate to personal experience What news stories have you heard about the Internet? Do you ever worry about using the Internet? Why or why not?

On your *ActiveBook* Self-Study Disc:
Extra Reading Comprehension Questions

NOW YOU CAN   Discuss the impact of the Internet

A Notepadding With a partner, discuss each statement. Write at least one good change and one bad change for each.

1	**The Internet has changed the way people find information.**
	Good changes:
	Bad changes:

2	**The Internet has changed the way people work in offices.**
	Good changes:
	Bad changes:

3	**The Internet has changed the way people shop.**
	Good changes:
	Bad changes:

4	**The Internet has changed the way people communicate.**
	Good changes:
	Bad changes:

B Discussion Do you think that computers and the Internet have brought more benefits or more problems? Support your opinions with examples.

Text mining (optional)
Underline language in the Reading on page 106 to use in the Discussion. For example: "We're losing the battle against ___ ."

❝ In my opinion, there are more benefits than problems. The Internet has really changed the way we do things ...❞

❝ I think the Internet is good, but there are really too many problems. First of all, ...❞

107

Review

A 5:16 🔊 **Listening comprehension** Listen to the conversations. Check the box if the person recommends the product. Then listen again and infer how to complete each statement.

Recommended?
☐ the C40 computer
☐ the Hip web camera
☐ the new Mundite CD drive
☐ the Play Zone 3 game

1 The C40's monitor is ...... the X8's.
   a the same size as   **b** larger than   **c** smaller than

2 The Hip web camera is ...... the Pentac web camera.
   a the same price as   **b** cheaper than   **c** more expensive than

3 Mundite's new CD drive is ...... Mundite's old CD drive.
   a the same as   **b** faster than   **c** slower than

4 Play Zone 3 is ...... Play Zones 1 and 2.
   a the same as   **b** less fun than   **c** more fun than

B Answer each question in your own words, using infinitives of purpose.

1 Why do people join social networking sites? ....

2 Why do people send instant messages? ....

3 Why do people surf the Internet? ....

4 Why do people shop online? ....

5 Why are you studying English? ....

C Complete each statement.

1 If you want to print a document, click on the print icon on the ....

2 To read more text on your screen, use the scroll .... to scroll down.

3 Click on File on the toolbar so you can see the .... menu.

4 When you're finished working on a document, don't forget to .... it before you close the file.

5:17 / 5:18
🎵 **Top Notch Pop**
"Life in Cyberspace"
Lyrics p. 150

D Unscramble the letters of the words in the box to complete each sentence.

chatated	clorls	doalwond	esmou	rekcha	rusvi

1 Last year, a .... got into the company's computer systems and stole important information.

2 Use the .... to click on a file and open it.

3 It isn't difficult to .... songs from the Internet.

4 Use the .... bar to see more text on the screen.

5 Her computer isn't working now because she downloaded a .... from a piece of junk e-mail.

6 I .... the photos to the e-mail I sent this morning.

E **Writing** On a separate sheet of paper, write two paragraphs about the benefits and the problems of the Internet. Use your notepads from page 107.

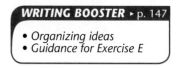

WRITING BOOSTER ▸ p. 147
• *Organizing ideas*
• *Guidance for Exercise E*

Contest Look at the photos for one minute. Then close your books. Who can name all the computer parts and activities in the photos? For example:

There's a printer and ... OR

He's trying to print photos ...

Pair work

1 Create a conversation for the man and the woman. They are troubleshooting a problem. Start like this:

Could you take a look at this?

2 Create a conversation for the two men. One is asking for a product recommendation. Start like this:

I'm thinking about getting a new ...

3 Create a conversation for the two women on the phone. One is asking the other about what she is doing on the computer. Start like this:

Am I interrupting you?

NOW I CAN... ✔

☐ Troubleshoot a problem.
☐ Recommend a better deal.
☐ Describe how I use computers.
☐ Discuss the impact of the Internet.

Ethics and Values

GOALS   After Unit 10, you will be able t

1 Discuss ethical choices.
2 Return someone else's property.
3 Express personal values.
4 Discuss acts of kindness and honesty.

MORAL DILEMMAS
What should they do?

This box has the wrong price.

$17 $10⁰⁰

$17⁰⁰

Uh-oh. Someone forgot that watch.

I think this total is wrong.

But I only ordered one!

Guest Check

TABLE NO.	NO. PERSONS	SERVER NO.	CHECK NO. 2651		
1	shrimp cocktail			9	50
1	tomato bisque			4	50
1	garden salad			6	75
1	sirloin			18	95
1	bottle sparkling water			3	00
1	espresso			2	50
	TOTAL			22	20

Thank You - Call Again

GUEST RECEIPT NO. PERSONS	DATE	CHECK NO. 2651	AMOUNT

AJ's OUTDOOR GEAR   **INVOICE**

DESCRIPTION	QUANTITY	UNIT PRICE
Nylon windbreaker	1	$52.99
	TOTAL	$52.99

A Group work Have you ever been faced with a moral dilemma similar to the ones in the pictures? Tell your classmates what happened.

B 🔊 5:19 **Photo story** Read and listen to a conversation about a moral dilemma.

Matt: I can't believe it! I just picked this up to look at it and the thing broke in two. And with these ridiculous prices, it's going to cost me an arm and a leg.

Noah: Oh, forget it. I'll bet it was already broken.

Matt: You're probably right.

Noah: Just put it back on the shelf. The place is empty. No one saw. Let's just split.

Matt: I couldn't do that.

Noah: Why not? You said it yourself. The prices are ridiculous.

Matt: Well, put yourself in the owner's shoes. Suppose the plate were yours? How would you feel if someone broke it and didn't tell you?

Noah: Well I'm *not* the owner. And, anyway, for him it would be just a drop in the bucket. To *you* it's a lot of money.

Matt: Maybe so. But if I ran out without telling him, I couldn't face myself.

C **Focus on language** Replace the underlined part of each sentence by substituting an underlined word or expression from the Photo Story.

1 I know this painting is a little expensive, but we have a lot of other expenses. Compared with the rest, the painting is only a small amount of money. ....

2 It's really getting late and I'm tired. Let's leave. ....

3 I would feel bad about it. ....

4 These boots were so expensive! They cost me a lot of money. ....

5 Imagine how you would feel if this were your store. ....

D **Think and explain** Answer the following questions. Support your answers with quotations from the Photo Story.

1 Was it Matt's fault that the plate broke?

2 Why does Noah think they can leave without saying anything?

3 What opinion does Matt have about the prices in the store?

4 Why does Noah think the broken plate won't be a problem for the owner?

5 What reason does Matt have for telling the owner?

E **Class survey** Poll the class and complete the chart. Then discuss and explain your reasons. (Students who choose "other" should present their solution.)

How many classmates think . . .	
Matt should put the plate back and leave?	
Matt should tell the owner what happened and offer to pay for the plate?	
Matt should tell the owner but say it wasn't his fault?	
Other:	

GOAL Discuss ethical choices

GRAMMAR BOOSTER ▸ p. 137

GRAMMAR *The real and unreal conditional*

- *Present factual conditionals: usage*
- *Future factual conditionals: usage and common errors*
- *Order of clauses: punctuation*

Remember: Conditional sentences express the results of actions or conditions.

if-clause (the condition)　　**result clause**
If I don't use English in class, I won't learn to speak it.

Real conditional sentences express factual or future results.
If I do the right thing, I can sleep at night. (factual: a result that <u>always</u> occurs if "I do the right thing")
If they don't make a reservation, they won't get a table. (future: a result that <u>will</u> occur if "they don't make a reservation")

The unreal conditional
Unreal conditional sentences describe what happens if a condition that doesn't exist actually does occur.

unreal action or condition　　**result (if it were true)**
If I found a wallet in the street, I'd look for the name of the owner. (unreal: I haven't found a wallet.)

In the <u>if</u>-clause, use the simple past tense. For the verb <u>be</u>, always use <u>were</u>.
In the result clause, use <u>would</u> and a base form.

unreal action or condition	result (if it were true)
If I **had** to make a hard decision,	I **would try** to do the right thing.
If she **knew** how to speak French,	she **would help** them.
If you **broke** something in a store,	**would** you **pay** for it?
If you **were** Matt,	what **would** you **do**?
If I **were** there,	I'**d know** what to do.
If you **weren't** my friend,	I **wouldn't tell** you what happened.

Be careful! Don't use <u>would</u> in the if- clause.
If I knew his name, I would tell you.
NOT If I ~~would know~~ his name…

Note: In real and unreal conditional sentences the clauses can occur in either order.
If I knew, I would tell you. OR I would tell you if I knew.

A Understand the grammar Check the sentences that describe an unreal condition or action and its results.

- ☐ 1 If we ate in a restaurant, I would pay the bill.
- ☐ 2 I'll pay the bill if we eat in a restaurant.
- ☐ 3 If we eat in a restaurant, I pay the bill.
- ☐ 4 If you get a haircut, you can charge it to your room.
- ☐ 5 His wife would worry if he came home really late.
- ☐ 6 If I were you, I'd tell him the truth.
- ☐ 7 If someone leaves a coat in her restaurant, the manager always tries to locate the owner of the coat.
- ☐ 8 If they sent me the wrong pants, I would return them.

B Grammar practice Complete each unreal conditional sentence with the correct forms of the verbs.

1 If they .... (put) the wrong price on the coat, ... you .... (buy) it without telling the clerk?

2 I'm sure you .... (say) something if the restaurant check .... (be) wrong.

3 If I .... (find) an expensive piece of jewelry in a public bathroom and .... (can not) find the owner, I .... (keep) it.

4 If you .... (be) friends with someone who did something wrong, ... you .... (say) something to him or her?

5 If you .... (have) two tickets, ... you .... (give) one to a friend?

6 What .... (happen) if it .... (snow) here tomorrow?

7 They .... (go) to India if they .... (have) the money.

8 If they .... (send) you two jackets instead of the one you ordered, ... you .... (call) the company and .... (send) one jacket back?

9 If they .... (be) here, I .... (tell) them what happened.

5:20

A 🔊 Read and listen to people discussing an ethical choice.

A: Look at this. They didn't charge us for the desserts.

B: Really? I think we'd better tell the waiter.

A: You think so?

B: Absolutely. If we didn't tell him, it would be wrong.

5:21

B 🔊 **Rhythm and intonation** Listen again and repeat. Then practice the Conversation Model with a partner.

5:22 🔊 **Confirming responses**
Absolutely.
Definitely.
Of course.
Sure.

Assimilation of <u>d</u> + y in <u>would you</u>

5:23

A 🔊 Notice how the /d/ and /y/ sounds assimilate to /dʒ/ in questions with "would you." Read and listen. Then listen again and repeat.

1 What would you do if the waiter didn't charge you for the dessert?

2 What would you do if you found a wallet on the street?

3 Who would you call if you were sick?

4 Where would you go if you wanted a great meal?

B Complete the following questions. Ask a partner the questions, using assimilation with <u>would you</u>. Then answer your partner's questions.

1 What would you do if ....?

2 Where would you go if ....?

3 When would you eat if ....?

NOW YOU CAN **Discuss ethical choices**

A **Pair work** Change the Conversation Model. Use the pictures to discuss ethical choices. Then change roles.

A: Look .... They ....

B: ....? I think ....'d better ....

A: You think so?

B: .... If ...., ...

B **Discussion** Tell your classmates about an ethical choice <u>you</u> had to make in the past.

They undercharged me.

They didn't charge us for the cake.

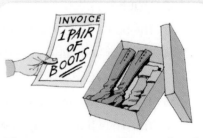
They gave me more than I ordered.

They gave me too much change.

GOAL   Return someone else's property

CONVERSATION MODEL

A 🔊 5:24 Read and listen to a conversation about returning property.

A: Excuse me. I think you forgot something.

B: I did?

A: Isn't this jacket hers?

B: Oh, you're right. It is. That's nice of you.

A: Don't mention it.

> 🔊 5:26 **Acknowledging thanks**
> Don't mention it.
> My pleasure.
> You're welcome.
> Not at all.

B 🔊 5:25 **Rhythm and intonation** Listen again and repeat. Then practice the Conversation Model with a partner.

GRAMMAR   *Possessive pronouns / Whose*

> **Be careful!**
> • Don't use a possessive adjective in place of a possessive pronoun.
>   Is this yours? NOT Is this ~~your~~?
> • Don't use a noun after a possessive pronoun.
>   These shoes are mine. NOT ~~They're mine shoes.~~

Possessive pronouns can replace nouns and noun phrases. They answer questions with <u>Whose</u> and clarify answers to questions with <u>Which</u>.

A: **Whose** coat is that?   B: It's **mine**. (=It's my coat.)
A: **Which** is <u>her cup</u>?   B: This one is **hers**.

GRAMMAR BOOSTER ▶ p. 138
• *Possessive nouns: review and expansion*
• *Pronouns: summary*

subject pronouns	possessive adjectives	possessive pronouns	
I	my	mine	That's <u>my jacket</u>. / It's **mine**.
you	your	yours	<u>Your dinner</u> was great. / **Yours** was great.
he	his	his	Are these <u>his keys</u>? / Are these **his**?
she	her	hers	She drives <u>her car</u> to work. / She drives **hers** to work.
we	our	ours	These are <u>our shoes</u>. / These are **ours**.
they	their	theirs	They finished <u>their assignment</u>. / They finished **theirs**.

A Grammar practice Replace the noun phrases with possessive pronouns.

1 Those gloves are ~~my gloves~~. *(mine)*

2 That is ~~her coat~~.

3 The books on that table are ~~Mr. Davison's~~.

4 Their car and ~~our car~~ are parked on the same street.

5 Are those my tickets or ~~her tickets~~?

6 The white house is ~~my mother's house~~.

7 Is this painting ~~your painting~~ or ~~her brother's painting~~?

8 The newspaper under the chair is ~~his daughter's paper~~.

9 Is this DVD ~~your DVD~~ or ~~your friends'~~?

10 Are these ~~your son's shoes~~?

B Grammar practice Complete the conversations. Circle the correct answers.

1 A: Whose umbrella is this, (he / his) or (her / hers)?

B: I'm not sure. Ask them if it's (their / theirs).

2 A: Who is more conservative? Your parents or Jerome's?

B: (He / His), I think. (My / Mine) parents are pretty liberal.

3 A: Is this (ours / our) suitcase?

B: No, I already got (our / ours) suitcase, so this one can't be (our / ours).

4 A: I found this necklace near Carrie's desk. Is it (her / hers)?

B: No, it's (my / mine) necklace. I'm so happy someone found it!

5 A: Is that (their / theirs) car?

B: No, (their / theirs) is the black one over there.

6 A: Where should we meet? At (your / yours) house or (my / mine)?

B: Neither. Let's meet at (my / mine) office.

C 🔊 **Listening comprehension** Listen to the conversations and complete each statement with a possessive pronoun.

5:27

1 The bag is ....

2 The phone is ...., but the keys belong to Brad's wife. They're ....

3 The coat isn't ....

4 The concert tickets aren't ....

NOW YOU CAN | **Return someone else's property**

A Pair work Change the Conversation Model to role-play
returning the items in the pictures. Then change roles.

A: Excuse me. I think you forgot something.

B: I did?

A: .... yours?

B: Oh, you're right. .... That's
nice of you.

A: ....

B Group work First, collect personal items
from your classmates. Then, role-play returning
someone else's property. Walk around the room
to find the owners. Use possessive pronouns.

C Extension Place all your classmates' personal
items on a table. Ask about each item. Identify
the owner, using possessive pronouns.

❝ Whose cell phone is this? ❞

❝ It's his. ❞

GOAL Express personal values

Explore your ideas Which actions would be OK, and which wouldn't be OK for the following people: you? your parents? your grandparents? your own teenaged child?

> ❝ It wouldn't be OK if my grandmother pierced her nose. Face piercing is for young people. She's too old. ❞

dye one's hair a wild color

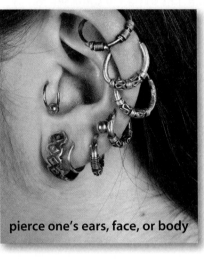

pierce one's ears, face, or body

get a tattoo

A 🔊 5:28 **Listen for the main ideas** Listen to each conversation. Then circle the correct word or phrase to complete each statement.

1 a Beth thinks it's (OK / not OK) to wear an earring to the office.
  b Beth (convinces / doesn't convince) Luke that it's OK.

2 a Celia's husband thinks it's (OK / wrong) for a woman to have a tattoo.
  b Celia's husband thinks it's (OK / wrong) for a man to have a tattoo.

3 a The first man is (happy / not happy) that his daughter is going to law school.
  b He wants his daughter to (stay home / go to work).

4 a Kate's dad is (worried / not worried) about what people think of Kate.
  b Kate is (worried / not worried) about what people think of her.

B **Understand vocabulary from context** Read the following quotations from the conversations. Then choose the correct definition for each underlined word or phrase. Listen again if necessary.

1 "But lots of people are <u>old-fashioned</u> and they don't think men should wear earrings."
  a prefer the way things were in the past
  b prefer the way things are now

2 "What <u>a double standard</u>!"
  a the same rules for everyone
  b different rules for different people

3 "That's a little <u>sexist</u>, if you ask me!"
  a You don't treat men and women equally.
  b You treat men and women equally.

4 "But <u>modesty</u> is very important for girls."
  a wearing clothes that cover one's body
  b wearing clothes that show one's body

C Apply new vocabulary Write an example for each word or phrase from your own experience. Compare examples with a partner.

old-fashioned	
a double standard	
sexist	
modesty	

D Pair work Discuss the picture. Use the following words and phrases in your discussion: <u>old-fashioned</u>, <u>sexist</u>, <u>double standard</u>, <u>modesty</u>.

> " He's measuring her swimsuit. If she were a man, he wouldn't measure it. That's a double standard. "

Man measuring the length of a woman's swimsuit (U.S., 1920s)

NOW YOU CAN Express personal values

A Idea framing Complete the Values Self-Test. Then compare answers with a partner. Do you have the same values?

B Notepadding Answer each question and explain your opinion, using examples.

Is it sometimes OK to have a double standard for men and women?
Can people be sexist when they talk about men, or only about women?
Are old-fashioned ideas usually better or worse than modern ideas?

C Group work Now discuss each question, expressing your personal values. Expect people to disagree with you!

♻ **Be sure to recycle this language.**

Agreement and disagreement	Likes and dislikes	Adjectives
I agree.	I like ___ .	liberal
I disagree.	I dislike ___ .	conservative
It depends.	I hate ___ .	strict
	I can't stand ___ .	modest
	I don't mind ___ .	
	___ drives me crazy!	

Values Self–Test

Check the boxes that best describe your values. Include a specific example.

1. ❑ I'm modern in my attitudes about modesty.
   ❑ I'm old–fashioned in my attitudes about modesty.
   Explain _____
   _____
   _____

2. ❑ I think tattoos and body piercing are OK for men.
   ❑ I think tattoos and body piercing are OK for women.
   Explain _____
   _____
   _____

3. ❑ I think it's OK to have a double standard for different people.
   ❑ I think the rules should be the same for everyone.
   Explain _____
   _____
   _____

4. ❑ Some people might say I'm sexist.
   ❑ Nobody would say I'm sexist.
   Explain _____
   _____
   _____

BEFORE YOU READ

Predict Look at the headlines of the three news stories. In what way do you think the stories will be similar?

READING   5:29

Man Risks Life to Save Another

Many people who ride a busy urban subway wonder, "What would happen if I fell off the platform and onto the tracks? What would I do?" Others wonder, "What would I do if someone else fell?"

That question was answered in a split-second decision made by "subway hero" Wesley Autrey, a fifty-year-old New York City construction worker on his way to work. Autrey jumped onto the tracks to save a fellow passenger from an oncoming New York City subway train.

The passenger, Cameron Hollopeter, 20, a film student at the New York Film Academy, had fallen between the tracks after suffering a seizure. Autrey rolled Hollopeter into a gap between the rails and covered him with his own body just as the train entered the station. Both men survived.

"I don't feel like I did something spectacular; I just saw someone who needed help," Mr. Autrey said. "I did what I felt was right."

Homeless Man Returns Wallet with $900

Posted on: Monday, 17 April

SANTA ANA, Calif. - A homeless man searching through trash bins for recyclable cans found a missing wallet and returned it to its owner. Kim Bogue, who works in the city, realized that her wallet was missing last week and doubted she'd ever get back the $900 and credit cards inside. "I prayed that night and asked God to help me," said Bogue, who was saving the money for a trip to her native Thailand.

Days later, a homeless man found the wallet wrapped in a plastic bag in the trash, where Bogue had accidentally thrown it away with her lunch. He gave it to Sherry Wesley, who works in a nearby building. "He came to me with the wad of money and said, 'This probably belongs to someone that you work with. Can you return it?'" Wesley said.

"He has a very good heart," said Bogue, who gave the man a $100 reward. "If someone else had found it, the money would have been gone."

An act of honesty by airport screener

NEW DELHI: In a display of honesty, a security agent at the Indira Gandhi International Airport handed over a small plastic bag with US $3,000 in cash to a passenger who had completely forgotten the bag after it passed through the airport screening machine.

Noticing that the bag had been left behind, Dalbir Singh made an announcement asking passengers to come forward to claim it. However, when no one claimed it, Singh inspected the baggage tag and guessed it probably belonged to a passenger en route to Mumbai. An announcement was made on the next flight to Mumbai and the owner of the bag came forward to collect it.

Singh was given a cash reward for his honesty.

Information sources: cbs.com, hinduonnet.com, ap.org

A Summarize Summarize one of the articles. Close your book and tell the story in your own words.

B Interpret information Discuss each person's motives for his or her actions.

1 Why did Kim Bogue give the homeless man a reward?

2 Why did Wesley Autrey risk his life to save a stranger?

3 Why do you think Dalbir Singh returned the money to the passenger?

C Relate to personal experience Think of a story you have heard about someone who helped a stranger in need. Tell it to the class.

On your *ActiveBook* Self-Study Disc:
Extra Reading Comprehension Questions

A Notepadding Answer the questions about each situation.

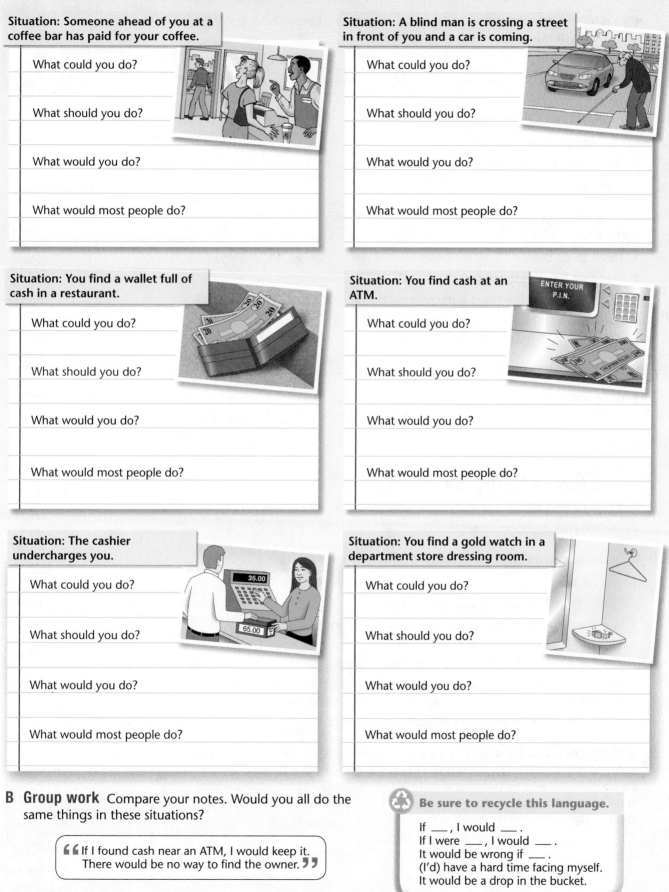

Situation: Someone ahead of you at a coffee bar has paid for your coffee.

What could you do?

What should you do?

What would you do?

What would most people do?

Situation: A blind man is crossing a street in front of you and a car is coming.

What could you do?

What should you do?

What would you do?

What would most people do?

Situation: You find a wallet full of cash in a restaurant.

What could you do?

What should you do?

What would you do?

What would most people do?

Situation: You find cash at an ATM.

What could you do?

What should you do?

What would you do?

What would most people do?

Situation: The cashier undercharges you.

What could you do?

What should you do?

What would you do?

What would most people do?

Situation: You find a gold watch in a department store dressing room.

What could you do?

What should you do?

What would you do?

What would most people do?

B Group work Compare your notes. Would you all do the same things in these situations?

> "If I found cash near an ATM, I would keep it. There would be no way to find the owner."

Be sure to recycle this language.

If ___ , I would ___ .
If I were ___ , I would ___ .
It would be wrong if ___ .
(I'd) have a hard time facing myself.
It would be a drop in the bucket.

Review

More Practice
ActiveBook Self-Study Disc

grammar · vocabulary · listening
reading · speaking · pronunciation

A ◀)) **Listening comprehension** Listen to the conversations. Check <u>Yes</u> or <u>No</u> to answer each question and explain your answers.

5:30

5:31 / 5:32

🎵 **Top Notch Pop**
"What Would You Do?"
Lyrics p. 150

	Yes	No
1 Do you think John has a double standard?	☐	☐

Explain your answer: ....

2 Do you think Jessica's mom is sexist? ☐ ☐

Explain your answer: ....

3 Do you think Alex's dad is old-fashioned? ☐ ☐

Explain your answer: ....

B Complete the questions with <u>Whose</u>. Then answer each question, using possessive pronouns. Follow the example.

1 Those shoes belong to my daughter. *Whose are* .... they? *They're hers.* ....

2 That coat belongs to my son. .... it? ....

3 The house across the street is my parents' house. .... it? ....

4 These coins are my husband's and mine. .... they? ....

5 The table over there is your table. .... it? ....

C Complete each conditional sentence in your own words.

1 If the weather were good, ...

2 If ...., I'd go out to eat tonight.

3 If I found your wallet, ...

4 If ...., I'd call home.

5 I'd be angry with my children if ....

6 If I had a new car, ...

7 I would choose a new career if ....

D What would you do? Complete each unreal conditional sentence.

1 You eat two sandwiches for lunch, but they only charge you for one.

(YOU) "If the restaurant undercharged me, I ...."

2 You pay for a newspaper that costs one dollar with a five-dollar bill. The merchant gives you nine dollars change.

(YOU) "If the merchant gave me too much change, I ...."

3 You buy a smart phone from a website. When the package arrives, you see that the company has sent you two MP3 players and the smart phone.

(YOU) "If the company sent me more items than I paid for, I ...."

E **Writing** On a separate sheet of paper, write three paragraphs about Matt's dilemma in the Photo Story on page 111. In the first paragraph, summarize the situation. In the second paragraph write about what Matt could or should do. In the third paragraph, write what you would do if you were Matt. Explain your reasons, using the unreal conditional.

WRITING BOOSTER ▸ p. 148

• *Introducing conflicting ideas* <u>On the one hand</u>; <u>On the other hand</u>
• *Guidance for Exercise E*

Contest Form teams. With your team, look at the two pictures for one minute. Then close your books and tell the story you saw in the pictures. The team that remembers more details wins.

Pair work

1 Tell your partner what you would do if you were the woman who found the lost object. Use the unreal conditional. Start like this:

If I found ..., I would ...

2 Create a conversation for the people in the second picture. Use possessive pronouns. Start like this:

Excuse me. Is this your ...

GATE 22 B

BAGGAGE →

departures

A few minutes later

NOW I CAN...

☐ Discuss ethical choices.
☐ Return someone else's property.
☐ Express personal values.
☐ Discuss acts of kindness and honesty.

121

Grammar Booster

The Grammar Booster is optional. It is not required for the achievement tests in the *Top Notch Complete Assessment Package.* If you use the Grammar Booster, there are additional Grammar Booster exercises in the Workbook in a separate labeled section.

UNIT 1 Lesson 1

The present perfect: information questions

Form information questions by inverting <u>have</u> and the subject of the sentence.
   What **have** you **seen** in Paris?
   What (OR Which) countries **have** you **visited**?
   Where **has** she **found** the best souvenirs?
   How **have** your parents **been**?
   How many cities **have** you **visited** this week?
   Who **have** you **traveled** with?

Note: When <u>Who</u> is the subject of the sentence, there is no inversion.
   Who **has traveled** to Miami in the last two months?

On a separate sheet of paper, write information questions. Use the present perfect.

1 what dishes / she / try / in Mérida
2 who / you / invite / to the party
3 where / he / work / before
4 which movies / they / see

5 how / your children / be
6 who / climb / Grouse Mountain
7 what / they / hear / about the new school
8 how many times / she / take / that class

UNIT 1 Lesson 2

The present perfect: use and placement of <u>yet</u> and <u>already</u>

Use <u>already</u> in affirmative statements. Place <u>already</u> before the main verb or at the end of the statement.
   I've **already** read the book. OR I've read the book **already**.

Use <u>yet</u> in negative statements. Place <u>yet</u> at the end of the statement or between <u>have</u> and the base form.
   I haven't read the book **yet**. OR I haven't **yet** read the book.

Use <u>yet</u> or <u>already</u> in questions.
   Have you read the book **yet**? OR { Have you **already** read the book?
                                          Have you read the book **already**?

Be careful!
Don't use <u>yet</u> in affirmative statements. Don't use <u>already</u> in negative statements.
   DON'T SAY Yes, I've read the book ~~yet~~. / No, I haven't ~~already~~ read the book.
Don't use <u>ever</u> with <u>yet</u> or <u>already</u>.
   DON'T SAY Have you ~~ever~~ read the book ~~yet~~? / Have you ~~ever~~ read the book ~~already~~?

A On a separate sheet of paper, rewrite each statement or question, using <u>already</u> or <u>yet</u>.

1 (yet) Has she finished the homework?
2 (yet) They haven't seen the movie.

3 (already) We've tried fried clams several times.
4 (already) Has your father left?

B On a separate sheet of paper, rewrite each sentence, using <u>already</u> or <u>yet</u>.

1 I haven't had dinner.
2 She's been to London, Berlin, and Rome.

3 They haven't called home.
4 We've finished our class.

The present perfect: ever, never, and before

Use ever in questions. Use never in negative statements and short answers. Do not use ever in affirmative statements.

Have you **ever** made sushi? ⎰ Yes, I have. OR Yes, I've made sushi. NOT Yes, I've ~~ever~~ made sushi.
                        ⎱ No, I **never** have. OR No, I've **never** made sushi.

You can also use before in negative statements with never.

I've **never** been to Thailand before.

In very informal speech, ever is sometimes used to strongly emphasize never. This meaning of ever is similar to "in my whole life."

I've **never ever** been to Thailand.

C On a separate sheet of paper, answer each question, using real information. If the answer is yes, write when this happened.

1 Have you ever gone on a cruise?
2 Have you ever tried Indian food?
3 Have you ever been to Hawaii?

4 Have you ever met a famous person?
5 Have you ever fallen in love?
6 Have you ever played golf?

UNIT 2 Lesson 1

The present perfect and the present perfect continuous: unfinished actions

Unfinished (or continuous) actions are those that began in the past, continue in the present, and may possibly continue into the future. Here are three ways to talk about unfinished actions:

1 the present perfect with since: Use since with a stated start time in the past.
I've lived here **since** 2001. (2001 is the stated start time. I still live here, so the action "continues.")

2 the present perfect with for: Use for to describe the period of time from its start until the present.
I've lived here **for** five years. (Emphasis is on the five-year period. I still live here, so the action "continues.")

3 the present perfect continuous with for or since. (Form the present perfect continuous with the present perfect of be and a present participle.)
I've **been living here** since 2001. OR I've **been living here** for five years. (In both cases, the action "continues.")

When describing continuing and unfinished actions with for and since, the present perfect and the present perfect continuous are both correct. Some people feel the present perfect continuous emphasizes the continuing time a bit more.

A Read the sentences with the present perfect. Check each sentence that describes an unfinished (or continuing) action.

☐ **1** The Grants have lived in Buenos Aires since the late seventies.

☐ **2** Carmen has been living in Buenos Aires since last year.

☐ **3** I've visited Paris three times.

☐ **4** Ted has been visiting Paris since the 1980's.

☐ **5** We have eaten in that great Indian restaurant for years.

☐ **6** They've eaten in that Indian restaurant before.

☐ **7** My brother has been playing tennis for many years.

☐ **8** Min-ji has played tennis twice.

B Complete each statement with the present perfect continuous.

1 Wall-E _____ (play) at the Children's Classics Cinema every Saturday since 2009.

2 Robert _____ (wait) in the ticket holders' line for a pretty long time.

3 People _____ (worry about) violence in movies since the sixties.

4 I'_____ (talk about) that movie for weeks.

5 We'_____ (come) to this classics movie theater for two years.

Spelling rules for the present participle: review

Add –ing to the base form of the verb
speak → speaking

If the base form ends in a silent –e, drop the –e and add –ing.
have → having

In verbs of one syllable, if the last three letters are a consonant-vowel-consonant (C-V-C) series, double the last consonant and then add –ing.

C V C
s i t → sitting

Be careful! Don't double the last consonant in words that end in –w, –x, or –y.
flow → flowing
fix → fixing
pay → paying

In verbs of more than one syllable that end in a consonant-vowel-consonant series, double the last consonant only if the stress is on the last syllable.

control → controlling BUT order → ordering

C On a separate sheet of paper, write the present participle for the following base forms.

1 find		**8** go		**15** come		**22** forget		**29** begin
2 be		**9** make		**16** leave		**23** eat		**30** tell
3 lose		**10** fix		**17** drive		**24** pay		**31** bring
4 put		**11** know		**18** meet		**25** stand		**32** take
5 get		**12** speak		**19** blow		**26** think		
6 say		**13** hear		**20** give		**27** buy		
7 write		**14** let		**21** run		**28** see		

UNIT 2   Lesson 2

Ways to express preferences: review

Use <u>like</u>, <u>prefer</u>, or <u>would rather</u> with a direct object to indicate preferences. The direct object can be a noun or noun phrase, a base form, or an infinitive, depending on the structure you use.

Nouns or noun phrases
She'd like tea.
We'd like an early breakfast tomorrow.

Sarah prefers coffee.
Would they prefer a horror film?

Base forms
They'd rather see a comedy.
Would you rather have coffee or tea?

I'd rather not go out tonight.

Infinitives
I'd like to go to the movies tonight.
I prefer (OR I'd prefer) to see something less bloody.

She'd prefer not to show her children that film.

A On a separate sheet of paper, write sentences and questions using the following words and phrases.

1 They / prefer / see / the Woody Allen film.

5 Jason / would like / have / a large container of popcorn.

2 What time / you / would rather / meet?

6 I'd prefer / rent / a sci-fi film tonight.

3 Who / would like / order / eggs for breakfast?

7 Her parents / would rather not / watch / anything too violent.

4 they / would rather / watch TV or go out?

8 Who'd prefer / not see / that silly animated film?

B On a separate sheet of paper, answer each question in a complete sentence, expressing your own preference.

1 What genre of movie do you usually prefer?

2 What would you like to have for dinner tonight?

3 Would you rather see a comedy or a horror film?

4 Would you prefer popcorn or potato chips from the refreshment stand?

5 Would you like to rent a DVD or go out to the movies?

UNIT 3   Lesson 1

Expressing obligation with have to and must

Use have to and must plus a base form to express obligation when there is no other choice of action available.

Students **must take** this exam.

You **have to take** the 6:00 train if you want to arrive on time.

She **has to make** a reservation before July 15th.

Be careful!

The negative form **must not** expresses prohibition, not obligation.

You **must not smoke** in your room. = Don't smoke there.

The negative forms **don't have to** and **doesn't have to** express a lack of obligation.

You **don't have to show** your passport. = It isn't necessary.

Note: Must is very formal and not very common in speaking. It is generally used by a person in authority (e.g. a teacher or boss) to state policy or law. Have to is much more common in both speaking and writing. The more informal have got to* is also common in spoken English.

Sorry. I've got to hurry. I'm going to be late.

*There is no negative form of have got to in American English. Use don't have to or doesn't have to.

A On a separate sheet of paper, write each of the following sentences two ways: with must and with have to.

1 Hotel guests / leave / their luggage at the front desk.

2 Hotel employees / arrive / before 9:00 A.M.

3 Hotel maids / close / the door / while cleaning a room.

4 Hotel guests / park / their cars in front of the hotel.

B On a separate sheet of paper, write each of the sentences in Exercise A again, using must not to express a prohibition. Make changes so the sentence makes sense.

Hotel guests must not leave their luggage at the front desk.

C On a separate sheet of paper, write each of the sentences in Exercise A again, using don't or doesn't have to to express a lack of obligation. Make changes so the sentence makes sense.

Hotel employees don't have to arrive before 9:00 A.M.

Suggestions and advice: <u>could</u>, <u>should</u>, <u>ought to</u>, and <u>had better</u>

Use <u>could</u> plus a base form to suggest or ask about an alternative. There is no negative form.
> They **could stay** at the Fiesta Hotel if the Milton is full.
> **Could** they **stay** at the Fiesta Hotel if the Milton is full?

Use <u>should</u> or <u>ought to</u> plus a base form to state an opinion or give advice.
> You **should** (or **ought to**) stay at the Milton. It's close to town and very cheap.
> You **shouldn't stay** at the Fairway Inn. It's too expensive.

Use <u>had better</u> to state an opinion or give advice. The meaning is similar to <u>should</u> and <u>ought to</u>, but <u>had better</u> expresses the idea that there is a consequence for not doing something.
> You'**d better stay** at the Milton. The other hotels are too far from town.
> You'**d better not stay** at the Fairway Inn if you want to save money.

Note: In American English it's very uncommon to use <u>ought to</u> in the negative. It's unusual to say: You ~~ought not stay~~ at the Fairway Inn.

<u>Ought to</u> has the same meaning as <u>should</u>, but <u>should</u> is slightly less formal.
Don't use <u>ought to</u> in questions or negative statements. Use <u>should</u> or <u>shouldn't</u> instead.

D On a separate sheet of paper, write five suggestions to a visitor to your city or country, using <u>could</u>, <u>should</u>, <u>shouldn't</u>, <u>had better</u>, and <u>had better not</u>.

> *You should stay at a hotel on the beach. The beaches are really beautiful, and the location is convenient.*

Expectation: <u>be supposed to</u>

Use <u>be supposed to</u> to mean that someone expects an action from another person.
> We'**re supposed to check out** of our room by twelve.
> (The hotel expects guests to check out at that time.)

The negative form is <u>be not supposed to</u>.
> Hotel guests **are not supposed to take** anything from their rooms.

E On a separate sheet of paper, write five sentences that describe actions your school expects from its students. Use <u>be supposed to</u>.

> *Students are supposed to come on time to class. They're not supposed to be late.*

F Choose the sentence closer in meaning to each numbered statement or question.

1 Do you think the Milton Hotel is a good place to stay?
  a Do you think I should stay at the Milton Hotel?
  b Do you think I have to stay at the Milton Hotel?

2 If you don't have your luggage ticket, the bellman won't give you your luggage.
  a You could give the bellman the ticket.
  b You must give the bellman the ticket.

3 They don't accept credit cards in this hotel. They only accept cash.
  a You have to pay with cash.
  b You'd better pay with cash.

4 When I made the reservation, I asked for a suite.
  a They could give me a suite.
  b They're supposed to give me a suite.

5 Don't wear shorts in the restaurant.
  a You must not wear shorts in the restaurant.
  b You don't have to wear shorts in the restaurant.

Will and be going to

Use will or be going to for predictions about the future. The meaning is the same.
It'll rain tomorrow.
It's going to rain tomorrow.

Use be going to when you already have a plan for the future.
A: Are you coming to class tomorrow?
B: No, I'm going to go to the beach instead. NOT No, I'll go to the beach instead.

Other uses of will

Use will to talk about the immediate future when you do not already have a plan.
Maybe I'll go to the beach this weekend. NOT Maybe I'm going to go to the beach this weekend.

Use will to show willingness.
I'll eat chicken, but I won't eat seafood. (expresses willingness)

Compare will with be going to:
I'm going to eat chicken, but I'm not going to eat seafood. (expresses a plan)

A On a separate sheet of paper, write five sentences about your plans for the weekend, using be going to.

B On a separate sheet of paper, write five sentences with will or won't for willingness on one of the following topics.

> **Topics**
> kinds of exercise you're willing (or not willing) to do
> kinds of food you're willing (or not willing) to eat for breakfast
> kinds of clothes you're willing (or not willing) to wear

The past continuous: other uses

The past continuous describes an action that was continuous until (and possibly after) the moment at which another action took place. The words when or while are often used in sentences that contrast continuing and completed actions.
He was talking on the phone when the storm began. (continuous action, then completed action)
While I was living in Chile, I got married. (continuous action, then completed action)

The past continuous also describes two continuing actions occurring in the same period of time.
While she was driving, her husband was reading the newspaper.
They were eating, and the music was playing.

On a separate sheet of paper, use the prompts to write logical sentences. Use the past continuous and the simple past in each sentence.

1 She / take a test at school / when / she / hear the fire alarm

2 While I / talk to my mother on the phone / the TV show / start

3 Mr. Park / cook dinner / when / Mrs. Park / finish the laundry

4 Mr. Kemp / work in the garden / when / the rain / begin

5 While / Claudia / pick up / their rental car / Alex / call / their hotel

6 While / Nancy / shop at the grocery store / she / see / an old friend

Nouns and pronouns: review

A <u>noun</u> is a word that names a person, a place, or a thing. Nouns are either common or proper. A proper noun is capitalized.
    common nouns: car, windshield, doctor, woman, father
    proper nouns: Martin, Caracas, Carla's Restaurant

Two functions of nouns in sentences are subjects and direct objects. The subject performs the action of the verb. The object receives the action.

       subject   **direct object**
    Carla's Restaurant serves breakfast all day long.

A <u>pronoun</u> is a word that represents or replaces a noun. Pronouns also function as subjects and direct objects.
    subject pronouns: I, you, he, she, it, we, they
    object pronouns: me, you, him, her, it, us, them

    subject   **direct object**
    My parents   the car
           They   drove   it   to the airport.

First, underline the subjects and circle the objects in the following sentences. Then label each noun either "common" or "proper." Finally, write a checkmark above each pronoun. (Note: Not every sentence contains a pronoun.)

   proper   *common*
<u>Italians</u> drive fast (cars.)

1 We love big vans.

2 The children broke the side-view mirror.

3 Ms. Workman picked up the car this morning.

4 Rand loves sports cars, and his wife loves them, too.

5 A man driving a sports car hit our minivan.

6 I returned the rental car at the airport.

7 A-1 Rental Agency called me about the reservation.

Some and any: review

<u>Some</u> and <u>any</u> are indefinite quantifiers. They indicate an indefinite number or amount.
    There are some toothbrushes in aisle 2. (We don't know how many.)
    They are buying some shaving cream. (We don't know how much.)
    Could I get some nail files? (We're not asking for a specific number of nail files.)
    Do they have any makeup in this store? (We're not asking specifically how much.)

Be careful to use <u>some</u> and <u>any</u> correctly with count and non-count nouns:
<u>Some</u>: **with non-count nouns and plural count nouns in affirmative statements**
        non-count noun   **plural count noun**
    We need some sunscreen and some combs. They have some here.
<u>Any</u>: **with non-count nouns and plural count nouns in negative statements**
        non-count noun   **plural count noun**
    A: She doesn't want any shampoo, and he doesn't need any nail clippers.
    B: Good! We don't have to buy any, then. I'm out of cash.
<u>Any</u> or <u>some</u>: **with count and non-count nouns in questions**
    Do they need any toothpaste or sunscreen for the trip?
    Do we need any razors or toothbrushes?

> **Remember:** Count nouns name things you can count individually. They have singular and plural forms (1 nail file, 3 combs). Non-count nouns name things you cannot count individually. They don't have plural forms. Use containers, quantifiers, and other modifiers to make non-count nouns countable.
> **a bottle of** shampoo / aftershave
> **a jar of** face cream / deodorant
> **a tube of** toothpaste / lipstick
> **a bar of** soap
> **a can of** hairspray / deodorant / shaving cream
> **250 milliliters of** sunscreen

A On a separate sheet of paper, change the following sentences from affirmative to negative. Follow the example.

There is some shampoo in the shower. *There isn't any shampoo in the shower.*

1 There are some razors next to the sink.

2 We have some nail clippers.

3 They need some brushes for the children.

4 She's buying some mascara.

5 The salon needs some nail polish for the manicurists.

6 I want some sunscreen on my back.

7 There is some dental floss in aisle 4.

8 They need some deodorant for the trip.

B Complete each sentence with <u>some</u> or <u>any</u>.

1 I don't need _____ more hand lotion.

2 There isn't _____ makeup in the bag.

3 We don't see _____ scissors in the whole store.

4 They need _____ soap to wash their hands.

5 It's too bad that there isn't _____ toothpaste.

6 I don't see _____ combs or brushes on those shelves.

7 I know I had _____ nail files in my bag. Now I can't find them.

Too many, too much, and enough

The word <u>too</u> indicates a quantity that is excessive—more than someone wants or needs. Use <u>enough</u> to indicate that something is satisfactory.

Use <u>too many</u> and <u>not too many</u> for count nouns.
There are too many customers waiting in line.

Use <u>too much</u> and <u>not too much</u> for non-count nouns.
There's too much toothpaste on the toothbrush.

Use <u>enough</u> and <u>not enough</u> for both count and non-count nouns.
There's enough shampoo, but there aren't enough razors.

C Complete each sentence with <u>too many</u>, <u>too much</u>, or <u>enough</u>.

1 Let's do our nails. Do we have _____ nail polish for both of us?

2 This shampoo has _____ perfume. It smells awful!

3 It's not a good idea to buy _____ fruit. We're not going to be home for a few days.

4 This menu has _____ choices. I can't make up my mind.

5 Check the bathroom shelf to see if we have _____ soap. Mom and Dad are coming to visit.

6 I don't like when there are _____ brands. I can't decide which one to buy.

7 There's no way to get a haircut today. _____ people had the same idea!

8 They don't want to spend _____ money on makeup. They're trying to save money.

Comparative quantifiers fewer and less

Use <u>fewer</u> for count nouns. Use <u>less</u> for non-count nouns.
The Cosmetique store has fewer brands of makeup than the Emporium.
There's less hand lotion in this jar than in that bottle.

D Complete each sentence with <u>fewer</u> or <u>less</u>.

1 Which class has _____ students—the early class or the late one?

2 The recipe calls for _____ cheese than I thought.

3 It has _____ ingredients, too.

4 Don't rent from Cars Plus. They have _____ kinds of cars than International.

5 The Cineplus has _____ movies this weekend than usual.

6 Is there _____ shampoo in the large size or the economy size?

Indefinite pronouns: <u>something</u>, <u>anything</u>, and <u>nothing</u>

Use <u>something</u> in affirmative statements.

There's **something** in this box.

Use <u>anything</u> in negative statements.

There isn't **anything** in the fridge.

Use <u>something</u> or <u>anything</u> in <u>yes</u> / <u>no</u> questions.

Is there **something** we should talk about? Is **anything** wrong?

<u>Nothing</u> is the equivalent of <u>not anything</u>. Don't use <u>nothing</u> in negative statements.

There isn't **anything** in the fridge = There's **nothing** in the fridge. NOT There ~~isn't nothing~~ in the fridge.

Choose the correct indefinite pronoun to complete each sentence.

1 I need to go to the store to buy (something / anything).

2 There is (something / anything) I can do to help.

3 There isn't (something / anything) you can do to make yourself taller.

4 I went on the Internet to find (something / anything) about how to use sunscreen.

5 They have (something / anything) that helps you lose weight.

6 There's (anything / nothing) that can make you look young again.

7 They can't get (anything / nothing) to eat there after ten o'clock.

Use to / used to: use and form

The simple past tense can express a past habitual action if there is a reference to a period of time in the past.

When I was a kid, I **didn't eat** vegetables. I still don't today.

<u>Use to</u> and <u>used to</u> also express a past habitual action, but one that is no longer true today.

When I was a kid, I **didn't use to eat** vegetables. But now I do.

Remember: In <u>yes</u> / <u>no</u> questions and negative statements, use <u>use to</u> NOT <u>used to</u>.

I **used to** stay up late. Now I don't.

I **didn't use to** (NOT ~~used~~ to) get up early. Now I do.

Did you **use to** (NOT ~~used~~ to) go dancing more often?

A   **On a separate sheet of paper, change each statement into a <u>yes</u> / <u>no</u> question.**

I used to go running every day. *Did you use to go running every day?*

1 There used to be a large tree in front of your house.

2 Mr. and Mrs. Palmer used to go dancing every weekend.

3 Their grandmother used to put sugar in their orange juice.

4 Luke used to be very overweight.

B   **Use the prompts to write logical sentences with negative or affirmative forms of <u>use to</u> / <u>used to</u>.**

1 Jason and Trish / get lots of exercise, but now they go swimming every day.

2 There / be a movie theater on Smith Street, but now there isn't.

3 No one / worry about fatty foods, but now most people do.

4 English / be an international language, but now everyone uses English to communicate around the world.

5 Women / wear pants, but now it's very common for them to wear them.

Be used to means be accustomed to. Compare use to / used to + base form and be used to.

Used to + base form

I didn't use to like the food. But now I do.

Be used to

I'm used to the noise now. But when I first came here, it really bothered me.

Get used to means to become accustomed to.

You'll get used to the new schedule after a few days.

Be careful! With be used to, don't change used in negative statements or questions.

He wasn't used to the weather there. NOT He wasn't use to . . .

Are you used to the life here? NOT Are you use to . . .

C Check the sentences in which used to means accustomed to something.

☐ **1** When the school term ended, I was finally used to the new teacher.

☐ **2** In our other class, the teacher used to be very strict.

☐ **3** They used to like seafood, but now they don't.

☐ **4** Because we lived in the mountains, we weren't used to fresh seafood.

☐ **5** I'm sure she'll get used to her new apartment soon.

☐ **6** These shoes used to be comfortable, but now they're too loose.

☐ **7** I'm sure she'll get used to wearing high-heeled shoes.

D Write ✓ if the sentence is correct. Write ✗ if it is incorrect and make corrections.

☐ **1** I'll never get use to the traffic here.

☐ **2** We didn't use to take vacations very often.

☐ **3** Is he use to his new roommate yet?

☐ **4** Will she ever get use to life in the city?

☐ **5** What did you used to do on weekdays when you weren't working?

E On a separate sheet of paper, write two sentences about something you're used to and two sentences about something you're not used to.

You can also use would + the base form of a verb to describe repeated past actions. In this use, would has the same meaning as used to.

When we were young, our parents would go camping with us. (= used to go camping with us.)

Be careful! Use used to, not would, to describe possession, likes and dislikes, situations, or location in the past.

I used to have a lot of clothes. NOT I would have a lot of clothes.

My hometown used to be Dakar. NOT My hometown would be Dakar.

I used to be a terrible English student. NOT I would be a terrible English student.

F If it is possible, complete the sentence with would. If not, use a form of used to.

1 They _____ go to the beach every Saturday in the summer.

2 I _____ have a really large kitchen in my old house.

3 My husband never _____ like coffee, but now he can't get enough of it.

4 Almost every evening of our vacation we _____ eat at a terrific outdoor restaurant.

5 Before the microwave, people _____ heat up soup on the top of the stove.

6 Sigrid _____ be a tour guide, but now she's a professional chef.

7 There _____ be three or four Italian restaurants in town, but now there aren't any.

Negative yes / no questions: short answers

Answer negative yes / no questions the same way as you would answer affirmative yes / no questions.

Is Jane a vegetarian?
Isn't Jane a vegetarian? } Yes, she is. / No, she isn't.

Do they have two sons?
Don't they **have** two sons? } Yes, they do. / No, they don't.

A Answer each negative question with a short answer. (Use the information for your answer.)

1 A: Isn't Hank a lawyer?
 B: _____. He's not a lawyer.

2 A: Doesn't Bob have two brothers?
 B: _____. He has two younger brothers.

3 A: Haven't you been to Siberia before?
 B: _____. I've never been here before.

4 A: Aren't you learning English right now?
 B: _____. I'm studying English at the institute.

5 A: Wasn't Nancy at the movies last night?
 B: _____. She didn't go to the movies.

6 A: Don't Sachiko and Tomofumi have a car?
 B: _____. They own a minivan.

Suggestions with Why don't...? and Why doesn't...?

You can make suggestions with both Why don't . . . ? or Why doesn't . . . ?

A: Your daughter looks really cold.
 Why doesn't she **put** on a sweater?
B: Good idea.

A: Your kids are so nice. **Why don't** they **come**
 and play with mine sometime?
B: That would be great.

B On a separate sheet of paper, continue each statement with a suggestion using Why don't . . . ? or Why doesn't . . . ?

Your husband doesn't look like he feels very well. *Why doesn't he go see a doctor?*

1 Wouldn't you love to have a cup of coffee right now?

2 Did you say your father hasn't taken a vacation in two years?

3 It's such a beautiful day! We shouldn't stay indoors.

4 Your sister looks so bored!

5 We shouldn't just watch TV tonight.

6 Mr. García needs a ride to the airport.

7 Nina's English teacher suggested that she work on her listening skills.

Gerunds and infinitives: as subjects, subject complements, and objects

Gerunds (–ing form of a verb) and infinitives (to + base form) function as nouns within sentences.
Gerunds can be subjects, subject complements, or objects.
   Painting is my favorite leisure-time activity. (subject)
   My favorite activity is **painting**. (subject complement; usually follows <u>be</u>)
   I enjoy **painting**. (direct object)
   I read a book about the history of **painting**. (object of the preposition <u>of</u>)

Infinitives can be subjects, subject complements, and direct objects.
   To paint well is a talent. (subject)
   The only thing he needs is **to paint**. (subject complement; usually follows <u>be</u>)
   I want **to paint**. (direct object)

Underline the gerunds and circle the infinitives in the following sentences. Then write *subject* (s), *subject complement* (c), *direct object* (do), **or** *object of a preposition* (op) **on the line next to each one.**

_____ **1** I enjoy watching movies every night on DVD.

_____ **2** Her greatest dream was to see all of her children attend college.

_____ **3** What's the point of creating a nice environment at home if genetics is the only thing that counts?

_____ **4** Avoiding too much pressure helps children become less critical.

_____ **5** My niece plans to study personality development next semester.

Negative gerunds

A gerund can be made negative by using a negative word before it.
   I like **not going** to bed too late.
   They complained about **never having** enough time.

Complete the paragraph with affirmative and negative gerunds.

I really want to do something to improve my appearance and lose weight. I'm sick of _____ able to fit into my
_{1 be}
clothes. I know it's not enough to complain about _____ weight—I need to do something about it! I plan to spend
_{2 gain}
every afternoon _____ my bike. Also, I want to go on a diet, but I'm afraid of _____ hungry all the time.
_{3 ride} _{4 feel}
I worry about _____ enough energy to exercise if I'm _____ enough to eat.
_{5 have} _{6 get}

The passive voice: transitive verbs and intransitive verbs

Remember: The subject of a sentence performs the action of the verb. A direct object receives the action of the verb.

A transitive verb can have a direct object. Transitive verbs can be used in the active voice or passive voice.

active voice	passive voice
Picasso **painted** *Guernica* in 1937. →	*Guernica* **was painted** in 1937.

An intransitive verb cannot have a direct object. With an intransitive verb, there is no "receiver" of an action.
   The painting **arrives** tomorrow.
   The *Mona Lisa* **will stay** at the Louvre.
   That new sculpture **seems** like a Botero.

Common intransitive verbs

arrive	happen	sit
come	laugh	sleep
die	live	stand
fall	rain	stay
go	seem	walk

A Check each sentence that has an intransitive verb.

☐ **1** Pedro Almodóvar's new film about women arrives in theaters this fall.

☐ **2** A Canadian art collector has bought two of Michelangelo's drawings.

☐ **3** Someone stole Edvard Munch's painting *The Scream* in 2004.

☐ **4** The painter Georgia O'Keeffe lived in the southwestern part of the United States.

☐ **5** The Van Gogh Museum in Amsterdam sent *Sunflowers* on a world tour.

☐ **6** The traveling collection of ancient Roman sculpture is coming to San Diego this week.

☐ **7** The Metropolitan Museum of Art opened a new gallery last year.

The passive voice: form

Form the passive voice with a form of <u>be</u> and the past participle of a verb.

	Active voice	Passive voice
Simple present tense	Art collectors **buy** famous paintings all over the world.	Famous paintings **are bought** by art collectors all over the world.
Present continuous	The Film Center **is showing** Kurosawa's films.	Kurosawa's films **are being shown** at the Film Center.
Present perfect	Some world leaders **have bought** Yu Hung's paintings.	Yu Hung's paintings **have been bought** by some world leaders.
Simple past tense	I.M.Pei **designed** the Grand Pyramid at the Louvre.	The Grand Pyramid at the Louvre **was designed** by I.M.Pei.
Past continuous	Last year, the museum **was selling** copies of Monet's paintings.	Last year, copies of Monet's paintings **were being sold** by the museum.
Future with <u>will</u>	Ang Lee **will direct** a new film next year.	A new film **will be directed** by Ang Lee next year.
Future with <u>be going to</u>	The Tate Modern **is going to show** Van Gogh's drawings next month.	Van Gogh's drawings **are going to be shown** at the Tate Modern next month.

B On a separate sheet of paper, rewrite each sentence in the passive voice. Use a <u>by</u> phrase only if it is important to know who is performing the action.

1 Someone actually stole the *Mona Lisa* in 1911.

2 Paloma Picasso designed these pieces of silver jewelry.

3 Someone will repair the sculpture when it gets old.

4 People have paid millions of U.S. dollars for some of Van Gogh's paintings.

5 They are showing some new paintings at the Smith Gallery this week.

6 The Malcolm Museum is going to exhibit ten sculptures by Asian artists.

7 Frida Kahlo was painting these pieces while she was married to Diego Rivera.

8 People built great pyramids throughout Central America during the height of the Mayan civilization.

C On a separate sheet of paper, rewrite the sentences in Exercise A that have a transitive verb, changing the active voice to the passive voice.

The passive voice: <u>yes</u> / <u>no</u> questions

To form <u>yes</u> / <u>no</u> questions in the passive voice, move the first auxiliary verb before the subject.

Simple present tense	Are famous paintings ~~are~~ bought by art collectors?
Present continuous	Are Kurosawa's films ~~are~~ being shown at the Film Center?
Present perfect	Have Yu Hung's paintings ~~have~~ been bought by some world leaders?
Simple past tense	Was the Grand Pyramid at the Louvre ~~was~~ designed by I.M. Pei?
Past continuous	Were copies of Monet's paintings ~~were~~ being sold by the museum?
Future with <u>will</u>	Will a new film ~~will~~ be directed by Ang Lee next year?
Future with <u>be going to</u>	Is a collection of Van Gogh's drawings ~~is~~ going to be shown at the Tate Modern next month?

On a separate sheet of paper, rewrite the sentences as <u>yes</u> / <u>no</u> questions in the passive voice.

1 That new film about families is being directed by Gillian Armstrong.

2 One of da Vinci's most famous drawings has been sold by a German art collector.

3 A rare ceramic figure from the National Palace Museum in Taipei will be sent to the Metropolitan Museum of Art in New York.

4 A new exhibit is going to be opened at the Photography Gallery this week.

5 Some new paintings have been bought by the Prado Museum for their permanent collection.

6 *Las Meninas* can be seen at the Prado Museum in Madrid.

7 The *Jupiter* Symphony was written by Mozart.

8 Some of Michelangelo's work was being shown around the world in the 1960s.

Other ways to express a purpose

<u>In order to</u>

You can use <u>in order to</u> with a base form of a verb to express a purpose. The following three sentences have the same meaning.

I scrolled down in order to read the text.

I scrolled down because I wanted to read the text.

I scrolled down to read the text.

<u>For</u>

You can use <u>for</u> to express a purpose before a noun phrase or gerund phrase.

She e-mailed me for some advice.

They shop online for electronic products.

I use my smart phone for e-mailing clients.

Be careful! Don't use <u>for</u> before an infinitive of purpose.

DON'T SAY She e-mailed me ~~for~~ to ask a question.

A On a separate sheet of paper, rewrite the sentences with <u>in order to</u>.

1 She joined Facebook to meet new people.

2 Jason surfs the Internet to see what's new.

3 Alison uses online banking to pay all her bills.

4 They always print their documents first to read them carefully.

5 I never use the pull-down menu to open files.

6 He used an online telephone service to call his family.

B Complete each sentence with <u>for</u> or <u>to</u>.

1 My friend e-mailed me _____ say he's getting married.

2 Matt created a web page _____ keeping in touch with his family and friends.

3 I went online _____ find a new keyboard.

4 Jane shops online _____ clothing.

5 When Gina's computer crashed, her brother came over _____ help her.

6 Sometimes I use my computer _____ download movies.

7 We both log on to the Internet _____ information.

8 Just click the icon _____ open the file.

UNIT 9 *Lesson 2*

Comparison with adjectives: review

<u>As</u> … <u>as</u>

Use <u>as</u> … <u>as</u> to indicate how two things are equal or the same. Use <u>not as</u> … <u>as</u> to indicate how two things are different.

The new Jax 10 monitor is just as good as the Jax 20.

The Jax 10 monitor is not as big as the Jax 20.

Comparatives

Use comparatives to show how two things are not equal. Use <u>than</u> if the second item is mentioned.

My laptop is heavier than John's (is).   OR My laptop is heavier.

Regular mail is less convenient than e-mail. OR Snail mail is less convenient.

Superlatives

Use superlatives to show how one thing is different from two or more other things. Remember to use <u>the</u> with the superlative.

The M2, LX, and Bell printers are all good. But the Bell is the best.

The Gatt 40 monitor is the least expensive one you can buy.

A Correct the error in each sentence.

1 The Orca speakers aren't as heavier as the Yaltas.

2 My old laptop didn't have as many problems than my new laptop.

3 I checked out the three top brands, and the Piston was definitely the better.

4 Maxwell's web camera is much more expensive as their digital camera.

5 Of all the monitors I looked at, the X60 is definitely larger.

6 The Cray Jaguar is most powerful computer in the world.

Comparison with adverbs

Comparatives

My new computer runs faster than my old one.

The X20 operates more quietly than the X30.

<u>As</u> … <u>as</u>

My new phone works as well as my old one.

The Macro laptop doesn't run as slowly as the Pell does.

Superlatives

Of these three laptops, the MPro starts up the most slowly.

Remember: Adverbs often give information about verbs.
My phone works well.   My printer prints fast.

Many adjectives can be changed to adverbs by adding **–ly**.

loud → loudly   quick → quickly   quiet → quietly
poor → poorly   bad → badly   slow → slowly

B On a separate sheet of paper, rewrite each pair of sentences into a single sentence using comparatives. Then write single sentences using <u>as ... as</u>.

1 My brother's MP3 player downloads music quickly. My MP3 player doesn't download quickly.

2 My new computer doesn't log on slowly. My old computer logs on slowly.

3 Your old monitor works well. My new monitor doesn't work well.

4 The Rico printer prints quickly. The Grant printer doesn't print quickly.

5 The Pace scanner doesn't run quietly. The Rico scanner runs quietly.

UNIT 10   *Lesson 1*

Present factual conditionals: usage

Use the present factual conditional to express general and scientific facts.
Use the simple present tense or the present tense of <u>be</u> in both clauses.

    If it **rains**, flights **are** late. [fact]
    If you **heat** water to 100 degrees, it **boils**. [scientific fact]

In present factual conditional sentences, <u>when</u> (or <u>whenever</u>) is often used instead of <u>if</u>.

    When (or **Whenever**) it rains, flights are late.
    When you heat water to 100 degrees, it boils.

Note: For a review of the concept of clauses, see Units 4 and 6 of the Writing Booster.

A On a separate sheet of paper, write present factual conditional sentences.

1 Water (freeze) when you (lower) its temperature below zero degrees.

2 Whenever my daughter (take) her umbrella to school, she (forget) to bring it home.

3 She (go) on vacation every August if she (not have) too much work.

4 He (run) in the park if the weather (be) dry.

5 In my company, if cashiers (make) a mistake, they have to (repay) the money.

Future factual conditionals: usage and common errors

Use the future factual conditional to express what you believe will happen in the future under certain conditions or as a result of certain actions. Use the simple present tense or the present of <u>be</u> in the <u>if-</u> clause. Use a future form (<u>will</u> or <u>be going to</u>) in the result clause.

    If I **go** to sleep too late tonight, I **won't be able to** get up on time. (future condition, future result)
    If she **comes** home after 8:00, I'm **not going to make** dinner. (future condition, future result)

Be careful! Don't use a future form in the <u>if-</u> clause.
    If I see him, I'll tell him.
    NOT If I ~~will~~ see him, I'll tell him.
    NOT If I'm ~~going to~~ see him, I'll tell him.

B Circle the correct form to complete each future factual conditional sentence.

1 If they (like / will like) the movie, they (see / will see) it again.

2 I ('m going to talk / talk) to her if she (does / 's going to do) that again.

3 If you (buy / are going to buy) some eggs, I (make / 'll make) you an omelet tonight.

4 If they (see / will see) her tomorrow, they (drive / 'll drive) her home.

5 (Are you going to study / Do you study) Italian if they (offer / will offer) it next year?

Order of clauses: punctuation

In all conditional sentences, the clauses can be reversed with no change in meaning. In writing, use a comma between the clauses when the <u>if-</u> clause comes first.

    If you don't return the bracelet, you'll feel bad.
    You'll feel bad if you don't return the bracelet.

C On a separate sheet of paper, complete each present unreal conditional sentence with true information. Use a comma when the <u>if-</u> clause comes first.

1 If I lived to be 100 …

2 My family would be angry if …

3 If I didn't study English …

4 If I went to my favorite restaurant …

5 If I were a child again …

6 The English class would be better if …

UNIT 10 *Lesson 2*

Possessive nouns: review and expansion

Add <u>'s</u> (an apostrophe + <u>s</u>) to a name or a singular noun.

Where is Glenn's car?

This is Ms. Baker's class.

What's your daughter's married name?

I love Dickens's novels.

Add an apostrophe to plural nouns that end in <u>s</u>. For irregular plurals, such as <u>women</u> or <u>children</u>, add <u>'s</u>.

the boys' clothes   the Jacksons' car   the women's room

Add <u>'s</u> to the name or noun that comes last in a list of two or more.

Jean and Ralph's house

A Correct the following sentences, adding an apostrophe or an apostrophe + <u>s</u> to the possessive nouns.

Carmen's jacket is under the table.

1 The two girls keys are lost.

2 Mr. Stiller English is really fluent.

3 The doctor office is downstairs.

4 Sarah and Tom children are at the Taylor School.

5 That man car is parked in a no-parking zone.

6 Julia friend brother is going to get married tonight.

7 The Smiths garden is beautiful.

Pronouns: summary

Subject Pronouns

Subject pronouns represent subject nouns and noun phrases. The subject pronouns are <u>I</u>, <u>you</u>, <u>he</u>, <u>she</u>, <u>it</u>, <u>we</u>, and <u>they</u>.

Matt didn't break the plate = He didn't break the plate.

Object Pronouns

Object pronouns represent nouns (and noun phrases) that function as direct objects, indirect objects, and objects of prepositions. The object pronouns are <u>me</u>, <u>you</u>, <u>him</u>, <u>her</u>, <u>it</u>, <u>us</u>, and <u>them</u>.

They gave Susan the toy car for the children.

They gave it to her for them.

B On a separate sheet of paper, rewrite the sentences, replacing the underlined nouns and noun phrases with pronouns.

<u>Matt</u> didn't break <u>the plate</u>. *He didn't break it.*

1 <u>Our children</u> love <u>TV</u>.

2 <u>Janet and I</u> never buy <u>food</u> at that store.

3 Do <u>you and I</u> have <u>the car</u> this afternoon?

4 <u>Sylvia's family</u> laughs at <u>her jokes</u>.

5 <u>My friends</u> are speaking with <u>Ms. Rowe</u> today.

6 <u>Mr. Harris</u> is teaching <u>the class</u> with <u>Mr. Cooper</u>.

7 <u>All the students</u> are speaking English very well this year.

8 Does <u>Carl</u> need to give <u>the paper</u> to <u>his teachers</u>?

9 <u>Martin and Larry</u> returned <u>the money</u> to <u>the woman</u>.

Writing Booster

The Writing Booster is optional. It is intended to teach students the conventions of written English. Each unit's Writing Booster is focused both on a skill and its application to the Writing topic from the Unit Review page.

UNIT 1 *Avoiding run-on sentences*

An independent clause is a sentence with a subject and a verb.

subject	verb
I	saw a photo of the mountain.
It	looked very high.

Remember: A sentence …
* begins with a capital letter and ends with a period.
* has a subject and a verb.
* expresses a complete idea.

In writing, a run-on sentence is when we forget to use a coordinating conjunction, such as <u>and</u> or <u>but</u>, to combine independent clauses.

Run-on sentence   ✗ I saw a photo of the mountain it looked very high.

Correct a run-on sentence by (a) using a period to separate it into two sentences, or (b) using a coordinating conjunction to combine the two independent clauses. A comma before the conjunction is optional.

✓ I saw a photo of the mountain. It looked very high.
✓ I saw a photo of the mountain, and it looked very high.

Be careful! Do not use a comma to combine independent clauses. Use a period to separate them.

Run-on sentence   ✗ A new student arrived yesterday, he is from Santos.
✓ A new student arrived yesterday. He is from Santos.

A Write ✗ if the item contains a run-on sentence. Write ✓ if the item is written correctly.

☐ **1** Ann is Canadian she doesn't speak French.

☐ **2** They're good students they work very hard.

☐ **3** My brother is a lawyer, he lives in Hong Kong.

☐ **4** Victor and Lisa came home late last night. They stayed up until 4:00 A.M.

☐ **5** Some people think cities are beautiful I don't agree.

☐ **6** I have been to three foreign countries, I have never been to the United States.

☐ **7** We haven't tried Polish food, but we have tried Hungarian food.

☐ **8** I have never been to the top of the Empire State Building in New York, I have been to the top of Taipei 101 in Taipei.

☐ **9** I visited Jeju in Korea and it was really beautiful.

B On a separate sheet of paper, write each of the run-on sentences in Exercise A correctly.

C Guidance for Writing (page 12) After you write about your experience in Exercise D, check carefully to see if you have written any run-on sentences. Use a period to separate the independent clauses or use the coordinating conjunctions <u>and</u> or <u>but</u> to combine them.

A **paragraph** is a group of sentences that relate to a topic or a theme. When your writing contains sections about a variety of topics, it is a good idea to divide it into separate paragraphs.

When there is more than one paragraph, it is customary, though not required, to include **a topic sentence** in each paragraph that summarizes or announces the main idea of the paragraph. The other sentences in the paragraph traditionally include details or facts that support the main idea. Using topic sentences makes paragraphs clearer and easier to understand.

In the writing model to the right there are two paragraphs, each beginning with a topic sentence (highlighted in yellow):

In the first paragraph, the topic sentence informs us that the paragraph will contain details about violence in movies "before the 1960s."

In the second paragraph, the topic sentence informs us that the paragraph will shift focus. The word "Today" lets the reader know what the focus of the paragraph will be.

Without the topic sentences, the ideas would run together and be difficult to follow.

Remember: Indent the first word of each new paragraph so readers know that a new section of the writing is beginning.

Before the 1960s, most movies did not show much graphic violence. When fighting or shooting occurred on the screen, it was clean: Bang! You're dead! The victim fell to the ground and died, perhaps after speaking a few final words. The viewer never saw blood or suffering. But in the late 60s, filmmakers such as Arthur Penn and Sam Peckinpah began making movies with more graphic violence, such as *Bonnie and Clyde* and *The Wild Bunch*. They believed that if audiences could see how truly horrible real violence was, people would be less violent in their own lives.

Today, special-effects technology has made it possible to create very realistic images of bloodshed and violence. Steven Prince, author of *Savage Cinema: Sam Peckinpah and the Rise of Ultraviolent Movies*, describes the difference between early movies and the movies of today: "... filmmakers can create any image that they can dream up." So, Prince believes, because of technology, movies today are more and more violent and bloody.

A Choose a topic sentence for each of the following paragraphs.

1

Some people are worried that viewing a lot of violence in movies and video games can be dangerous. They feel that it can make violence seem normal and can cause people to imitate the violent behavior, doing the same thing themselves. Other people disagree. They believe that showing violence is honest and can even be helpful.

a Many people say violence in movies can be harmful.
b People have different opinions about how violence can affect viewers.
c People imitate violent behavior they see in movies.

2

The 1967 Arthur Penn movie is about a real gang of violent bank robbers who terrorized the U.S. Southwest in the 1930s. Bonnie (Faye Dunaway) and Clyde (Warren Beatty), and their gang were believed to be responsible for thirteen deaths and many robberies before they were finally killed.

a *Bonnie and Clyde* is based on a true story.
b Arthur Penn is one of the most famous directors of the 1960s.
c There were a lot of bank robberies in the 1930s.

3

The U.S. documentary *Spellbound* visits the homes of eight finalists for the National Spelling Bee and then follows them to the finals in Washington. We get to know the kids and their families.

a Spelling bees are popular in the U.S., and there have been a number of them in Washington.
b The finals of the National Spelling Bee take place in Washington.
c Some documentaries give us an intimate view of people and their lives.

B On a separate sheet of paper, write two paragraphs of three to five sentences each with details about the following topics. Then make sure you have included a topic sentence for each paragraph that summarizes or announces the main idea of the paragraph.

Paragraph 1 The story of a time you (or someone else) were late to meet someone for an event	**Paragraph 2** The story of what you (or the others) did after the event

C Guidance for Writing (page 24) On the notepad, write notes about why some people think watching violence is harmful and why others think it isn't. Use your notes as a guide for your paragraphs about violence in Exercise D. Include a topic sentence for each paragraph to summarize the main ideas.

Harmful:

Not harmful:

UNIT 3 *Avoiding sentence fragments with because or since*

Remember: You can use the subordinating conjunctions <u>because</u> or <u>since</u> to give a reason. <u>Because</u> and <u>since</u> answer the <u>Why</u> question. A clause that begins with <u>because</u> or <u>since</u> is called a dependent clause. A dependent clause gives information about an independent clause.

—— independent clause ——   ——— dependent clause ———————

I prefer the Hotel Casablanca   because (or since) it looks very interesting.

A dependent clause with <u>because</u> or <u>since</u> can also come at the beginning of a sentence. If it comes first, use a comma.
   Because it looks very interesting, I prefer the Hotel Casablanca.

In writing, a dependent clause alone is an error called a "sentence fragment." It is not a sentence because it does not express a complete idea. Avoid writing sentence fragments.
   Sentence fragment   ✗ I prefer the Hotel Casablanca. ~~Because it looks very interesting~~.

To correct a sentence fragment with <u>because</u> or <u>since</u>, make sure it is combined with an independent clause. Or rewrite the sentence without <u>because</u> or <u>since</u> to create an independent clause.
   ✓ I prefer the Hotel Casablanca because it looks very interesting.
   ✓ I prefer the Hotel Casablanca. It looks very interesting.

A In the following paragraph, underline four sentence fragments with <u>because</u> or <u>since</u>.

> When I was a child, I had three very important dreams. Because I was young, I thought they would all come true. The first one was that I wanted to be an architect. Because I loved modern buildings. Since I wanted to help people. The second dream was to be a doctor. The last one was to be a flight attendant. Since I liked to travel. Only one of my dreams became a reality. I am an architect today. Because I really love my job. I think it was really the right choice for me.

B On a separate sheet of paper, write the paragraph again. Correct all the sentence fragments. Combine the dependent clauses with independent clauses to make complete sentences.

C Guidance for Writing (page 36) In your paragraph about a hotel in Exercise D, include at least three reasons using <u>because</u> or <u>since</u>. Then check carefully to make sure that there are no sentence fragments.

<u>And</u>

<u>And</u> connects two or more words in a series. Use commas to separate words when there are more than two in the series. (The last comma is optional.)

I'm concerned about aggressive and inattentive driving. (no comma: <u>and</u> connects two adjectives.)

Inattentive drivers sometimes eat and talk on their cell phones while they are driving. (no comma: <u>and</u> connects two verbs of the same subject.)

Gesturing, staring, and multitasking are three things aggressive drivers often do. (A comma is necessary: <u>and</u> connects more than two words in a series. The comma after <u>staring</u> is optional.)

<u>And</u> can also combine two separate complete sentences into one sentence. In the new sentence, the two original sentences are called "independent clauses." The comma is common but optional.

——————— complete sentence ——————— —— complete sentence ——
Aggressive drivers do many dangerous things. They cause a lot of crashes.

——————— independent clause——————— —— independent clause ——
Aggressive drivers do many dangerous things, **and** they cause a lot of crashes.

A Insert commas where necessary or optional in the following sentences.

1 She enjoys swimming hiking and fishing.

2 I don't like SUVs and other large cars.

3 We're traveling to France Italy and Spain.

4 Marianne and Sally are coming with us.

5 I'm renting a car and I'm driving it to Chicago.

6 This agency has nice convertibles vans and sports cars.

B On a separate sheet of paper, combine each pair of sentences into one sentence consisting of two independent clauses. Use <u>and</u>.

1 They made a call to a car rental company. They reserved a minivan for the weekend.

2 The left front headlight is broken. It won't turn on.

3 We rented a full-size sedan with a sunroof. We opened it because the weather was beautiful.

4 I hit the car in front of me. A passenger in the back seat was hurt.

5 You can drop the car off at nine o'clock. You can pick it up in the late afternoon.

<u>In addition</u>, <u>Furthermore</u>, and <u>Therefore</u>

Use <u>In addition</u> and <u>Furthermore</u> to add to the ideas in a previous sentence. <u>In addition</u> and <u>Furthermore</u> are approximately equal in meaning, but <u>Furthermore</u> is a little more formal. You can use both in the same writing to avoid a repetitive style.

People should pay attention to their own driving. In addition, they should be aware of the driving of others.

I think defensive driving makes sense. Furthermore, it has been proven to reduce the number of accidents.

<u>Therefore</u> introduces a result.

——————————— result ———————————————
Ron has had a lot of accidents. Therefore, the rental company said he couldn't rent one of their cars.

Note: It's customary to use a comma after <u>In addition</u>, <u>Furthermore</u>, and <u>Therefore</u>.

C Complete the statements with <u>In addition</u> or <u>Therefore</u>.

1 The other driver was speeding. _____, she wasn't paying attention.

2 No one was hurt. _____, we didn't have to go to the hospital after the crash.

3 I was taking a business trip with a lot of equipment. _____, I rented a car with a lot of trunk space.

4 They need to rent a minivan for their trip to Montreal. _____, they have to stay in a pet-friendly hotel because they plan to bring their pet dog.

D Guidance for Writing (page 48) In your paragraph about good and bad drivers in Exercise E, use <u>And</u>, <u>In addition</u>, <u>Furthermore</u>, and <u>Therefore</u>. Then check your paragraph carefully to see if you have used commas to separate words correctly.

E-mails and handwritten social notes are informal ways to communicate with others. They don't have many rules. Formal letters, such as business letters, are generally typed and have conventions and rules. For these, be sure to include the following elements:

- your address
- the recipient's name (and / or position) and address
- the date of the letter
- a salutation
- a complimentary close
- your typewritten name <u>and</u> your handwritten signature

Note: If you know the recipient's name, the salutation should use the following format: <u>Dear</u> [title + last name]. It's common in a formal letter to use a colon (:) after the name. In less formal letters, a comma is appropriate.

Dear Mr. Smith:

Dear Marie,

If you don't know the recipient's name or gender, use this format:

Dear Sir or Madam: OR

To whom it may concern:

Follow the layout and punctuation in the writing model to the right.

your address { 657 Boulevard East
New Compton, Fortunia

date { December 14, 2012

Manager
The Tipton Spa
Tipton Hotel } recipient's address
2200 Byway
Sylvania, Sorrento

Dear Sir or Madam: } salutation

I'm writing to tell you that I was very happy with the service provided by the staff of the Tipton Spa when I was in Sylvania last week. The hair stylist gave me a wonderful haircut and the masseur was really top notch. I particularly enjoyed the relaxing music that played over the public address system. Finally, the prices were fair, and I left the spa feeling great.

I want you to know that I am recommending the Tipton Spa to all my friends and have told them that they should visit you even if they are staying in another hotel or if they are in Sylvania for the day. In fact, I have told them that it's worth traveling to Sylvania just to visit the spa. Congratulations on such a wonderful spa.

Sincerely, } complimentary close

Francine Classon } signature

Francine Classon } typewritten name

Other common complimentary closes
Cordially,
Sincerely yours,
Best regards,

A Think of a business such as a hotel, a store, a salon, a gym, or a restaurant where you have received good service. On the notepad, write notes about the business.

Name of business:
Address:
Why you are happy with the service:

B On a separate sheet of paper, write a letter of thanks to the manager of the business in Exercise A. Explain what you like about the service. Use your notes and the writing model above as a guide.

C Guidance for Writing (page 60) Using the letter from page 56 that you chose, list three methods on the notepad below which a person could use to improve his or her appearance. Make notes of the advantages and disadvantages of each method. Then use your notes as a guide to help you write your response letter in Exercise E. Be sure to include your name and address, the date, a salutation, and a complimentary close in your letter.

Method	Advantages	Disadvantages
1.		
2.		
3.		

A subordinating conjunction connects a dependent clause to an independent clause.

——— independent clause ———   ——— dependent clause ———
People are eating more fast foods today **because** they want to save time.
I generally avoid carbohydrates **even though** it isn't easy.

Subordinating conjunctions	
because	unless
since	although
if	(even) though

A dependent clause can also come at the beginning of a sentence. Use a comma after the dependent clause when it comes first.

——— dependent clause ———   ——— independent clause ———
Because people want to save time, they are eating more fast foods today.
Even though it isn't easy, I generally avoid carbohydrates.

Use the subordinating conjunction <u>if</u> to express a condition. Use <u>unless</u> to express a negative condition.

You will be healthy   **if** you eat right and exercise regularly.
You will gain weight   **unless** you eat right and exercise regularly. (= if you don't)

Use the subordinating conjunctions <u>although</u>, <u>even though</u>, or <u>though</u> to express a contradiction.

Although
Even though } they knew fatty foods were unhealthy, people ate them anyway.
Though

Remember: Use <u>because</u> or <u>since</u> to give a reason.

A Choose the best subordinating conjunction to complete each sentence.

1 (Though / If / Unless) I learn to speak English well, I will be very happy.

2 (Even though / Because / If) she is an artist, she is interested in science.

3 Studying English is important (although / because / unless) it can help you do more.

4 (Unless / Although / Since) English grammar isn't easy, I like studying it.

5 They have to go on a diet (because / unless / though) they're overweight.

6 He cut back on desserts and sodas (even though / if / because) he didn't want to.

7 (Even though / Because / Unless) my grandmother is 80 years old, she is in very good health.

8 (Unless / Because / Though) I think I'm going to get sick, I don't want to change my eating habits.

9 She won't eat red meat (because / unless / although) she has to.

10 (Unless / Even though / Since) she's a vegetarian, she sometimes eats fish.

B Read each sentence. Then, on a separate sheet of paper, write and connect a clause to the sentence, using the subordinating conjunction.

1 Most people don't want to change their eating habits. (even though)

2 Children become overweight. (if)

3 Obesity will continue to be a global problem. (unless)

4 Eating too much fast food is bad for you. (because)

5 Most people continue to eat unhealthy foods. (although)

1 Most people don't want to change their eating habits
even though they have health problems.

C Guidance for Writing (page 72) Using four different subordinating conjunctions, write four sentences: two about eating habits in the past and two about eating habits in the present. Use your sentences in your paragraph about eating habits in Exercise F.

When writing a series of words or phrases in a sentence, be sure that all items in the series are in the same grammatical form. This feature of good writing is called parallel structure.

parallel structure (all items in the series are gerunds)
Lucy is creative. She likes painting, playing the piano, and dancing.

Be careful! Don't combine gerunds and infinitives in the same series.
Don't write: Lucy is creative. She likes painting, to play the piano, and dancing.

In a series of infinitives, it is correct to use <u>to</u> before each item in the series or to use <u>to</u> only before the first item.
✓ I decided to study medicine, to get married, and to have children before my thirtieth birthday.
✓ I decided to study medicine, get married, and have children before my thirtieth birthday.
✗ I decided to study medicine, get married, and to have children before my thirtieth birthday.

Remember: When a sentence includes a series of more than two words or phrases, separate them with commas. Use <u>and</u> before the last item in the series. The comma before <u>and</u> is optional.

no comma (two items)   commas (three items)
Jake and May have three favorite activities: painting, singing, and dancing.

A **Correct the errors in parallel structure in the following sentences.**

1 I have begun studying psychology and to learn about personality development.

2 They continue arguing about the nature-nurture controversy and to disagree about which is more important.

3 The Bersons love to run, to swim, and lift weights.

4 She's both responsible and social. She prefers to study early in the evening and going out afterwards.

5 Introverts hate to talk about their feelings and being with a lot of people.

6 Marjorie is a classic extrovert. She likes to be very active, knowing a lot of people, and to seek excitement.

7 To be quiet, be hard to know, and to seek peace are traits typical of the introvert's personality.

8 Psychologists of the nineteenth century continued believing in the importance of genetics and to write about it in books and articles.

B Guidance for Writing (page 84) **On a separate sheet of paper, write sentences to answer some or all the following questions about a person you know well. If appropriate, use verbs and phrases from the lists below. Be careful to use parallel structure. Use the sentences in your paragraphs about a person in Exercise E.**

- Who is the person?
- What is the person's relation to you?
- Who are the people in the person's family?
- How many siblings does the person have?
- What kind of personality does the person have?
- What are the person's likes and dislikes?
- Are there some things the person is excited about, bored with, angry about, or worried about right now?

Words to describe likes / dislikes	
avoids	hopes
hates	would like
can't stand	is happy about
doesn't mind	is excited about
enjoys	is bored with
expects	is sick and tired of

Remember: A good paragraph has a topic sentence that states clearly what the main idea of the paragraph is.

In addition, a paragraph should have **supporting details**—that is, information that provides support for, and is clearly tied to, the topic sentence.

Be careful! If a detail doesn't support the topic sentence or isn't tied to it clearly, then it may not belong in the paragraph.

In the writing model to the right, the topic sentence of the paragraph is highlighted in yellow. The sentences that follow are details. Two of the sentences are crossed out because they do not support the topic sentence and should not be included in the paragraph. These two sentences do not provide information about the chair and do not indicate why the writer likes the chair. The remaining sentences are supporting details—they all support the topic sentence and are clearly tied to it. They provide more information about the chair and they explain why the writer likes the chair.

In my living room, I have many things.
My favorite possession is an old wooden chair. My parents gave it to me when I left home. ~~A wooden chair can be very expensive if it is an antique.~~ It has lots of memories for me because it was in my parent's bedroom when I was growing up. ~~It's important to take very good care of wooden furniture.~~ The chair is very comfortable, and I used to sit in it a lot as a child.

A **Read each topic sentence. Circle the detail that does not support the topic sentence.**

1 Many French artists in the nineteenth century were influenced by Japanese art and printmaking.
   a Today, the work of Hokusai, Japan's most famous printmaker, is popular in Western countries.
   b Looking at the work of the French impressionists, it is clear that they chose to imitate the Japanese artistic styles of the time.
   c A number of French artists had collections of Japanese art.

2 I love my poster of Reinaldo, the Brazilian soccer star, but my wife hates it.
   a I think Reinaldo is the greatest player in the world.
   b My wife doesn't think I should keep it in our bedroom.
   c Reinaldo is a right-footed soccer player.

3 Rodin's statue, *The Thinker*, is probably one of the most famous sculptures in the world.
   a This metal and stone sculpture of a man deep in thought is recognized all over the world.
   b Rodin was born on November 12, 1840.
   c The image of *The Thinker* can be seen in popular art and advertisements.

4 On a side table in my dining room, I have two small ceramic figures of lions from my trip to Taipei.
   a They have beautiful colors including red, green, blue, and yellow.
   b You should visit the National Palace Museum when you are in Taipei.
   c I bought them together from a small shop at a temple I was visiting.

5 My sister has always shown a lot of talent in the performing arts.
   a We've had our differences and we haven't always agreed on everything.
   b She has acted in school plays since she was about ten years old.
   c I think she's going to follow a career as an actor or dancer.

6 I think artistic talent is something you're born with.
   a I've tried many times to improve my ability at drawing, but it hasn't worked.
   b I have friends who are very talented in art, but they've never taken any special classes.
   c My aunt studied art at the Art Institute of Chicago for four years.

B Guidance for Writing (page 96) On the notepad, write the favorite object you chose in Exercise E. Create a topic sentence that states the most important thing you want to say about that object. Then write five supporting details to use in your paragraph.

Favorite object:

Topic sentence:

Details to support my topic sentence:

1.

2.

3.

4.

5.

UNIT 9 *Organizing ideas*

When you want to describe the benefits and problems of an issue, there are different ways you can organize your ideas. Here are some approaches.

Approach 1: In one paragraph
One way is to describe all the advantages and disadvantages in one paragraph. Following are notes of the details that will be included in the paragraph.

> THE ADVANTAGES AND DISADVANTAGES OF CELL PHONES
>
> Advantages: are easy to carry, don't miss calls, keep you connected with family and friends
>
> Disadvantages: bother other people, make people dependent, are easy to lose

This approach is good for a short piece of writing consisting of only a few sentences. However, if you want to develop those ideas in more than just a few sentences, it is easier for the reader to follow if you can organize the details in one of the following ways.

Approach 2: In two paragraphs
In this approach, you can use a first paragraph to describe all the advantages. Then you can use a second paragraph to describe all the disadvantages. Following are notes of the details that will be included in each paragraph.

> Paragraph 1: CELL PHONES HAVE ADVANTAGES
>
> are easy to carry, don't miss calls, keep you connected with family and friends
>
> Paragraph 2: BUT THEY ALSO HAVE DISADVANTAGES
>
> bother other people, make people dependent, are easy to lose

Approach 3: In two or more paragraphs
In this approach, you can use a separate paragraph to focus on each different topic. In each paragraph, you can describe both advantages and disadvantages. Following are notes of the details that will be included in each paragraph.

> Paragraph 1: (THEY'RE SMALL.) cell phones easy to carry, but also easy to lose
>
> Paragraph 2: (THEY'RE CONVENIENT.) won't miss calls, but you can also bother other people
>
> Paragraph 3: (THEY'VE CHANGED OUR LIVES.) keep people connected with family and friends, but also can
>
> make people dependent

A Below are ideas for a piece of writing about renting a car during a vacation overseas. Using Approach 2, you can organize the ideas into two paragraphs, one about the benefits of renting and one about the problems. Write 1 next to the sentences that belong in paragraph 1. Write 2 next to the sentences that belong in paragraph 2.

__ It gives you the freedom to go wherever you want to go whenever you want.

__ There are advantages and disadvantages to renting a car while you're on vacation overseas.

__ You might see places you can't see by bus or train.

__ You could have an accident during your trip.

__ You have more control over whether or not you will have an accident during your trip.

__ You can carry more luggage and other things you might need.

__ To drive safely, you have to become familiar with the local driving rules.

__ If you're traveling with a group of people, it could cost less than paying for bus and train tickets.

__ You may have to understand road signs that are in a different language.

__ If you have to do all the driving, it can be very stressful and tiring.

__ If you're traveling alone or with one other person, it could cost a lot of money in rental fees and gas.

B Now, on a separate sheet of paper, practice using Approach 3. Choose sentences from Exercise A that you can organize into two or more separate topics.

C Guidance for Writing (page 108) Use your notes on page 107 to write your paragraphs in Exercise E about the benefits and problems of the Internet. Choose Approach 2 or Approach 3 to organize your writing.

UNIT 10 *Introducing conflicting ideas: On the one hand; On the other hand*

Use <u>On the one hand</u> and <u>On the other hand</u> to present conflicting ideas or two sides of an issue. The following two sentences present the two sides together, one right after the other.

> On the one hand, I would want to tell the truth. On the other hand, I wouldn't want to get in trouble.

Remember: You can also present conflicting or contradictory information with <u>Even though</u>, <u>Although</u>, and <u>However</u>.

> Even though I'm basically an honest person, I don't always tell the truth.
> Although Matt didn't think he broke the dish, it's possible that he did.
> Matt wanted to tell the owner of the store what happened. However, Noah didn't agree.

When one paragraph presents one side of an issue and the next one presents the other, writers don't usually use <u>On the one hand</u> in the first paragraph. Instead, they just begin the next paragraph with <u>On the other hand</u> to let the reader know that the conflicting idea will follow. Look at the writing model to the right.

> Being honest has many advantages. If you always tell the truth, you don't have to remember an untruth you said before. People who tell the truth don't have trouble sleeping. They can look at themselves in the mirror and feel good.
>
> On the other hand, there are times when telling a lie makes sense. For example, if a friend asks you what you think of a new piece of clothing and you hate it, telling him or her that you think it's ugly would be very hurtful. It's possible that not being absolutely truthful might make more sense.

A Reread the Photo Story on page 111. Write a summary of the story in three to five sentences. Answer the questions below.

- Where was Matt?
- What happened?
- Who was he with?
- What did the two friends discuss?

B Answer the questions below. Write three to five sentences about Matt's choices. Then write the consequences of each choice. Use <u>If</u> and the unreal conditional in at least one sentence.

- What should he do?
- What could he do?
- What would most people do?

C Write three to five sentences about what you would do if you were Matt. Answer the questions below.

- What would you do?
- What would happen if you did that?
- What would happen if you didn't?

D Guidance for Writing (page 120) In your paragraphs about Matt's dilemma in Exercise E, use <u>On the one hand</u>, <u>On the other hand</u>, <u>Even though</u>, <u>Although</u>, and <u>However</u> to connect conflicting ideas.

Top Notch Pop Lyrics

1:15/1:16
🔊 Greetings and Small Talk [Unit 1]
You look so familiar. Have we met before?
I don't think you're from around here.
It might have been two weeks ago, but I'm
not sure.
Has it been a month or a year?
I have a funny feeling that I've met you twice.
That's what they call déjà vu.
You were saying something friendly, trying to
be nice—and now you're being friendly, too.
One look, one word.
It's the friendliest sound that I've ever heard.
Thanks for your greeting.
I'm glad this meeting occurred.

(CHORUS)
Greetings and small talk
make the world go round.
On every winding road I've walked,
this is what I've found.

Have you written any letters to your friends
back home?
Have you had a chance to do that?
Have you spoken to your family on the
telephone?
Have you taken time for a chat?
Bow down, shake hands.
Do whatever you do in your native land.
I'll be happy to greet you
in any way that you understand.

(CHORUS)

Have you seen the latest movie out of
Hollywood?
Have you read about it yet?
If you haven't eaten dinner, are you in the
mood for a meal you won't forget?
Bow down, shake hands.
Do whatever you do in your native land.
I'll be happy to greet you
in any way that you understand.

(CHORUS)

1:33/1:34
🔊 Better Late Than Never [Unit 2]
Where have you been? I've waited for you.
I'd rather not say how long.
The movie began one hour ago.
How did you get the time all wrong?
Well, I got stuck in traffic, and when I arrived
I couldn't find a parking place.
Did you buy the tickets? You're kidding—
for real?
Let me pay you back, in that case.

(CHORUS)
Sorry I'm late.
I know you've waited here forever.
How long has it been?
It's always better late than never.

When that kind of movie comes to the
big screen,
it always attracts a crowd,
and I've always wanted to see it with you—
but it looks like we've missed it now.
I know what you're saying, but actually,
I would rather watch a video.
So why don't we rent it and bring it
back home?
Let's get in the car and go.

(CHORUS)

Didn't you mention, when we made our
plans, that you've seen this movie recently?
It sounds so dramatic, and I'm so upset,
I'd rather see a comedy!
Well, which comedy do you recommend?
It really doesn't matter to me.
I still haven't seen 'The World and a Day'.
I've heard that one is pretty funny.

(CHORUS)

2:16/2:17
🔊 Checking Out [Unit 3]
Ms. Jones travels all alone.
She doesn't need much space—
a single room with a nice twin bed
and a place for her suitcase.
Her stay is always satisfactory,
but in the morning she's going to be
checking out.
Mr. Moon will be leaving soon,
and when he does I'll say,
"Thank you, sir, for staying with us.
How do you want to pay?"
And in the end it isn't hard.
He'll put it on his credit card. He's
checking out.
Would you like to leave a message?
Could you call back later?
Do you need some extra towels
or today's newspaper?
Can I get you anything?
Would you like room service?
I'm so sorry.
Am I making you nervous?
Good evening.
I'll ring that room for you.
Is that all?
I'll be glad to put you through.
I'm sorry, but he's not answering.
The phone just rings and rings.
The couple in room 586
have made a king-size mess.
Pick up the laundry. Turn down the beds.
We have another guest
coming with his family.
You'd better hurry or they will be
checking out. . .

2:33/2:34
🔊 Wheels around the World [Unit 4]
Was I going too fast
or a little too slow?
I was looking out the window,
and I just don't know.
I must have turned the steering wheel
a little too far
when I drove into the bumper
of that luxury car.
Oh no!
How awful!
What a terrible day!
I'm sorry to hear that.
Are you OK?

(CHORUS)
Wheels around the World
are waiting here with your car.
Pick it up.

Turn it on.
Play the radio.
Wheels around the World—
"helping you to go far."
You can drive anywhere.
Buckle up and go.

Did I hit the red sedan,
or did it hit me?
I was talking on the cell phone
in my SUV.
Nothing was broken,
and no one was hurt,
but I did spill some coffee
on my favorite shirt.
Oh no!
Thank goodness you're still alive!
I'm so happy that
you survived.

(CHORUS)
What were you doing when you hit that tree?
I was racing down the mountain, and the
brakes failed me.
How did it happen? Was the road still wet?
Well, there might have been a danger sign,
But I forget.
The hood popped open and the door fell off.
The headlights blinked and the
engine coughed.
The side-view mirror had a terrible crack.
The gearshift broke. Can I bring the
car back?
Oh no!
Thank goodness
you're still alive!
I'm so happy that
you survived.

(CHORUS)

3:17/3:18
🔊 Piece of Cake [Unit 5]
I need to pick up a few things
on the way back to school.
Feel like stopping at a store with me?
I'd like to, but I think I'll pass.
I don't have time today.
It's already nearly a quarter to three.

(CHORUS)
Don't worry. We'll be fine.
How long can it take?
It's easy. It'll be a piece of cake.

I need a tube of toothpaste and
a bar of Luvly soap,
some sunscreen, and a bottle of shampoo.
Where would I find makeup?
How about a comb?
Have a look in aisle one or two.

(CHORUS)

I have an appointment
for a haircut at The Spa.
On second thought, they're always
running late.
My class starts in an hour.
I'll never make it now.
How long do you think we'll have to wait?

(CHORUS)
They say there's someone waiting
for a trim ahead of me.
Can I get you some coffee or some tea?
OK. In the meantime,
I'll be getting something strong
for this headache at the pharmacy!

(CHORUS)

3:37/3:38

🔊 A Perfect Dish   [Unit 6]

I used to eat a lot of fatty foods,
but now I just avoid them.
I used to like chocolate and lots of sweets,
but now those days are gone.
To tell you the truth,
it was too much trouble.
They say you only live once,
but I'm not crazy about feeling sick.
What was going wrong?
Now I know I couldn't live without this.
Everything's ready.
Why don't you sit down?

(CHORUS)
It looks terrific,
but it smells pretty awful.
What in the world can it be?
It smells like chicken,
and it tastes like fish—
a terrific dish
for you and me—
a perfect dish for you
and me.

I used to be a big meat eater,
now I'm vegetarian,
and I'm not much of a coffee drinker.
I can't stand it anymore.
I'm avoiding desserts with sugar.
I'm trying to lose some weight.
Some things just don't agree with me.
They're bad for me, I'm sure.
Would you like some?
Help yourself.
Isn't it so good for you health?

(CHORUS)

Aren't you going to have some?
Don't you like it?
Wasn't it delicious?
Don't you want some more?

(CHORUS)

4:14/4:15

🔊 The Colors of Love   [Unit 7]

Are you sick and tired of working hard day
and night?
Do you like to look at the world in shades of
black and white?
Your life can still be everything that you were
dreaming of.
Just take a look around you and see all the
colors of love.
You wake up every morning and go through
the same old grind.
You don't know how the light at the window
could be so unkind. If blue is the color that
you choose when the road is rough, you know
you really need to believe in the colors of love.

(CHORUS)
The colors of love
are as beautiful as a rainbow.

The colors of love
shine on everyone in the world.
Are negative thoughts and emotions painful
to express?
They're just tiny drops in the ocean of
happiness.
And these are the feelings you must learn to
rise above.
Your whole life is a picture you paint with the
colors of love.

(CHORUS)

4:30/4:31

🔊 To Each His Own   [Unit 8]

He doesn't care for Dali.
The colors are too bright.
He says that Picasso
got everything just right.
She can't stand the movies
that are filmed in Hollywood.
She likes Almodóvar.
She thinks he's really good.
He's inspired by everything
she thinks is second-rate.
She's moved and fascinated
by the things he loves to hate.
He's crazy about art that only
turns her heart to stone.
I guess that's why they say
to each his own.
He likes pencil drawings.
She prefers photographs.
He takes her to the the art museum,
but she just laughs and laughs.
He loves the Da Vinci
that's hanging by the door.
She prefers the modern art
that's lying on the floor.
"No kidding! You'll love it. Just wait and see.
It's perfect in every way."
She shakes her head. "It's not for me.
It's much too old and gray."
She thinks he has the worst taste
that the world has ever known.
I guess that's why they say
to each his own.
But when it's time to say goodbye,
they both feel so alone.
I guess that's why they say
to each his own.

5:17/5:18

🔊 Life in Cyberspace   [Unit 9]

I'm just fooling around.
Am I interrupting you?
Well, I wanted to know—
what are you up to?
I tried to send some photos,
but it's been so long
that I almost don't remember
how to log on.
So I'm thinking about getting a
new computer.
I don't know what kind. I should have done
it sooner.
But I heard the Panatel is as good as
the rest.
Check it out. Check it out.
You should really check it out.

(CHORUS)

Let's face it—that's life.
That's life in cyberspace.
When you download the pictures,
then you open the files.
If your computer's slow,
then it can take a little while.
From the pull-down menu,
you can print them, too.
But don't forget to save
everything you do.
Scroll it up. Scroll it down.
Put your cursor on the bar.
Then click on the icon,
and you'll see my new car!
The car goes as fast
as the one I had before.
Check it out. Check it out.
You should really check it out.

(CHORUS)

Am I talking to myself, or are you still there?
This instant message conversation's
going nowhere.
I could talk to Liz.
She isn't nearly as nice.
It isn't quite as much fun.
I've done it once or twice.
What's the problem?
Come on. Give it a try.
If you don't want to be friends,
at least tell me why.
Did you leave to make a call
or go out to get some cash?
Did the photos I sent make your
computer crash?

(CHORUS)

5:31/5:32

🔊 What Would You Do?   [Unit 10]

What would you do
if I got a tattoo with your name?
What would you say
if I dyed my hair for you?
What would you do
if I sang outside your window?
What would you think
if I told you I loved you?

(CHORUS)
I hate to say this,
but I think you're making a big mistake.
By tomorrow,
I'm sure you'll be sorry.

What would you do
if I sent you a love letter?
Would you say it was wrong
and send it back to me?
What would you think
if I pierced my ears? Would you care?
Would you think
that I had lost all my modesty?

(CHORUS)

Well, give it some thought.
I know I could make you happy.
Are you kidding?
You'd have to be nuts to ask me.
It's no mistake. I'm sure
that my heart is yours.
I have to find a way
to make you mine.

(CHORUS)